W9-ADJ-897

THE SILVER SPOON
PASTA

Φ

CONTENTS

Pasta is the most popular of Italy's many culinary delights. Its almost infinite variety means that it can take pride of place on the most sophisticated tables and also satisfy the need for fast yet tasty food. One thing is certain: This "absurd Italian culinary religion," as Marinetti referred to it in the 1930s in his drive toward wide-ranging futurist renewal, remains the most Italian of all foods. It is synonymous with Italy, playing a huge part in its worldwide fame, and it is a symbol of the ingenuity of the Italian people.

A BALANCED DIET

There is no more natural and simple food than pasta, which is made from two ingredients only – flour and water. Preservatives and artificial colors are not required. Simply drying the product makes it last for much longer, while its natural coloring is already full of the sun's brightness, absorbed by the wheat grains as they grow in the fields. Furthermore, pasta is one of the most balanced foods in terms of human nutrition. Starch, which makes up the highest percentage of the carbohydrates in pasta, is an excellent source of energy and easy to digest. Nutritionists recommend that the main part of the daily supply of calories for adults should come from carbohydrates, the rest from lipids and proteins. The composition of durum wheat pasta is 74 percent carbohydrates, 1.2 percent fats, and 11.5 percent proteins. Other nutritional needs are then completed by traditional ways of serving pasta. Sprinkling pasta with cheese, for example, supplies the essential amino acid that balances the proteins already in pasta, tossing it with tomatoes and vegetables provides vitamins. It has only to be combined with richer sauces to make it into a single course meal.

THE HISTORY OF PASTA

Who invented pasta? Countless stories and legends surround this famous food. The truth is as simple as its ingredients and is linked to the discovery and use of cereals. Some 7,000 years ago, people began to abandon their nomadic existence and to farm the land. With each harvest, they learned to improve the process, grinding wheat, mixing it with water, rolling it out into thin sheets on hot stones and, eventually, boiling it in sea water. The oldest evidence dates back to 3,000 years BC. The ancient Greeks and Etruscans produced and ate the first types of pasta many years before the birth of Jesus. After varying fortunes, the foundations for pasta's shining future were laid in the eleventh century in Sicily, which became the first center for the production of dried pasta and was responsible for its great popularity and spread. From Sicily pasta traveled across the Mediterranean sea, arriving in Amalfi in the south of Italy and Genoa in the northwest. The oldest documentary evidence for the use of dried pasta dates back to 1316 and was found in Genoa, naming the first pasta maker in history, Maria Borgogno, owner of a house in which "faciebat lasagnas"—"lasagna was made." In 1363, in the inventory of a house in Recco, near Genoa, the first colander is mentioned. When the power of Genoa declined, its famous pasta faded in comparison with that of other areas, notably Naples. For centuries pasta was a luxury foodstuff, and it was only in the seventeenth century that noble maccherone, the generic name for all types of pasta became a common dish among the general population. Its consumption was boosted by the introduction into Europe of tomatoes, used sporadically in the sixteenth century. The unusual appearance of this food, the pasta makers' stalls, and, above all, their entertaining customers, were a source of great curiosity. Despite its fragile structure, spaghetti soon became as strong as only a legend can, and synonymous with Italy and the Italians

CHANGES IN TASTE

For Italians the only way pasta can be cooked is "al dente" or "vierde vierde", as they say in Naples, and overcooked pasta is considered uneatable. "Al dente" literally means "to the tooth", while "vierde vierde" means "very green" or "unripened", both describing pasta that is tender but still firm to the bite. Nowadays, historical recipes for pasta provoke mixed feelings of disapproval and amusement, even those of recognized "masters" such as Martino, cook to a distinguished prelate, who in 1450 recommended very long cooking times—up to two hours—and sauces with salt, cheese, and sweet spices. The same is true for the authors of magnificent sixteenth-century recipe books, such as Cristoforo da Messisbugo or Bartolomeo Scappi, the former specifying one hour's cooking time for dried vermicelli and the latter 30 minutes for maccaraoni alla romanesca, a type of fresh pasta. It was the famous cookbook writer Artusi at the end of the nineteenth century who advised draining spaghetti while it still had some bite. The first ingredients for pasta sauces were still sweet—honey, spices, and cinnamon sugar—although they do not really constitute sauces as they were added raw and after cooking. The only savory ingredient that has always been used is cheese: Cacio, provolone, and Parmesan. It was only in the eighteenth century that savory sauces become known. The first real recipe in which tomatoes are used with pasta dates from 1839 and is by Ippolito Cavalcanti, Duke of Buonvicino in southern Italy.

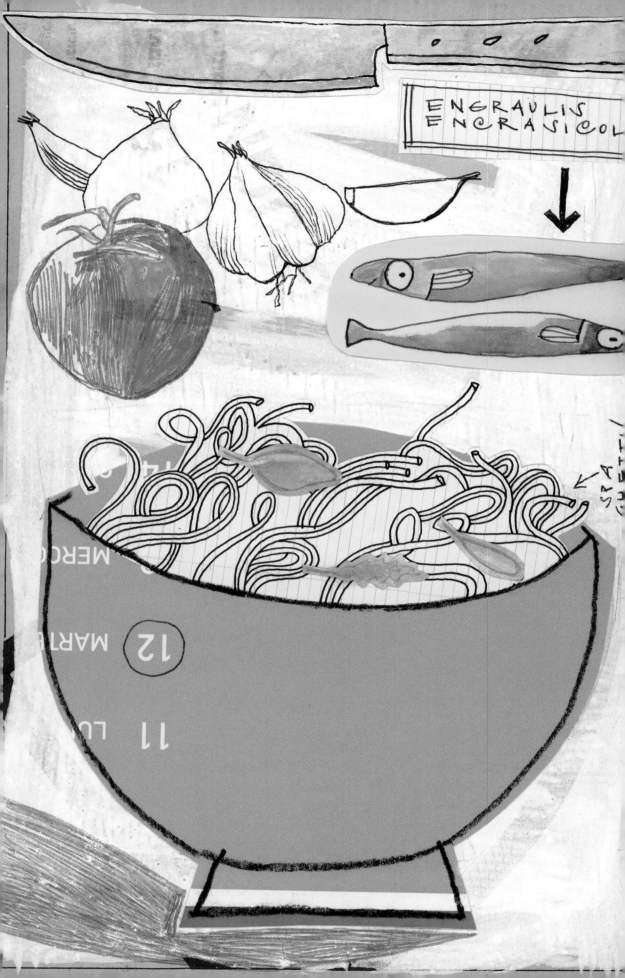

DRIED PASTA

PASTA SECCA

HOW DRIED PASTA
IS PRODUCED

From the time of Roman writer and architect Vitruvius (first century BC) until almost the end of the eighteenth century, flour mills remained virtually unchanged: two wheel-shaped grindstones turned to produce semolina flour from durum wheat. This flour was then added to the tank of a kneading machine, the most important part of the pasta factory, and kneaded with warm water, first by hand and later with a grinding stone. Increased demand led to the invention of the first hydraulic presses in about 1870. Mechanization was gradual, producing hydraulic or steam-powered machines toward the end of the nineteenth century. The first machine able to carry out all phases of the production process was patented in 1933. It was only when artificial drying was introduced that pasta could become a truly industrialized product that could be manufactured throughout Italy. Until then, newly extruded spaghetti was collected, hung on long wooden rods, and exposed to the sun and air to dry, giving pasta factories located in areas with a favorable climate an advantage. This problem vanished with the advent of the drying units of the modern pasta factory, where the semolina flour is hydrated with 30 to 35 percent water to make the dough. Mixing and kneading are then carried out in a vacuum to produce a more compact and translucent dough, which is then driven toward metal cutters to make long strands of pasta. These strands are then hung over rods. Finally, each strand is cut cleanly to the required size, and the resulting pasta is immediately collected on other rods, moving toward the enormous drying unit where the pasta remains for about eight hours until the total moisture content is reduced to below 12.5 percent.

COOKING INSTRUCTIONS

QUANTITY As a general rule, allow 3 ounces per serving for a first course and 3½ ounces per serving for a main course.

PAN Use a large pan, preferably made from aluminum or steel, which should be taller than it is wide.

WATER AND SALT Allow 4 cups water and 2½ teaspoons salt for 3½ ounces pasta.

TIMING Follow the packet instructions but check the pasta at least twice to avoid overcooking.

WATER Only add the pasta when the salted water has reached a rolling boil. If using spaghetti, fan out a handful in the pan then stir immediately. Cover the pan, and as soon as the water comes back to a boil remove the lid and leave uncovered.

COOKING AND PREPARATION TIME The times indicated for both pasta and sauces in the recipes have been calculated as an average. Times vary depending on the type of heat, the quality of the ingredients and the skill of the cook.

SAUCE AND CHEESE If you require cheese, always use fresh and grate it just before sprinkling it on the pasta. Do not overdo the quantity. Those who wish may add more at the table from the cheese dish. It is worth pointing out that metal spoons may rust on contact with fatty particles, so it is better to serve the cheese with a spoon made from another material, such as wood.

LONG
PASTA

BAVETTE

Bavette, along with its smaller relation bavettine, is a type of dried pasta that originated in the city of Genoa in northwest Italy. The name means "little threads" in Italian, as bavette closely resembles slightly convex, flattened spaghetti. It is about 10 inches long, ¹⁄₁₅ inch thick, and ¼ inch wide. Bavette is very similar to linguine, a Ligurian cousin, and is traditionally accompanied by sauces without meat, such as pesto in particular. It also goes well with vegetable and fish sauces. It can be substituted with any other type of long, flat pasta.

SPRING BAVETTE

BAVETTE PRIMAVERILI

Preparation time: 30 minutes
Cooking time: 30 minutes
Serves 4

4 tablespoons butter
2 tablespoons olive oil
2 scallions, chopped
3½ cups shelled peas
14 ounces asparagus, trimmed and cut into short lengths
⅔ cup hot water
12 ounces bavette
⅔ cup grated Parmesan cheese
salt and pepper

Melt half the butter with the oil in a shallow pan. Add the scallions and cook for 3–5 minutes until soft and translucent. Add the peas and asparagus, season with salt and pepper, stir in the hot water, and simmer for 25 minutes. Meanwhile, cook the bavette in plenty of salted boiling water until al dente. Drain, tip into the pan with the vegetables, and mix. Stir in the remaining butter and the Parmesan and serve immediately.

BAVETTE WITH CLAMS AND ZUCCHINI

Preparation time: 30 minutes

Cooking time: 45 minutes

Serves 4

1¾ pound live clams, scrubbed

3 tablespoons olive oil

1 shallot, chopped

1 garlic clove

½ fresh chile, seeded and chopped

11 ounces zucchini, cut into strips

1 tablespoon chopped fresh flat-leaf parsley

scant ½ cup dry white wine

3 tomatoes, peeled and diced

12 ounces bavette

salt

Discard any clams with broken shells or that do not shut immediately when sharply tapped. Put the clams in a dry skillet and cook over high heat for about 5 minutes until they open. Discard any that remain closed. Remove the clams from their shells and set aside. Heat the oil in a pan, add the shallot, the garlic clove and chile and cook over low heat, stirring occasionally, for 5 minutes until soft. Remove and discard the garlic clove, add the clams, zucchini and flat-leaf parsley and cook for 5 minutes. Pour in the wine and cook until it has evaporated. Add the tomatoes, season with salt, and cook for 20–30 minutes until thickened. Cook the bavette in a large pan of salted, boiling water until al dente. Drain, add to the clam and zucchini mixture and toss well. Serve immediately.

PASTA MISTA

BUCATINI

A type of dried pasta from the Lazio region in central Italy, bucatini looks like thick spaghetti and is so called because it is hollow, "buco" meaning "hole" in Italian. Approximately ⅛ inch in diameter, it is made from durum wheat semolina flour. The hole allows air to circulate inside the pasta, which facilitates the slow drying process. It also means that the pasta can absorb a large quantity of sauce, and bucatini is therefore best combined with smooth and aromatic sauces such as Amatriciana (see page 20), the traditional tomato-based recipe from Amatrice, near Rome. In central and southern Italy, where bucatini goes by the name "perciatelli," it is common to combine it with more robust and full-flavored sauces such as ragù (meat sauce), whereas in Sicily it is usually combined with a traditional sardine and wild fennel sauce. Bucatini can be substituted with other types of long, thick pasta.

BUCATINI WITH MOZZARELLA AND EGGPLANT

BUCATINI ALLA MOZZARELLA E MELANZANE

Preparation time: 35 minutes

Cooking time: 35 minutes

Serves 4

1 eggplant, cut into julienne strips

5 tablespoons olive oil

⅓ cup diced pancetta or bacon

4 tomatoes, peeled, seeded and chopped

3½ ounces mozzarella cheese, diced

½–1 fresh chile, seeded and chopped

12 ounces bucatini

1 egg, hard-cooked and finely chopped

salt

Layer the eggplant strips in a colander, sprinkling each layer with salt, and let drain for 30 minutes, then rinse, and pat dry. Heat the oil in a skillet. Add the eggplant strips and cook over medium heat, stirring occasionally, for 5–8 minutes until lightly browned. Remove from the skillet with a slotted spoon and drain. Meanwhile, cook the pancetta or bacon in another skillet over medium-low heat, without adding any oil, for 5 minutes, stirring occasionally. Add the tomatoes and chopped chile to taste to the pancetta and season with salt. Lower the heat and simmer, stirring occasionally, for 15 minutes. Add the eggplant strips and simmer for a few minutes more. Remove the skillet from the heat and stir in the mozzarella. Cook the bucatini in plenty of salted boiling water until al dente. Drain and tip into a warmed serving dish, then pour over the sauce. Sprinkle with the chopped egg and serve immediately.

BUCATINI AMATRICIANA

BUCATINI ALL'AMATRICIANA

Preparation time: 20 minutes

Cooking time: 30 minutes

Serves 4

2 tablespoons olive oil

½ onion, chopped

1 fresh chile, seeded and chopped

3 ounces pig's cheek or pancetta, diced

4 tomatoes, peeled, seeded, and sliced

12 ounces bucatini

½ cup grated pecorino cheese

salt

Heat the oil in a shallow pan. Add the onion and cook over low heat, stirring occasionally, for 5 minutes. Add the chile and pork, increase the heat to medium and cook, stirring frequently, for 5–8 minutes until the meat has browned. Remove the meat from the pan with a slotted spoon and keep warm. Add the tomatoes to the pan and cook, stirring occasionally, for 5 minutes. Cook the bucatini in plenty of salted boiling water until al dente. Drain and tip into a warmed serving dish. Add the meat and the tomato sauce, sprinkle with the pecorino, and toss well. Serve immediately.

Tip: the bucatini can be replaced by other types of pasta— spaghetti, macaroni, vermicelli or rigatoni.

A local and ancient speciality in Lazio in central Italy, this popular dish is still causing controversy. There is wide and fierce debate over whether the sauce is named Matriciana or Amatriciana. Either way most sources agree that it is named after Amatrice, a small town in the province of Rieti. However since Amatrice once belonged to the neighboring region of L'Aquila it is argued that this dish belongs to the cuisine of Abruzzo rather than Lazio.

BUCATINI WITH BREAD CRUMBS

BUCATINI CON LA MOLLICA

Preparation time: 15–20 minutes

Cooking time: 20 minutes

Serves 4

5 salted anchovies

4 tablespoons olive oil

1 tablespoon capers, drained and chopped

1¼ cups black olives, pitted and halved

12 ounces bucatini

3½ ounces coarse bread crumbs, preferably whole wheat

salt and pepper

Pinch the heads of the anchovies between your thumb and index finger and pull them off. Pinch along the top edge of each anchovy and pull out the backbones. Put them into a dish, add water to cover, and let soak for 10 minutes to remove some of the salt. Heat 2 tablespoons of the oil in a pan. Drain the anchovies, add to the pan, and cook, mashing with a wooden spoon until they have disintegrated. Add the capers and olives and cook for 5 minutes more. If you like, you can add ½ ounces pitted green olives and freshly chopped flat-leaf parsley to the sauce. Cook the pasta in plenty of salted boiling water and when it is almost ready, heat the remaining oil in a pan, add the bread crumbs, and cook, stirring frequently, until golden brown. Drain the pasta and tip into a serving dish. Spoon the bread crumb mixture on top, add the anchovy sauce, and toss. Serve immediately.

BUCATINI WITH GREEN TOMATOES

Preparation time: 15 minutes

Cooking time: 45 minutes

Serves 4

2 tablespoons olive oil

generous ½ cup diced pancetta or bacon

½ garlic clove, crushed

1 sprig fresh flat-leaf parsley, chopped

4 green tomatoes, seeded and chopped

3 ounces canned tuna in oil, drained and flaked

12 ounces bucatini

salt

Heat the oil in a pan, add the pancetta or bacon, garlic, and parsley, and cook over medium heat for 5 minutes until lightly browned. Add the tomatoes and tuna, season with salt if necessary, and cook over low heat for 40 minutes. Cook the bucatini in a large pan of salted, boiling water until al dente, then drain, and tip into the pan of sauce. Mix well and serve.

BUCATINI WITH MANTIS SHRIMP

Preparation time: 30 minutes

Cooking time: 40 minutes

Serves 4

1 pound 2 ounces tomatoes, peeled, seeded and diced

8–12 raw mantis shrimp or Mediterranean shrimp

2 tablespoons olive oil

1 garlic clove

pinch of chile powder

scant 1 cup dry white wine

12 ounces bucatini

1 tablespoon finely chopped fresh flat-leaf parsley

salt

Put the tomatoes into a dish, sprinkle with salt, tilt the dish and let drain. Pull the heads off the shrimp if this has not already been done and cut a slit along the back of each down to the tail. Drain the tomatoes and pat dry with paper towels.

Heat the oil in a large pan. Add the garlic clove and chile powder and cook over low heat, stirring frequently, for a few minutes until the garlic is golden brown. Remove the garlic clove with a slotted spoon and discard. Add the tomatoes to the pan, increase the heat to medium-high, and cook, gently stirring occasionally, until softened but not mushy. Add the shrimp and cook for 5 minutes. Pour in the wine, cover, and cook for another 5 minutes.

Meanwhile, cook the pasta in plenty of salted boiling water until al dente. Remove the shrimp from the pan and keep warm. Drain the pasta, tip into the pan with the sauce, and stir. Transfer to a warmed serving dish, put the shrimp on top, sprinkle with the parsley, and serve immediately.

BUCATINI WITH MORTADELLA SAUCE

BUCATINI CON SUGO DI MORTADELLA

Melt the butter in a skillet. Add the mortadella and cook over medium-low heat, stirring frequently, for a few minutes. Beat the egg yolks with the cream in a bowl and season with salt and pepper. Cook the bucatini in plenty of salted boiling water until al dente. Drain, tip into the skillet and toss with the mortadella. Remove the skillet from the heat, sprinkle with the pecorino, pour in the egg and cream mixture, and toss again. Serve immediately.

Preparation time: 15 minutes

Cooking time: 10 minutes

Serves 4

2¼ tablespoons butter

scant 1 cup diced mortadella

2 egg yolks • 2 tablespoons heavy cream

12 ounces bucatini

½ cup grated pecorino cheese • salt and pepper

BUCATINI WITH FENNEL

BUCATINI AL FINOCCHIETTO SELVATICO

Put the raisins into a heatproof bowl, pour in warm water to cover, and let soak. Blanch the fennel in boiling water for 3–4 seconds, then drain, and chop. Heat the oil in a pan. Add the onion and cook over low heat, stirring occasionally, for 5 minutes. Add the fennel and cook, stirring occasionally, for another 10 minutes. Drain the raisins and squeeze out the excess liquid, then add to the pan with the pine nuts and saffron. Cook the bucatini in plenty of salted boiling water until al dente. Drain, tip into a warmed serving dish and pour the sauce on top. Serve immediately.

Preparation time: 15 minutes

Cooking time: 20 minutes

Serves 4

⅓ cup raisins

3½ ounces fennel, trimmed

2 tablespoons olive oil

1 onion, very thinly sliced

¼ cup pine nuts

pinch of saffron threads

12 ounces bucatini • salt

BUCATINI WITH BELL PEPPER SAUCE

BUCATINI CON SALSA AI PEPERONI

Heat the oil in a pan, add the onion and garlic and cook over low heat, stirring occasionally, for 10 minutes until lightly browned. Add the bell peppers, mix well, and cook for another 10 minutes until tender. Transfer to a food processor and process to a purée. Return to the pan, stir in the cream, and season with salt and pepper to taste. Keep warm over very low heat. Cook the bucatini in a large pan of salted, boiling water until al dente, then drain, and tip into the sauce. Cook for 1 minute, stir in the marjoram, and serve.

Preparation time: 20 minutes

Cooking time: 30 minutes

Serves 4

2 tablespoons olive oil

1 pearl onion, chopped

½ garlic clove, chopped

3 red or yellow bell peppers, halved,

seeded and sliced

1 scant ½ cup heavy cream

12 ounces bucatini

2 teaspoons chopped fresh marjoram

salt and pepper

BUCATINI TIMBALE

Cook the bucatini in plenty of salted boiling water until al dente, then drain and tip into a bowl. Preheat the oven to 350°F and grease an ovenproof dish with butter. Melt half the butter in a small pan. Add the onion and cook over low heat, stirring occasionally, for 8–10 minutes until golden brown. Stir in the flour and cook, stirring constantly, for 2 minutes. Gradually stir in the hot stock, season with salt and pepper, and add the cayenne pepper and Worcestershire sauce. Pour the sauce over the pasta and add the ham and Gruyère. Mix well and transfer to the prepared dish. Dot with the remaining butter and bake for 20 minutes. Serve immediately.

Preparation time: 40 minutes
Cooking time: 35 minutes
Serves 4
12 ounces bucatini
4 tablespoons butter, plus extra for greasing
1 onion, finely chopped
¼ cup all-purpose flour
2¼ cups hot stock
pinch of cayenne pepper
dash of Worcestershire sauce
generous 1 cup diced ham
1¼ cups grated Gruyère cheese
salt and pepper

SPICY RED BUCATINI

Heat 2 teaspoons of the oil in a skillet. Add 2 of the garlic cloves and cook over low heat, stirring frequently, until lightly browned. Add the whole chiles and cook, stirring frequently, until they are puffed up and shiny. Remove the chiles and garlic from the skillet with a slotted spoon, transfer to a mortar, and pound to a paste with a pestle. Cook the pasta in plenty of salted boiling water until al dente, then drain. Heat the remaining oil in a pan with the remaining garlic clove until it is lightly browned. Remove and discard the garlic, add the chile and pasta to the pan and quickly toss together. Transfer to a warmed serving dish and serve immediately.

Preparation time: 20 minutes
Cooking time: 25 minutes
Serves 6
½ cup olive oil
3 garlic cloves
6 fresh red chiles
1 pound bucatini
salt

This is a recipe from the rugged, sun-drenched region of Basilicata in southern Italy, an area fragrant with the aromatic herbs that grow wild on the hills and the bright strings of red chiles drying on the doors and walls of houses. Wheat is farmed intensively, leading to a rich tradition of pasta making with many original shapes created by skillful, local hands. The inclusion of the "forte," the ubiquitous chile, is virtually compulsory in every dish.

BUCATINI WITH OLIVES

Preparation time: 15 minutes

Cooking time: 30 minutes

Serves 4

2 tablespoons olive oil

1½ tablespoons butter

1 garlic clove

4 anchovy fillets

2 ounces capers, drained and chopped

9 ounces canned tomatoes, coarsely chopped

scant 1 cup green olives, pitted and cut into rounds

12 ounces bucatini

1 tablespoon black olive paste

salt

chopped fresh flat-leaf parsley, to serve

Heat the oil and butter with a pinch of salt in a pan. Add the garlic and cook over low heat, stirring frequently, until golden brown, then remove, and discard. Add the anchovies, capers, and tomatoes to the pan and cook over low heat, stirring occasionally, for 15 minutes. Add the olives and season lightly with salt if necessary. Mix well and simmer for another 15 minutes. Meanwhile, cook the bucatini in plenty of salted boiling water until al dente. Drain, tip into the pan with the sauce, and stir in the olive paste. Transfer to a warmed serving dish, sprinkle with the parsley, and serve immediately.

BUCATINI WITH PANCETTA

Preparation time: 15 minutes

Cooking time: 20 minutes

Serves 4

1 tablespoon olive oil

2 tablespoons butter

generous ½ cup pancetta

or bacon, diced

3 eggs, lightly beaten

1 cup grated pecorino cheese

1 tablespoon heavy cream

10 ounces bucatini

salt and pepper

Heat the oil with the butter in a large skillet. Add the pancetta or bacon and cook over medium heat, stirring occasionally, for a few minutes until lightly browned. Beat together the eggs, pecorino, and cream in a bowl and lightly season with salt. Cook the bucatini in plenty of salted boiling water until al dente. Drain, tip into the skillet, toss with the pancetta or bacon, and remove the skillet from the heat. Pour the egg mixture over the pasta and toss well. Season with plenty of pepper and serve immediately.

BUCATINI WITH MUSHROOM SAUCE

BUCATINI ALLA SALSA DI FUNGHI

Place the dried mushrooms in a bowl, add warm water to cover, and let soak for 20 minutes, then drain, and squeeze out. Chop half the fresh porcini. Thinly slice the rest and reserve for later. Heat 3 tablespoons of the oil with 1 whole garlic clove in a pan, add the drained dried mushrooms and chopped porcini and cook for about 10 minutes until the mushrooms have released their liquid. Remove and discard the garlic. Add the water and cook for 20 minutes. Transfer the mixture to a food processor and process to a purée, then stir into the ricotta. Put the reserved sliced porcini into a pan with the remaining oil, the remaining garlic, and the tomato paste. Mix well, add 2 tablespoons water, and cook for 15 minutes. Season with salt and pepper. Meanwhile, cook the pasta in a large pan of salted, boiling water until al dente. Drain, place in a warmed serving dish and spoon the ricotta mixture and fried mushrooms on top.

Preparation time: 30 minutes
Cooking time: 45 minutes
Serves 4

½ cup dried mushrooms
7 ounces fresh porcini mushrooms
4 tablespoons olive oil
½ garlic clove, crushed, and 1 whole
garlic clove
⅔ cup water
¼ cup ricotta cheese
1 tablespoon concentrated tomato paste
12 ounces bucatini
salt and pepper

BUCATINI WITH MUSSEL SAUCE

BUCATINI AL SUGO DI COZZE

Scrub the mussels under cold running water and remove the "beards". Discard any with damaged shells or that do not shut immediately when sharply tapped. Put them into a pan, add 2 tablespoons of the oil, cover, and cook over high heat, shaking the pan occasionally, for 4–5 minutes until they open. Remove the pan from the heat and lift out the mussels with a slotted spoon. Discard any that remain shut. Set aside a few mussels in their shells for the garnish and remove the remainder from their shells. Pour the cooking liquid through a cheesecloth-lined strainer into a bowl. Melt the butter with the remaining oil in another pan. Mix the anchovy paste with 1 tablespoon water in a small bowl and stir into the pan. Add the olives, tomatoes, and 3–4 tablespoons of the reserved cooking liquid and simmer for 20 minutes. Stir in the garlic and parsley and simmer for a few minutes more, then remove from the heat. Cook the bucatini in plenty of salted boiling water until al dente. Drain and return to the pan, pour the sauce over, add the shelled mussels, and stir. Season with pepper and divide the mixture among warmed individual serving plates. Garnish with the reserved mussels in their shells and serve immediately.

Preparation time: 30 minutes
Cooking time: 35 minutes
Serves 4

2¼ pounds live mussels
4 tablespoons olive oil
4 tablespoons butter
1 tablespoon anchovy paste
scant 1 cup black olives, pitted and sliced
9 ounces tomatoes, peeled and diced
1 garlic clove, finely chopped
1 tablespoon finely chopped fresh
flat-leaf parsley
12 ounces bucatini
salt and pepper

ANGEL HAIR

Angel hair is a type of dried pasta called capellini or capelli d'angelo in Italian. Angel-hair pasta is very long and looks like thin spaghetti, with a diameter less than 1/15 inch thick. Because of the fineness of its texture, it is often served in a broth, or combined with light sauces. Angel-hair pasta is most suitable for oven-baked recipes including soufflés.

ANGEL HAIR IN CREAM AND CHEESE SAUCE

CAPELLINI IN BIANCO

Preparation time: 10 minutes

Cooking time: 10 minutes • Serves 4

3 tablespoons butter • scant ½ cup heavy cream

14 ounces angel-hair pasta

3 ounces diced Gruyère cheese

salt and freshly ground white pepper

Put the butter into a heatproof bowl set over a pan of simmering water and melt. Stir occasionally while the butter melts. Stir in the cream and heat through for a few minutes. Cook the angel hair in plenty of salted boiling water until al dente. Drain, tip into a warmed serving dish, pour the cream mixture over, add the Gruyère, and stir. Season with pepper and serve immediately.

SOUFFLÉ OF ANGEL HAIR

SOUFFLÉ DI CAPELLINI

Preparation time: 40 minutes

Cooking time: 45 minutes

Serves 4

3 tablespoons butter, plus extra for greasing

⅓ cup all-purpose flour

2¼ cups lukewarm milk

9 ounces angel-hair pasta

3 eggs, separated

¾ cup grated Gruyère cheese

salt

Preheat the oven to 325°F and grease a soufflé dish with butter. Melt the butter in a pan. Stir in the flour and cook over medium heat, stirring constantly, for 2–3 minutes until golden brown. Gradually stir in the milk, a little at a time. Bring to a boil, stirring constantly. Lower the heat, and simmer gently, stirring constantly, for 20 minutes until thickened and smooth. Meanwhile, cook the pasta in plenty of salted boiling water until al dente, then drain. Remove the pan of béchamel sauce from the heat. Beat in the egg yolks, one at a time, then stir in the Gruyère and the pasta, mixing with two forks. Stiffly whisk the egg whites in a grease-free bowl, then fold into the mixture. Gently spoon or pour the pasta mixture into the prepared dish, filing it three-quarters full to allow room for it to rise. Bake for about 20 minutes until well risen and golden. Remove from the oven and serve immediately straight from the dish.

ANGEL HAIR MOLD

SFORMATO DI CAPELLINI

Preparation time: 40 minutes

Cooking time: 1 hour 25 minutes

Serves 4

11 ounces angel-hair pasta

6 tablespoons butter, plus extra for greasing

3 tablespoons all-purpose flour

2 eggs, separated

salt and pepper

For the tomato sauce

9 ounces canned tomatoes

or fresh tomatoes, peeled

pinch of sugar

2 garlic cloves

2 tablespoons olive oil

10 fresh torn basil leaves

salt

Cook the angel hair in plenty of salted boiling water until al dente. Drain, reserving the cooking water, and set aside. Melt ¾ oz of the butter in a small pan. Stir in the flour and cook, stirring constantly, for 2–3 minutes until lightly browned. Gradually stir in scant 1 cup of the reserved cooking water, a little at a time. Bring to a boil, stirring constantly, and lower the heat. Simmer gently, stirring constantly, for 20 minutes until thickened and smooth. Remove from the heat and season with salt. Pour the sauce over the angel hair, add the remaining butter, and season with pepper. Let cool.

To make the tomato sauce, put the tomatoes, with their juice if using canned tomatoes, into a pan, and add the sugar, garlic, and a pinch of salt. Cover and cook over very low heat for about 30 minutes without stirring. Mash the tomatoes with a wooden spoon and, if using canned tomatoes, cook for another 15 minutes. Remove the garlic with a slotted spoon and discard. Remove the pan from the heat and let cool. Stir in the olive oil and basil. Preheat the oven to 350°F and generously grease a cake pan with butter. Stiffly whisk the egg whites in a grease-free bowl. Stir the egg yolks into the cooled pasta mixture, then fold in the egg whites. Pour the mixture into the prepared pan and bake for 10–15 minutes, or until light golden brown. Remove the tin from the oven, turn out onto a warmed serving dish, and serve with the hot tomato sauce on the side.

LINGUINE

Linguine, meaning "little tongues" in Italian, is a type of dried pasta produced industrially or by hand from durum wheat semolina flour and water. It is flat and thick in the center, about 10½ inches long and ⅛ inch wide. It originates from the Liguria region in the northwest of Italy, where the very similar bavette and trenette are also found. Linguine is ideal combined with sauces based on oil and aromatic herbs, but is rarely served with meat. The most traditional dishes are Linguine al Pesto Genovese (Linguine with Genoese Pesto, see page 38), and Linguine ai Frutti di Mare (Seafood Linguine, see page 39) from the Calabria region in the south.

LINGUINE WITH ANCHOVIES

LINGUINE ALLE ACCIUGHE

Pinch the head of an anchovy between your thumb and index finger and pull it off—the innards should come away with it. Pinch along the top edge of the anchovy and pull out the backbone. Repeat with the remaining fish, then rinse them, and pat dry. Heat the oil in a skillet. Add the anchovies and cook over medium heat, turning occasionally, for 4–5 minutes. Remove with a slotted spoon and drain on paper towels. Stir the anchovy paste into the skillet, add the garlic and tomatoes, and cook, stirring occasionally, for 10 minutes. Season to taste with salt and pepper and sprinkle with the parsley. Cook the pasta in plenty of salted boiling water until al dente. Drain, tip into the skillet, add the anchovies and toss gently. Serve immediately.

Preparation time: 30 minutes

Cooking time: 30 minutes

Serves 4

20 fresh anchovies

3 tablespoons extra virgin olive oil

1 teaspoon anchovy paste

2 garlic cloves, crushed

4 plum tomatoes, peeled, seeded, and chopped

2 tablespoons chopped fresh flat-leaf parsley

12 ounces linguine

salt and pepper

LINGUINE WITH BROCCOLI AND PANCETTA

Preparation time: 30 minutes

Cooking time: 30 minutes

Serves 4

2 tablespoons olive oil

2/3 cup diced pancetta or bacon

1 garlic clove, finely chopped

1 pound 5 ounces broccoli, cut into florets

1 tablespoon concentrated tomato paste

2/3 cup vegetable stock

12 ounces linguine

1/2 cup grated Parmesan cheese

salt

Heat the oil in a pan. Add the pancetta or bacon and cook over medium-low heat, stirring occasionally, for 4–5 minutes. Stir in the garlic and half the broccoli and cook, stirring occasionally, for 5 minutes. Stir in the tomato paste and stock, lower the heat, and simmer for 10 minutes until the broccoli is tender but firm. Cook the pasta with the remaining broccoli in plenty of salted boiling water until al dente. Drain, tip into the pan with the sauce, and toss over the heat for a few minutes. Transfer to a warmed serving dish, sprinkle with the Parmesan, and serve immediately.

LINGUINE WITH ARTICHOKES AND HAM

Preparation time: 20 minutes

Cooking time: 30 minutes

Serves 4

4 tablespoons olive oil

1/2 onion, finely chopped

4 baby globe artichokes, trimmed and sliced

5 ounces ham, cut into strips

12 ounces linguine

2/3 cup grated Parmesan cheese

salt and pepper

Heat the oil in a shallow pan. Add the onion and cook over low heat, stirring occasionally, for 5 minutes. Add the artichokes, cover, and cook, stirring occasionally, for 25 minutes, until tender. Stir in the ham, increase the heat to medium, and cook for another 2 minutes. Remove the pan from the heat. Cook the linguine in plenty of salted boiling water until al dente. Drain, tip into a warmed serving dish, and toss with the artichokes and ham. Sprinkle with the Parmesan and serve immediately.

LINGUINE WITH CAVIAR

Melt the butter in a shallow pan. Add the onion and cook over low heat, stirring occasionally, for 5 minutes. Drizzle with the vodka and cook gently until the alcohol has evaporated, then season with salt and pepper. Cook the linguine in plenty of salted boiling water until al dente. Drain, tip into the pan with the sauce, and stir well. Transfer to individual warmed plates, form a "nest" in the middle of each and add a heaping teaspoon of caviar or lumpfish roe. Alternatively, you can mix the caviar or lumpfish roe in the pasta. Sprinkle with the finely chopped parsley and serve immediately.

Tip: Fresh caviar should never have a fishy smell or piquant taste. The eggs should be whole and individual, not sticky or dry.

Preparation time: 15 minutes

Cooking time: 25 minutes

Serves 4

4 tablespoons butter

1 small onion, thinly sliced

scant ½ cup vodka

12 ounces linguine

2 tablespoons caviar or lumpfish roe

finely chopped fresh flat-leaf parsley, to garnish

salt and pepper

LINGUINE WITH CUTTLEFISH

To clean the cuttlefish, cut off the tentacles just in front of the eyes, squeeze out the beak from the center, and discard. Separate and skin the tentacles and pull off the skin from the body. Cut along the back and remove and discard the cuttlebone. Open out the body sac and carefully remove the ink sac, and reserve. Remove and discard the innards and head. Cut the body sacs and tentacles into strips. Heat the oil in a pan. Add the cuttlefish and onion and cook over low heat, stirring occasionally, for 5 minutes. Pour in the wine and cook until the alcohol has evaporated. Add the tomato, season with salt and pepper, cover, and simmer for about 20 minutes. Squeeze the ink into the pan, discarding the ink sacs, and cook for 5 minutes. Stir in the parsley and cook for another 20 minutes until the sauce has thickened. Cook the linguine in plenty of salted boiling water until al dente. Drain, tip into a warmed serving dish, add the cuttlefish sauce, and serve.

The coastal region of Liguria in northwest Italy has mild temperatures throughout the year. The Gulf Stream brings cooling breezes in summer and the surrounding mountains protect the area from low temperatures during the winter. Therefore the tomato season begins here in May, rather than running from June to September as in other regions.

Preparation time: 1 hour

Cooking time: 50 minutes

Serves 4

12 ounces small cuttlefish,
about 4–4½ inches long

2 tablespoons olive oil

1 onion, chopped

scant 1 cup dry white wine

3 tablespoons peeled and diced tomato

1 tablespoon chopped fresh flat-leaf parsley

12 ounces linguine

salt and pepper

LINGUINE WITH CRAB AND SALMON

LINGUINE AL GRANCHIO E SALMONE

Melt the butter in a small pan. Add the crab meat and cook over low heat for a few minutes, then add the tomatoes, and cook, stirring occasionally, for another 10 minutes. Add the strips of salmon, sprinkle with vodka, and cook until the alcohol has evaporated. Stir and remove the pan from the heat. Cook the linguine in plenty of salted boiling water until al dente. Drain, toss with the sauce, and serve immediately.

Preparation time: 10 minutes

Cooking time: 20 minutes

Serves 4

4 tablespoons butter

4 ounces canned crab meat, drained

4 plum tomatoes, peeled and diced

3 ounces smoked salmon, cut into strips

dash of vodka

10 ounces linguine

salt

LINGUINE WITH CHAMPAGNE

LINGUINE ALLO CHAMPAGNE

Melt the butter in a shallow pan over low heat. Add the onion and pancetta or bacon and cook over low heat, stirring occasionally, for 5 minutes. Pour in the champagne, increase the heat to medium, and cook until the alcohol has evaporated. Stir in the cream, season with salt and pepper, and heat through for a few minutes. Cook the linguine in plenty of salted boiling water until al dente. Drain, transfer to a warmed serving dish, pour the sauce over, and sprinkle with the Parmesan. Serve immediately.

Preparation time: 20 minutes

Cooking time: 20 minutes

Serves 4

3 tablespoons butter

1 onion, finely chopped

1/3 cup finely chopped pancetta or bacon

scant 1 cup champagne

2 tablespoons heavy cream

12 ounces linguine

1/2 cup grated Parmesan cheese

salt and pepper

SOUR CREAM LINGUINE

LINGUINE ALLA PANNA ACIDA

Melt the butter in a shallow pan over low heat. Stir in the sour cream and cook for 1 minute, then sprinkle with the paprika and nutmeg. Cook the linguine in plenty of salted boiling water until al dente. Drain, tip into the sauce, and toss over the heat for a few minutes. Serve immediately with the Parmesan.

Preparation time: 5 minutes

Cooking time: 15 minutes

Serves 4

4 tablespoons butter

scant 1 cup sour cream

1 tablespoon paprika • pinch of freshly grated nutmeg

12 ounces linguine

grated Parmesan cheese, to serve • salt

SEAFOOD LINGUINE

37

LINGUINE WITH GENOESE PESTO

LINGUINE AL PESTO GENOVESE

Preparation time: 10 minutes

Cooking time: 10 minutes

Serves 4

12 ounces linguine

2 potatoes, cut into thin batons

2 ounces French green beans

For the pesto

25 fresh basil leaves

2 garlic cloves, crushed

5 tablespoons olive oil

⅓ cup grated pecorino cheese

⅓ cup grated Parmesan cheese

salt

To make the pesto, put the basil, garlic, a pinch of salt and the oil into a food processor and process briefly at medium speed. Add both cheeses and process again until blended. Alternatively, pound the ingredients in a mortar with a pestle until a smooth paste is obtained. Cook the linguine, potatoes and beans together in a large pan of salted boiling water until al dente, then drain. Toss with the pesto and serve.

Tip: Instead of linguine, you can also make this recipe with reginette, another traditional type of pasta from the Liguria region in northwest Italy.

LINGUINE WITH LOBSTER

LINGUINE ALL'ARAGOSTA

Preparation time: 1 hour

Cooking time: 40 minutes

Serves 4

1 live lobster, about 1½ pounds

2 tablespoons olive oil

1 garlic clove

1 onion, finely chopped

5 ounces tomatoes, peeled, seeded and chopped

pinch of dried oregano

12 ounces linguine

salt

If you put the lobster into the freezer for 2 hours before cooking, it will die painlessly from hypothermia. Plunge the lobster into a large pan of boiling salted water, cover, bring back to a boil, and boil for 10 minutes. Remove from the pan and let cool. Put the lobster, belly side down, on a cutting board and cut it in half. Open it out and remove the tail meat from both halves of the shell. Remove the dark intestinal tract with the point of the knife and discard. Snap off the claws and break them into pieces at the joints, then crack the shells with a heavy knife. Remove the meat. Cut all the lobster meat into small pieces. Heat the oil in a shallow pan. Add the garlic clove and cook over low heat, stirring frequently, until lightly browned. Remove with a slotted spoon and discard. Add the onion, tomatoes, and oregano to the pan, season with salt, and simmer, stirring occasionally, for 10–15 minutes until thickened. Cook the linguine in plenty of salted boiling water until al dente. Drain, tip into the sauce, and toss. Add the diced lobster, toss again, and serve immediately.

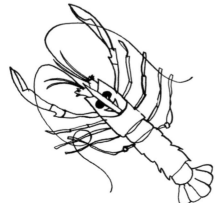

LINGUINE WITH SMOKED SALMON AND TOMATO SAUCE

LINGUINE AL SALMONE E SALSA DI POMODORO

Preparation time: 25 minutes

Cooking time: 30 minutes

Serves 4

3 tablespoons butter

½ onion, chopped • ½ cup brandy

1 pound 2 ounces fresh tomatoes, peeled and diced, or canned chopped tomatoes

4 ounces smoked salmon, cut into strips

scant ½ cup heavy cream

12 ounces linguine • salt and pepper

Melt the butter in a pan. Add the onion and cook over low heat, stirring occasionally, for 5 minutes. Pour in the brandy and cook until the alcohol has evaporated. Add the tomatoes and simmer, stirring occasionally, for about 10 minutes until thickened. Add the salmon, season with pepper, stir in the cream and heat gently. Meanwhile, cook the linguine in plenty of salted boiling water until al dente. Drain, tip into the pan with the sauce and toss for a few seconds. Transfer to a warmed serving dish and serve immediately.

SEAFOOD LINGUINE

LINGUINE AI FRUTTI DI MARE

Preparation time: 30 minutes

Cooking time: 25 minutes

Serves 4

11 ounces live mussels

14 ounces live clams

5 tablespoons olive oil

3 garlic cloves, crushed

pinch of dried oregano

12 ounces linguine

14 ounces canned chopped tomatoes

1 tablespoon chopped fresh basil

salt and pepper

Scrub the mussels and clams under cold running water and pull off the "beards" from the mussels. Discard any with broken shells or that do not shut immediately when sharply tapped. Preheat the oven to 425°F. Heat 1 tablespoon of the oil in a skillet. Add 1 of the chopped garlic cloves and the oregano. When hot, add the clams and cook over high heat, shaking the skillet occasionally, for 3–5 minutes until they open. Remove the skillet from the heat and lift out the clams with a slotted spoon. Reserve the cooking juices. Heat 1 tablespoon of the remaining oil in another skillet. Add the mussels and cook over high heat, shaking the skillet occasionally, for 5 minutes until they open. Remove from the heat and lift out the mussels with a slotted spoon. Discard any shellfish that remain shut and remove the remainder from their shells.

Cook the pasta in plenty of salted boiling water until al dente, then drain. Heat the remaining oil in a large pan. Add the garlic and cook over low heat, stirring frequently, for 1 minute, then add tomatoes, linguine, shellfish, basil, and 1 tablespoon of the reserved cooking juices. Season with salt and pepper and tip the mixture into the center of a large sheet of aluminum foil. Bring up the sides of the aluminum foil and fold over the edges securely to close. Put the parcel on a cookie sheet and bake for 5 minutes. Serve immediately.

REGINETTE

Reginette is a type of dried pasta originating from Naples in the south of Italy. It is long, flat and ½ inch wide, similar to tagliatelle, but with at least one side curled. The name, meaning "little queens," refers to Princess Mafalda of Savoy (1125–1158), in whose honor the shape was created. This type of pasta is also known as mafaldine, after her. In the Liguria region, in the northwest, the term reginette can also be used for tagliolini and linguine. Reginette is thought to complement any sauce, but its shape suits thicker and full-bodied sauces particularly well.

DELICATE REGINETTE

REGINETTE DELICATE

Preparation time: 20 minutes
Cooking time: 25 minutes
Serves 4

scant 1 cup baby peas • 3 tablespoons olive oil
1 small shallot, very finely chopped
16 small langoustines, shelled and deveined
(see Spaghetti with Langoustines, page 63)
12 ounces reginette • 2 tomatoes, peeled and diced
salt and freshly ground white pepper

Cook the peas in lightly salted boiling water for about 10 minutes until tender, then drain. Meanwhile, heat the oil in a pan. Add the shallot and cook over medium heat, stirring occasionally, for 3 minutes. Add the langoustines, season with salt and white pepper, lower the heat, and cook for 6–7 minutes. Cook the reginette in plenty of salted boiling water until al dente. Drain, tip into the pan with the langoustines, add the peas, and stir. Add the tomatoes and cook for 2 minutes, shaking the pan. Transfer to a warmed serving dish and serve immediately.

REGINETTE WITH ONION AND ARTICHOKE SAUCE

REGINETTE ALLA SALSA DI CIPOLLE E CARCIOFI

Preparation time: 30 minutes
Cooking time: 35 minutes
Serves 4

2 tablespoons lemon juice
4 young globe artichokes
2 tablespoons olive oil
7 ounces onions, chopped
scant 1 cup dry white wine
½ cup hot water
12 ounces reginette • ½ cup butter
salt and pepper
grated Parmesan cheese, to serve

Half fill a bowl with water and stir in the lemon juice. Trim the artichokes, slice, and put into the bowl to prevent discoloration. Heat the oil in a large pan. Add the onions, season with salt, and cook over low heat for 5 minutes. Drain the artichokes, add to the pan, and cook for 5–8 minutes until softened. Pour in the wine and cook until the alcohol has evaporated. Pour in the hot water, cover, and simmer for about 25 minutes until the artichokes are tender and the sauce is thicker. Meanwhile, cook the pasta in plenty of salted boiling water until al dente. Drain, tip into the pan with the sauce, add the butter, and season with pepper. Toss over the heat for a few minutes, then transfer to a warmed serving dish. Serve immediately with the Parmesan.

SPAGHETTI

Spaghetti is the classic dried pasta shape. The name means "small strings" and is Italy's favorite dish, with Italians eating an average of 62 pounds each per year. Annual production in Italy reaches almost three million tons, of which half is exported. According to Italian law, only durum wheat semolina flour is to be used for making spaghetti. However, European laws now permit the use of soft wheat flour, so check the label carefully. The thickness of spaghetti varies, but it is usually about ¹⁄₁₂ inch thick with a length of 10 inches. Thinner versions include spaghettini, which is ¹⁄₁₅ inch thick and is often called vermicelli in southern Italy. Good quality spaghetti can be recognized by its appearance and texture before tasting it. It should be an amber yellow color, with a shiny surface, and a firm consistency. Many Italian cooks believe spaghetti should not be drained in a colander, but simply lifted out of the water to keep it moist before the sauce is added. Spaghetti goes well with tomato-based sauces, fish and shellfish sauces, but surprisingly not Bolognese sauce, which is traditionally served with tagliatelle. Perhaps the best-known and most widely cooked spaghetti recipe is Spaghetti alla Carbonara (Spaghetti Carbonara, see page 51), from the central Italian region of Lazio.

SPAGHETTI FROM CIOCIARA

SPAGHETTI ALLA CIOCIARA

Preparation time: 20 minutes
Cooking time: 25 minutes
Serves 4

2 tablespoons olive oil
2 ripe tomatoes, chopped
1 red bell pepper, seeded and cut into julienne strips
scant ½ cup green olives, pitted
12 ounces spaghetti
½ cup grated Parmesan cheese
salt and pepper

Heat the oil in a pan. Add the tomatoes, red bell pepper and olives and season with salt and pepper. Cook over low heat, stirring occasionally and adding a little hot water if necessary, for 15 minutes. Cook the spaghetti in plenty of salted boiling water until al dente. Drain, tip into the pan with the sauce, and toss well over the heat for 1 minute. Sprinkle with the Parmesan and serve immediately.

It was not until the end of the eighteenth century that growing tomatoes as a food crop became common in Europe, mainly in France and southern Italy. However, in France tomatoes were eaten only at the royal court, whereas in Naples they quickly became popular amongst ordinary people, who had long suffered from food shortages.

GREEN SPAGHETTI

SPAGHETTI VERDI

Heat the oil with 1 tablespoon water in a skillet. Add the zucchini and cook over medium-low heat, stirring occasionally, for 15 minutes. Add a sprig of parsley, the basil leaves, and oregano and season with salt and pepper. Cook the spaghetti in plenty of salted boiling water until al dente. Drain, tip into a warmed serving dish, add the zucchini and Parmesan, and toss well. Garnish with the remaining parsley sprigs and serve immediately.

Preparation time: 25 minutes
Cooking time: 25 minutes
Serves 4
2 tablespoons olive oil
3 cups sliced zucchini
4–5 sprigs fresh flat-leaf parsley
4 fresh basil leaves, torn
pinch of dried oregano
12 ounces spaghetti
½ cup grated Parmesan cheese
salt and pepper

PIQUANT SPAGHETTI

SPAGHETTI PICCANTI

Pinch the heads of the anchovies between your thumb and index finger and pull them off. Pinch along the top edge of each anchovy and pull out the backbones. Put them into a dish, add water to cover, and let soak for 10 minutes to remove some of the salt. Meanwhile, heat the oil in a skillet. Add the garlic cloves and cook over low heat, stirring frequently, until golden brown. Remove the garlic with a slotted spoon and discard. Add the capers and olives to the skillet and cook, stirring occasionally, for 5 minutes. Drain the anchovies, and cook, mashing with a wooden spoon until they have disintegrated. Meanwhile, cook the spaghetti in plenty of salted boiling water until al dente. Drain, tip into the skillet, and toss well. Sprinkle with the parsley and serve immediately.

Preparation time: 20 minutes
Cooking time: 15 minutes
Serves 4
3½ ounces salted anchovies
4 tablespoons olive oil
2 garlic cloves
2 ounces capers, drained
scant 1 cup black olives, pitted and sliced
12 ounces spaghetti
chopped fresh flat-leaf parsley, to garnish
salt

PEPERONCINO
PICCANTE

43

RED SPAGHETTI

SPAGHETTI ROSSI

Preparation time: 20 minutes
Cooking time: 1 hour 15 minutes
Serves 4

2¼ pounds plum tomatoes, diced
1 garlic clove, crushed
1 onion, chopped
1 carrot, chopped
1 celery stalk, chopped
2 tablespoons butter
2 tablespoons olive oil
14 ounces spaghetti
fresh basil leaves, to garnish
grated Parmesan cheese, to serve
salt and pepper

Put the tomatoes, garlic, onion, carrot, and celery into a pan and add a pinch of salt. Bring to a boil, stirring frequently, then lower the heat, and simmer, stirring occasionally, for 1 hour. Remove the pan from the heat and spoon the mixture into a food processor or blender. Process to a purée and season to taste with salt and pepper. Melt the butter with the oil in a skillet. Add the vegetable purée and cook over low heat, stirring constantly, for a few minutes. Cook the spaghetti in plenty of salted boiling water until al dente. Drain, tip into a warmed serving dish, and spoon the sauce over it. Garnish with a few small basil leaves and serve immediately with the Parmesan.

Tip: To enhance the flavor, return the spaghetti to the pan in which it was cooked after draining, pour the sauce over it and mix well. The residual heat of the pan will add to the creaminess.

RUSTIC–STYLE SPAGHETTI

SPAGHETTI RUSTICI

Preparation time: 15 minutes
Cooking time: 10 minutes
Serves 4

1 tablespoon olive oil
2 tablespoons hot mustard
2 tablespoons chopped fresh flat-leaf parsley
3½ ounces canned tuna, drained and flaked
1 small red onion, finely chopped
3¼ cup cooked or canned
borlotti beans, drained
1 garlic clove, crushed
12 ounces spaghetti
1 bell pepper, seeded and cut into strips
salt and pepper

Whisk together the oil, mustard, and parsley in a bowl and season with salt and pepper. Put the tuna, onion, beans, and garlic into a tureen. Cook the spaghetti in plenty of salted boiling water until al dente. Drain, tip into the tureen, and toss well. Pour the oil dressing over the pasta, garnish with the bell pepper strips, and serve immediately.

SAFFRON SPAGHETTI WITH YOGURT

SPAGHETTI GIALLI ALLO YOGURT

Melt the butter in a shallow pan. Add the shallots and cook over low heat, stirring occasionally, for 15 minutes. Add the cream and cook, stirring occasionally, for another 15 minutes. Stir in the yogurt, season with salt and pepper, and cook until thickened. Bring a large pan of salted water to a boil, stir in the saffron, add the spaghetti, and cook until al dente. Drain, tip into the pan with the sauce, and toss well. Transfer to a warm serving dish and serve immediately, handing the Parmesan separately.

Preparation time: 15 minutes

Cooking time: 45 minutes

Serves 4

3 tablespoons butter

3 shallots, thinly sliced

2 tablespoons heavy cream

5 tablespoons plain yogurt

pinch of saffron threads

12 ounces spaghetti

grated Parmesan cheese, to serve

salt and pepper

SPAGHETTI WITH HAM AND MASCARPONE

*SPAGHETTI AL PROSCIUTTO
E MASCARPONE*

Cook the spaghetti in plenty of salted boiling water until al dente. Meanwhile, beat together the egg yolks, mascarpone, Parmesan, and ham in a bowl and season with salt and pepper. If necessary, stir in a little of the pasta cooking water to give a creamy consistency. Drain the pasta, tip it into a tureen, pour the sauce over, and toss well. Serve immediately.

Preparation time: 10 minutes

Cooking time: 10 minutes

Serves 4

12 ounces spaghetti

2 egg yolks

⅓ cup mascarpone cheese

⅔ cup grated Parmesan cheese

generous ½ cup diced ham

salt and pepper

GOLDEN SPAGHETTI

SPAGHETTI DORATI

Cook the spaghetti in plenty of salted boiling water until al dente. Meanwhile, beat the cream with the Parmesan and saffron in a bowl. Melt the butter in a pan, add the cream mixture, and heat gently. Drain the spaghetti, add to the pan, and heat through for a few minutes, then serve.

Preparation time: 10 minutes

Cooking time: 15 minutes

Serves 4

12 ounces spaghetti

1 cup heavy cream

3 tablespoons grated Parmesan cheese

pinch of saffron threads

3 tablespoons butter

salt

SPAGHETTI FROM NORCIA

SPAGHETTI ALLA NURSINA

Preparation time: 15 minutes
Cooking time: 15 minutes
Serves 4
2 fresh anchovies
scant ½ cup olive oil
3½ ounces black truffles, sliced
12 ounces spaghetti
1 sprig chopped fresh flat-leaf parsley
salt

Pinch the heads of the anchovies between your thumb and index finger and pull them off, taking the innards with them. Pinch along the top edge of each anchovy and pull out the backbones. Cut each anchovy into 2 fillets. Heat the oil in a shallow pan. Add the anchovies and cook over medium heat for a couple of minutes until tender but not crisp. Remove from the heat and add the truffles to the pan. Cook gently for a few minutes, making sure that the mixture does not boil. Cook the spaghetti in plenty of salted boiling water until al dente. Drain, tip into a warmed serving dish, add the sauce, and toss. Sprinkle with the chopped parsley and serve.

Tip: Truffles must not be kept for long as the aroma quickly disappears or, at least, fades. Store for a maximum of 2 days in an airtight glass jar, after carefully brushing but not washing them. Add a handful of uncooked rice to the jar. This will absorb some of their aroma and if used later for risotto, will produce a very fragrant dish.

This is possibly the simplest dish in Umbrian cuisine, yet it is one that requires careful preparation. Using a little too much garlic, pan-frying rather than gently sautéing the anchovies, or using poor quality olive oil, can result in a mediocre dish. The choice of truffles is crucial. The most famous are black truffles from Norcia—which gives this dish its name—and Spoleto, on sale from Christmas Eve to March. During the rest of the year truffles have less flavor.

SPAGHETTI AND SHELLFISH PARCEL

SPAGHETTI AI FRUTTI DI MARE
NEL CARTOCCIO

Preparation time: 40 minutes

Cooking time: 35 minutes

Serves 4

10 live clams

2 tablespoons olive oil

2 garlic cloves

1 fresh chile

4 ripe tomatoes, peeled and chopped

4 baby octopuses, cleaned and sliced

10 baby squid, cleaned and sliced

8 large raw shrimp, peeled and deveined

(see Spaghetti with Langoustines, page 63)

12 ounces spaghetti

1 sprig fresh basil, torn

1 sprig chopped fresh flat-leaf parsley

salt and pepper

Scrub the clams under cold running water. Discard any with damaged shells or that do not shut immediately when sharply tapped. Heat the oil in a pan with the garlic cloves. When the garlic turns golden brown remove with a slotted spoon and discard. Add the whole chile and clams to the pan, cover, and cook over high heat, shaking the pan occasionally, for 4–5 minutes until the shells open. Lift out the shellfish with a slotted spoon and when cool enough to handle remove the clams from the shells. Discard any that remain shut. Remove the chile from the pan and discard. Add the tomatoes, octopuses, and squid to the pan, season with salt and pepper, and cook, stirring occasionally, for a few minutes. Stir in the clams and the shrimp. Preheat the oven to 350°F. Meanwhile, cook the spaghetti in plenty of salted boiling water until al dente. Drain, tip into the pan of seafood, sprinkle with the basil and parsley, and toss, then remove the pan from the heat. Tip the mixture onto the middle of a large sheet of wax paper. Bring up the sides and fold over the edges to seal. Transfer the parcel to a cookie sheet and bake for 5 minutes. Transfer the parcel to a warmed serving dish, open the top slightly, and serve immediately.

Tip: To add the characteristic flavor of garlic sautéed in oil and, at the same time, avoiding its indigestibility, lightly crush the unpeeled clove with a fork before adding it to the pan. Always remove and discard the clove before serving.

SPAGHETTI BAKED IN ALUMINUM FOIL

SPAGHETTI AL CARTOCCIO

Preparation time: 15 minutes

Cooking time: 35 minutes

Serves 4

11 ounces plum tomatoes, peeled and diced

2 tablespoons olive oil • 2 tablespoons lemon juice

1 tablespoon capers, drained

1 garlic clove, crushed

1 sprig finely chopped fresh basil

12 ounces spaghetti • salt and pepper

Preheat the oven to 350°F. Put the tomatoes, oil, lemon juice, and capers into a skillet, season with salt and pepper, and cook over low heat, stirring occasionally, for 15 minutes until thickened. Stir in the garlic and basil. Cook the spaghetti in plenty of salted boiling water until al dente. Drain, return to the pan, pour in the sauce, and toss. Tip the mixture on to the center of a large sheet of aluminum foil, bring up the sides, and fold over securely to seal. Put the parcel on a cookie sheet and bake for 15 minutes. Serve immediately straight from the parcel.

SPAGHETTI MARINARA

SPAGHETTI ALLA MARINARA

Remove and discard the skin from the fish and cut the flesh into pieces, then put them into a food processor, and process to a purée. Scrub the clams under cold running water and discard any with broken shells or that do not shut immediately when sharply tapped. Heat the oil in a pan. Add the garlic cloves and cook over low heat, stirring frequently, for a few minutes until browned. Remove with a slotted spoon and discard. Add the tomatoes to the pan, season with salt and pepper, and cook, stirring occasionally, for 15 minutes. Stir the puréed fish into the pan, followed by the clams and shrimp. Cook for another 10 minutes and discard any clams that remain shut. Cook the spaghetti in plenty of salted boiling water until al dente. Drain, toss with the sauce, and serve immediately, sprinkled with parsley.

Preparation time: 25 minutes
Cooking time: 30 minutes
Serves 4

1 scorpion fish or ocean perch, or rockfish cleaned and boned
7 ounces live clams
3 tablespoons olive oil
2 garlic cloves
6 plum tomatoes, peeled and diced
7 ounces raw shrimp, peeled and chopped
12 ounces spaghetti
chopped fresh flat-leaf parsley, to garnish
salt

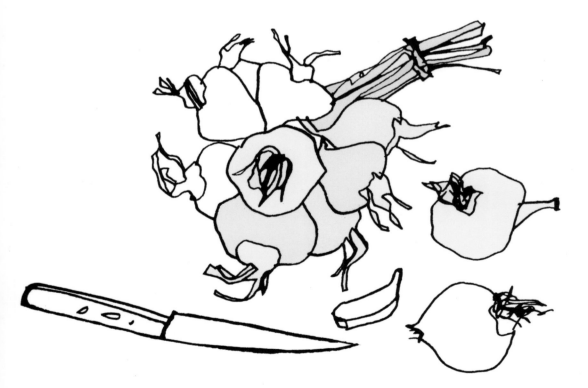

SPAGHETTI CARBONARA

Melt the butter in a pan, add the pancetta and garlic, and cook until the garlic turns brown. Remove and discard the garlic. Meanwhile, cook the spaghetti in a large pan of salted boiling water until al dente, then drain, and add to the pancetta. Remove the pan from the heat, pour in the eggs, add half the Parmesan and half the pecorino, and season with pepper. Mix well so that the egg coats the spaghetti. Add the remaining cheese, mix again, and serve.

Along with Bucatini Amatriciana (see page 20), this is among the best-known dishes of Lazio in central Italy. It is named "Carbonara" because it was a staple meal of the workers who collected wood in the Appenine Mountains to make charcoal or "carbone."

Preparation time: 30 minutes

Cooking time: 20 minutes

Serves 4

2 tablespoons butter

generous ½ cup diced pancetta

1 garlic clove

12 ounces spaghetti

2 eggs, beaten

½ cup grated Parmesan cheese

½ cup grated pecorino cheese

salt and pepper

SPAGHETTI WITH ANCHOVY AND BLACK TRUFFLE SAUCE

Heat the oil in a pan. Add the garlic clove and cook over low heat, stirring frequently, for a few minutes until lightly browned, then remove the garlic with a slotted spoon and discard. Stir the anchovy paste into the oil, then add the tomatoes and season with salt and pepper. Stir well and simmer for about 15 minutes until thickened. Cook the spaghetti in plenty of salted boiling water until al dente. Drain, return to the pan, pour the anchovy sauce over and sprinkle with the parsley. Transfer to a warmed serving dish, sprinkle with the truffle slices and serve immediately.

Preparation time: 10 minutes

Cooking time: 30 minutes

Serves 4

3 tablespoons olive oil

1 garlic clove

1 tablespoon anchovy paste

14 ounces tomatoes, peeled,

seeded and chopped

12 ounces spaghetti

1 tablespoon chopped fresh flat-leaf parsley

1 ounce black truffle, thinly sliced

salt and pepper

SPAGHETTI PARCEL WITH CLAMS AND BOTTARGA

SPAGHETTI AL CARTOCCIO
CON VONGOLE E BOTTARGA

Preparation time: 30 minutes

Cooking time: 40 minutes

Serves 4

2¼ pounds live clams

2 garlic cloves

1 fresh flat-leaf parsley sprig

scant 1 cup dry white wine

scant ½ cup olive oil

12 ounces spaghetti

1 ounce bottarga (salted pressed gray mullet
or tuna roe), grated

1 teaspoon chopped fresh flat-leaf parsley

salt and pepper

Preheat the oven to 425°F. Scrub the clams under cold running water. Discard any with damaged shells or that do not shut immediately when sharply tapped. Put them into a large pan with the garlic cloves and parsley sprig. Pour in the wine, cover, and cook over high heat, shaking the pan occasionally, for 3–5 minutes until the clams open. Drain, reserving the cooking liquid, and discard any clams that remain shut. Set aside a few whole clams for the garnish and remove the remainder from their shells. Pour the reserved cooking liquid through a cheesecloth-lined strainer into a clean pan. Add the olive oil, season lightly with salt and pepper, and bring to a boil over medium heat. Continue to boil until reduced and thickened. Cook the spaghetti in plenty of salted boiling water until al dente. Drain, tip into the reduced cooking liquid, and toss. Turn off the heat and stir in the bottarga, the parsley, and the shelled clams. Spoon the mixture into the center of a large sheet of wax paper, garnish with the whole clams, bring up the sides of the paper, and fold over the edges securely to seal. Put the parcel onto a cookie sheet and bake for 5 minutes. Transfer the parcel to a warmed serving dish, open slightly at the top, and serve immediately.

Tip: Chopped parsley should be added after the sauce is cooked, otherwise it loses some of its color and flavor. Use carefully in sautéed vegetables as it burns easily and becomes bitter.

SPAGHETTI WITH ANCHOVIES

SPAGHETTI CON ACCIUGHE

Preparation time: 30 minutes

Cooking time: 30 minutes

Serves 4

5 ounces salted anchovies

1 sprig fresh flat-leaf parsley

½ garlic clove

2 tablespoons olive oil

12 ounces spaghetti

salt and pepper

Pinch the heads of the anchovies between your thumb and forefinger and pull them off. Pinch along the top edge of each anchovy and pull out the backbones. Put them into a dish, add water to cover and let soak for 10 minutes to remove some of the salt. Chop the filleted anchovies very finely with the parsley and garlic, then put the mixture in a salad bowl and stir in the olive oil. Cook the spaghetti in a large pan of salted boiling water until al dente, then drain and tip into the salad bowl. Toss well and season with pepper.

SPAGHETTI WITH BLACK OLIVES AND LEMON

SPAGHETTI CON OLIVE NERE E LIMONE

Preparation time: 10 minutes

Cooking time: 5 minutes

Serves 4

10 ounces spaghetti

30 black olives, pitted and chopped

10 fresh basil leaves, torn

juice of 1 large lemon, strained

6–8 tablespoons extra virgin olive oil

salt

Cook the spaghetti in plenty of salted boiling water until al dente. Drain, return to the pan, and immediately add the olives, basil, lemon juice, and enough oil to season. Toss well and serve immediately or let cool, then chill in the refrigerator. This makes an excellent summery first course.

Extra virgin olive oil has been a feature in Italian cooking for over four thousand years. Its unique flavor and aroma have made it the king of vegetable oils. Whether used in salad dressings or in cooking, it is ideal because of its natural flavor, digestibility and nutritional value.

SPAGHETTI WITH BOTTARGA

SPAGHETTI ALLA BOTTARGA

Preparation time: 10 minutes

Cooking time: 10 minutes

Serves 4

¾ tablespoon olive oil • ½ garlic clove

2½ ounces tuna loin, diced

6 tablespoons white wine

4 plum tomatoes, peeled and diced

1 ounce bottarga

(salted pressed gray mullet or tuna roe), crumbled

10 ounces spaghetti or spaghettini

chopped fresh flat-leaf parsley, to garnish • salt

Heat the oil in a skillet. Add the garlic and cook for a few minutes until browned, then remove the garlic with a slotted spoon, and discard. Add the tuna to the skillet and stir. Pour in the wine and cook until the alcohol has evaporated. Add the tomatoes and bottarga and mix well. Cook the spaghetti in plenty of salted boiling water until al dente. Drain, tip into a warmed serving dish, and toss with the sauce. Sprinkle with parsley and serve immediately.

SPAGHETTI WITH CHEESE AND PEPPER

SPAGHETTI CACIO E PEPE

Preparation time: 5 minutes

Cooking time: 7 minutes

Serves 4

12 ounces spaghetti

generous 1 cup grated pecorino cheese

salt and pepper

Cook the spaghetti in plenty of salted boiling water until al dente. Drain, reserving a few tablespoons of the cooking liquid, and tip into a warmed tureen, sprinkle with the pecorino, and season well with pepper. Add the reserved pasta cooking water, toss, and serve immediately.

SPAGHETTI WITH CAPERS

Preparation time: 15 minutes

Cooking time: 20 minutes

Serves 4

4 tablespoons olive oil

1 salted anchovy

2 garlic cloves

2 tablespoons capers, rinsed and drained

12 ounces spaghetti

salt

Pinch the heads of the anchovy between your thumb and forefinger and pull them off. Pinch along the top edge of the anchovy and pull out the backbones. Put it into a dish, add water to cover and let soak for 10 minutes to remove some of the salt. Heat the oil in a pan, add the anchovy, and garlic and cook over low heat, stirring frequently, until the anchovy has disintegrated and the garlic has turned golden brown. Remove the pan from the heat, discard the garlic, and add the capers. Meanwhile, cook the spaghetti in a large pan of salted, boiling water until al dente, then drain, toss with the sauce, and serve.

In the Aeolian Islands of southern Italy caper bushes grow wild everywhere and are also intensively cultivated. The island of Salina produces the biggest quantity of capers, and the buds from Pollara (an area situated on the slopes of a dormant volcano) are particularly prized for their firm consistency and fragrance. The most common type of caper plant throughout the islands is the "tondino," which produces the firmest caper buds. Traditionally preserved in dried sea salt the capers are ready for consumption after a couple of months.

SPAGHETTI WITH CAULIFLOWER

Preparation time: 10 minutes

Cooking time: 15 minutes

Serves 4

1¾ pounds cauliflower, cut into florets

3 tablespoons olive oil

1 garlic clove

10 ounces spaghetti

grated Parmesan cheese, to serve

salt and pepper

Cook the cauliflower florets in plenty of lightly salted boiling water for 5–10 minutes until tender, then remove with a slotted spoon. Reserve the cooking water. Heat the oil in a skillet. Add the garlic clove and cook over low heat, stirring frequently, for a few minutes until browned. Remove with a slotted spoon and discard. Add the cauliflower florets to the skillet. Bring the reserved cooking water back to a boil, add the spaghetti, and cook until al dente. Drain, tip into the skillet, season with salt and pepper, and toss well. Serve immediately, handing the Parmesan separately.

SPAGHETTI WITH CHICKEN

SPAGHETTI AL POLLO

Preparation time: 20 minutes
Cooking time: 25 minutes
Serves 4
1 skinless boneless chicken breast portion
4 tablespoons butter
2 cups sliced cremini mushrooms
1 cup heavy cream
12 ounces spaghetti
½ cup grated Parmesan cheese
salt and pepper

Put the chicken into a pan and add water to cover. Bring just to a boil, then lower the heat so that it barely bubbles. Cover and poach for 25–30 minutes until cooked through and tender. Drain and let cool, then dice. Melt the butter in a skillet. Add the diced chicken and cook over medium heat, stirring frequently, for 5 minutes until lightly browned all over. Lower the heat, add the mushrooms, season with salt and pepper and cook, stirring occasionally, for 15 minutes. Stir in the cream and heat through gently. Meanwhile, cook the spaghetti in plenty of salted boiling water until al dente. Drain, tip into a serving dish, spoon the sauce on top, and sprinkle with the Parmesan. Serve immediately.

SPAGHETTI WITH ZUCCHINI FLOWERS

SPAGHETTI AI FIORI GIALLI

Preparation time: 25 minutes
Cooking time: 35 minutes
Serves 4
2 tablespoons olive oil
1 garlic clove
4 plum tomatoes, peeled, seeded, and chopped
16 zucchini flowers, cut into strips
12 ounces spaghetti
8 fresh basil leaves, torn
salt and pepper

Heat the oil in a pan. Add the garlic clove and cook over low heat, stirring frequently, for a few minutes until golden brown, then remove the garlic with a slotted spoon, and discard. Add the tomatoes and cook, stirring occasionally, for 15 minutes. Add the zucchini flowers and cook for 5 minutes more. Season with salt and pepper. Cook the spaghetti in plenty of salted boiling water until al dente. Drain, tip into a warmed serving dish, pour the sauce over, garnish with the basil, and serve immediately.

SPAGHETTI WITH ZUCCHINI

Heat the oil in a pan, add the garlic clove, whole onion, sage leaves, and celery stalk and cook over low heat for 5 minutes. Add the tomatoes and bring to a boil over medium heat, then add the zucchini. Season with salt and pepper, cover, and cook for 15 minutes, then remove the onion, garlic, celery, and sage. Meanwhile, cook the spaghetti in a large pan of salted water until al dente, then drain, and return to the pan. Toss with the sauce, mozzarella, and Parmesan and serve.

Preparation time: 20 minutes

Cooking time: 30 minutes

Serves 4

3 tablespoons olive oil • 1 garlic clove

1 small onion • 2 fresh sage leaves

1 celery stalk

3 plum tomatoes, peeled, seeded and chopped

2⅔ cups thinly sliced zucchini

12 ounces spaghetti

5 ounces mozzarella cheese, diced

⅓ cup grated Parmesan cheese

salt and pepper

SPAGHETTI WITH CUTTLEFISH SAUCE

Heat the oil in a skillet. Add the onion, celery, carrot, and garlic clove and cook over low heat, stirring occasionally, for 5 minutes. Once the garlic is lightly browned, remove it with a slotted spoon and discard. Add the cuttlefish to the skillet and cook, stirring occasionally, for 5 minutes more. Pour in the wine and cook until the alcohol has evaporated and season with salt and pepper. Cover and simmer, occasionally adding a little hot water or stock if necessary, for 20 minutes until the sauce has reduced. Remove from the heat and stir in the parsley. Cook the spaghetti in plenty of salted boiling water until al dente. Drain, tip into a warmed serving dish, and add the cuttlefish sauce. Garnish with parsley sprigs and serve immediately.

An added value of the artisanal production of spaghetti is sun drying, where the strands are hung up to dry like washing. This explains the high quality of pasta produced in areas with plenty of sea and sun such as Naples and Liguria. In modern manufacture however, where air conditioning replaces the warmth of the sun, the ultimate quality comes from the choice of durum wheat semolina flour, the quality of the water and flawless production techniques.

Preparation time: 40 minutes

Cooking time: 35 minutes

Serves 4

2 tablespoons olive oil

1 small onion, chopped

1 celery stalk, chopped

1 carrot, chopped

1 garlic clove

14 ounces cuttlefish, cleaned and cut into pieces or strips (see Linguine with Cuttlefish, page 35)

scant ½ cup dry white wine

3–5 tablespoons hot water or fish stock

3 tablespoons chopped fresh flat-leaf parsley

12 ounces spaghetti

1 sprig fresh flat-leaf parsley, to garnish

salt and pepper

SPAGHETTI WITH EGGS AND EGGPLANT

SPAGHETTI ALLE UOVA E MELANZANE

Preparation time: 1 hour
Cooking time: 20 minutes
Serves 4
2 eggplants, diced
2 tablespoons olive oil
1 tablespoon finely chopped fresh flat-leaf parsley
2 egg yolks
1 egg white
scant 1 cup ricotta cheese
12 ounces spaghetti • salt and pepper

Put the eggplants into a colander, sprinkle with salt, and let drain for 30 minutes, then rinse, and pat dry with paper towels. Heat the oil in a skillet. Add the eggplants and parsley and cook over medium heat, stirring frequently, for 15 minutes. Remove from the skillet with a slotted spoon and drain well. Beat together the egg yolks and egg white in a tureen, then beat in the ricotta until smooth. Season lightly with salt and pepper. Cook the spaghetti in plenty of salted boiling water until al dente. Drain, tip into the tureen, and mix well. Add the eggplants and serve immediately.

SPAGHETTI WITH GARLIC AND CHILE OIL

SPAGHETTI AGLIO, OLIO E PEPERONCINO

Preparation time: 5 minutes
Cooking time: 15 minutes
Serves 4
5 tablespoons olive oil
2 garlic cloves, thinly sliced
½ fresh chile, seeded and chopped
1 chopped fresh flat-leaf parsley sprig
12 ounces spaghetti • salt

Heat the oil in a small pan, add the garlic and chile, and cook over low heat for a few minutes until the garlic is golden brown. Season lightly with salt, remove the pan from the heat, and add the parsley. Cook the spaghetti in a large pan of salted, boiling water until al dente, then drain, toss with the garlic and chile oil, and serve.

SPAGHETTI WITH GORGONZOLA AND PANCETTA

SPAGHETTI AL GORGONZOLA E PANCETTA

Preparation time: 15 minutes
Cooking time: 20 minutes
Serves 4
2 tablespoons olive oil
12 ounces spaghetti
⅔ cup diced pancetta or bacon
¼–½ fresh chile, seeded and chopped
4 ounces mild Gorgonzola cheese
scant 1 cup heavy cream
salt • grated Parmesan cheese, to serve

Heat the oil in a shallow pan. Add the pancetta or bacon and chile to taste, and cook over low heat, stirring occasionally, for 5 minutes. Gradually crumble the Gorgonzola into the pan, stirring constantly, then pour in the cream. Cook the spaghetti in plenty of salted boiling water until al dente. Drain, tip into a warmed serving dish, and pour the sauce over. Serve immediately, handing the Parmesan separately.

SPAGHETTI WITH GREEN PEPPERCORNS

SPAGHETTI AL PEPE VERDE

Preparation time: 10 minutes
Cooking time: 7 minutes
Serves 4
2 egg yolks
⅔ cup grated Parmesan cheese
3 tablespoons butter, diced
2 tablespoons heavy cream
12 ounces spaghetti
10 green peppercorns
salt

Combine the egg yolks, ½ cup of the Parmesan, the butter, and cream in a tureen. Cook the pasta in plenty of salted boiling water until al dente. Drain, tip it into the tureen, and stir gently. Add the green peppercorns and the remaining cheese and serve immediately.

Tip: Green peppercorns are unripe and milder in flavor than either black or white pepper. They are preserved by freeze-drying, dehydrating, or bottling in brine or vinegar. If the peppercorns are preserved in brine, drain and rinse first. Avoid those preserved in vinegar.

SPAGHETTI WITH FISH, GREEN CHILES, AND OREGANO

SPAGHETTI CON PESCE AZZURRO, PEPERONI VERDI E OREGANO

Preparation time: 25 minutes
Cooking time: 20 minutes
Serves 6
scant ½ olive oil
2 garlic cloves
9 ounces oily fish fillets, such as anchovies, mackerel, or tuna, cut into cubes
scant 1 cup dry white wine
5 ounces mild green chiles, seeded and chopped
¼ cup chopped fresh oregano
15 ounces spaghetti
salt

Heat the oil in a pan. Add the garlic cloves and cook over low heat, stirring occasionally, for a few minutes until lightly browned. Remove with a slotted spoon and discard. Add the fish to the pan and cook for 3 minutes. Pour in the wine and cook until the alcohol has evaporated. Stir in the chiles and oregano and cook for a few minutes more. Cook the spaghetti in plenty of salted boiling water until al dente. Drain, tip into the pan, with the sauce and toss over the heat for a few minutes. Transfer to a warmed serving dish and serve immediately.

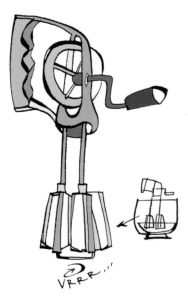

SPAGHETTI WITH GROUPER

Preparation time: 40 minutes

Cooking time: 45 minutes

Serves 4

2¼ pounds grouper, cleaned and boned

4 tablespoons olive oil

½ onion, thinly sliced

1 leek, thinly sliced

1 carrot, coarsely chopped

1 celery heart, coarsely chopped

3 small tomatoes, peeled and chopped

1 sprig fresh flat-leaf parsley, chopped

scant ½ cup dry white wine

12 ounces spaghetti

salt and pepper

Cut the fish into chunks. Heat the oil in a shallow pan. Add the onion and leek and cook over low heat, stirring occasionally, for 5 minutes. Increase the heat to medium, add the carrot and celery, and cook, stirring occasionally, for 5–7 minutes more, until lightly browned. Add the tomatoes and parsley, season with salt and pepper, and simmer, stirring occasionally, for about 15 minutes. Add the fish, lower the heat, and cook, occasionally stirring gently, for a few minutes until the fish is lightly browned. Drizzle with the white wine and cook until the alcohol has evaporated. Cover and simmer for 15 minutes. Cook the spaghetti in plenty of salted boiling water until al dente. Drain, tip into a warmed serving dish, pour the sauce over, toss well, and serve immediately.

SPAGHETTI WITH LANGOUSTINES

Preparation time: 40 minutes

Cooking time: 30 minutes

Serves 4

1 cup dry white wine

1 bay leaf

strip of thinly pared lemon rind

24 langoustines or lobsterettes

3 tablespoons olive oil

1 shallot, chopped

½ cup water

1 tablespoon pine nuts

2 fresh basil sprigs, chopped

12 ounces spaghetti

salt and pepper

Pour 8¾ cups of water into a pan and add half the wine, the bay leaf, lemon rind, and a pinch of salt. Add the langoustines, bring to a boil, and cook for 7 minutes. Drain and leave until cool enough to handle, then peel them, and remove the black intestinal vein. Heat the oil in a pan. Add the shallot and cook over low heat, stirring occasionally, for 5 minutes. Pour in ½ cup water, add the langoustines and pine nuts, drizzle with the remaining wine, and season with salt and pepper. Simmer for 5 minutes, then stir in the basil. Cook the spaghetti in plenty of salted boiling water until al dente. Drain, tip into a warmed serving dish, and top with the langoustine sauce.

SPAGHETTI WITH MASCARPONE

Preparation time: 10 minutes

Cooking time: 10 minutes

Serves 4

4 tablespoons butter • 1 cup heavy cream

⅔ cup mascarpone cheese

12 ounces spaghetti

½ cup grated Parmesan cheese

salt

Melt the butter with the cream in a heatproof dish over low heat. Add the mascarpone and stir until smooth and thoroughly incorporated. Cook the spaghetti in plenty of salted boiling water until al dente. Drain, tip into the dish and toss with the sauce. Increase the heat, sprinkle with the Parmesan, and serve.

SPAGHETTI WITH MUSHROOM SAUCE

Preparation time: 25 minutes

Cooking time: 45 minutes

Serves 4

2 tablespoons olive oil

2 garlic cloves

3⅔ cups sliced porcini mushrooms

1 pound 5 ounces tomatoes, peeled and diced

12 ounces spaghetti

2 tablespoons butter

1 tablespoon finely chopped fresh flat-leaf parsley

salt and pepper

Heat the oil in a shallow pan with the garlic cloves. When the garlic has turned golden brown, remove with a slotted spoon and discard. Add the mushrooms, increase the heat to medium-high, and cook until they have released their liquid. Lower the heat, add the tomatoes, season with salt and pepper, and simmer for 20 minutes. Cook the spaghetti in plenty of salted boiling water until al dente. Drain, tip into a warmed tureen, and pour over the mushroom sauce. Add the butter, sprinkle with the parsley, and serve immediately.

Tip: If fresh porcini mushrooms, also known as ceps, are not available, you can replace them with ⅓ cup dried mushrooms, soaked in lukewarm water for 30 minutes, rinsed, and drained.

SPAGHETTI WITH OLIVES

Preparation time: 15 minutes

Cooking time: 30 minutes

Serves 4

2 tablespoons extra virgin olive oil, plus extra for drizzling

2 leeks, sliced • scant 1 cup black olives, pitted

14 ounces spaghetti

2 tablespoons chopped fresh flat-leaf parsley

⅔ cup grated pecorino cheese • salt

Heat the oil in a pan. Add the leeks, cover, and cook over low heat, stirring occasionally, for 15 minutes. Stir in the olives and cook for another 5 minutes. Meanwhile, cook the pasta in plenty of salted boiling water until al dente. Drain, tip into the pan with the leeks, and toss. Sprinkle with the parsley and pecorino, drizzle with olive oil, and serve immediately.

SPAGHETTI WITH MUSHROOMS AND CAVIAR

SPAGHETTI AI FUNGHI E CAVIALE

Chop 1 parsley sprig and 1 garlic clove. Heat 2 tablespoons of the oil preferably in a heatproof earthenware dish or in a heavy pan. Add the mushrooms, chopped garlic, and chopped parsley and cook over very low heat, stirring constantly and gradually adding the wine, for 20 minutes. Chop the remaining parsley and remaining garlic together, put the mixture into a bowl, and stir in the caviar. Cook the spaghetti in plenty of boiling water until almost al dente but do not add salt as the caviar is already salty. About 2 minutes before the spaghetti is ready, stir in the tomato paste so that the pasta becomes slightly pink. Drain, tip onto a serving dish, pour the mushroom sauce over, and toss. Sprinkle with the parsley and caviar mixture and serve immediately.

Preparation time: 30 minutes

Cooking time: 30 minutes

Serves 4

2 sprigs fresh flat-leaf parsley

2 garlic cloves

scant 1 cup olive oil

5⅔ chopped mushrooms

scant 1 cup white wine

2 tablespoons caviar or lumpfish roe

12 ounces spaghetti

1 tablespoon concentrated tomato paste

salt

SPAGHETTI WITH NEEDLEFISH

SPAGHETTI CON LE AGUGLIE

Chop the fish. Heat the oil in a pan. Add the garlic, onion, and parsley and cook over low heat, stirring occasionally, for 5 minutes. Add the fish and cook for 3–5 minutes more. Pour in the wine and cook until the alcohol has evaporated, then add the tomatoes, and season with salt and pepper. Simmer gently for 12–15 minutes until thickened. Cook the spaghetti in plenty of salted boiling water until al dente. Drain and toss with the sauce. Transfer to a warmed serving dish, sprinkle with the bread crumbs, and serve immediately.

Preparation time: 20 minutes

Cooking time: 30 minutes

Serves 4

1 pound 5 ounces needlefish, cleaned and boned

3 tablespoons olive oil

2 garlic cloves, crushed

1 small onion, chopped

1 tablespoon chopped fresh flat-leaf parsley

3 tablespoons dry white wine

7 ounces canned chopped tomatoes

12 ounces spaghetti

½ cup bread crumbs

salt and pepper

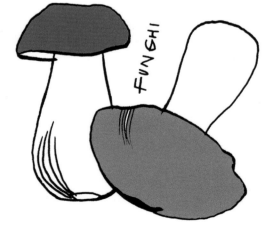

FUNGHI

SPAGHETTI WITH BROCCOLI

SPAGHETTI AI BROCCOLETTI

Preparation time: 15 minutes
Cooking time: 35 minutes
Serves 4
1 pound 2 ounces broccoli
3 tablespoons olive oil
2 tablespoons butter
1 onion, chopped
4 tablespoons heavy cream
12 ounces spaghetti
⅓ cup grated Parmesan cheese
salt and pepper

Parboil the broccoli in salted water for 8 minutes. Heat the oil and butter in a skillet, add the onion, and cook over low heat, stirring occasionally, for 5 minutes until softened. Drain the broccoli, add to the skillet, and mix well. Stir in the cream and simmer gently for 10 minutes. Transfer the mixture to a food processor and process to a purée. Season with salt and pepper to taste. Meanwhile, cook the spaghetti in a large pan of salted, boiling water until al dente, then drain, toss with the broccoli and cream mixture, sprinkle with the Parmesan, and serve.

SPAGHETTI WITH OCTOPUS SAUCE

SPAGHETTI AL SUGO DI POLPO

Preparation time: 50 minutes
Cooking time: 35 minutes
Serves 4
2¼ pounds small octopuses, cleaned
4 tablespoons olive oil
2 garlic cloves
7 ounces tomatoes, peeled and chopped
12 ounces spaghetti
1 sprig chopped fresh flat-leaf parsley
salt and pepper

Rinse the octopuses and, without draining all the water, put them into a heatproof earthenware dish or heavy pan and set over medium heat until the water has dried out. Add the oil and garlic cloves and cook, stirring frequently, for a few minutes until the garlic is lightly browned. Remove the garlic with a slotted spoon and discard. Add the tomatoes to the dish or pan, season with salt and pepper, lower the heat, and simmer for 20 minutes. Cook the spaghetti in plenty of salted boiling water until al dente. Drain, tip into a warmed serving dish, and pour the sauce over. Sprinkle with the parsley and serve immediately.

SPAGHETTI WITH SHRIMP AND GLOBE ARTICHOKES

SPAGHETTI CON GAMBERI E CARCIOFI

Half fill a bowl with water and stir in the lemon juice. Trim the artichokes, cut into thin wedges, and put them into the acidulated water. Heat the oil in a large pan. Add the shallot, celery, and carrot and cook over low heat, stirring occasionally, for 5–8 minutes until softened. Sprinkle with the wine and cook for a few minutes until the alcohol has evaporated. Add the warm water and cook for 5 minutes. Add the artichokes stalk ends up, season with salt and pepper, and cook, adding a few tablespoons of warm water if necessary, for 20 minutes, until tender but firm. Meanwhile, rinse the shrimp, set 4 of them aside, and peel and devein the remainder. When the artichokes are almost cooked add the 4 whole shrimp, cook for another 2 minutes, and add the peeled shrimp. Cook, stirring constantly, for 5 minutes, then remove the whole shrimp, and keep warm. Cook the pasta in plenty of salted boiling water until al dente. Drain, tip into the pan with the artichokes, and toss over low heat. Transfer to a warmed serving dish, garnish with the whole shrimp, parsley, and bottarga, and serve immediately.

Tip: Even when cooked in a sauce (for example, in a broth of oil and water with a garlic clove), artichokes should be cooked with the stalk ends uppermost so that only the leaves are cooked in the liquid, while the more tender parts are steamed.

Preparation time: 40 minutes

Cooking time: 35 minutes

Serves 4

2 tablespoons lemon juice

4–5 young globe artichokes, trimmed

2 tablespoons olive oil

1 shallot, finely chopped

1 celery stalk, finely chopped

½ carrot, finely chopped

1 tablespoon white wine

4 tablespoons warm water

1 pound 2 ounces raw shrimp

12 ounces spaghetti

salt and pepper

To garnish

chopped fresh flat-leaf parsley

grated bottarga (salted pressed gray mullet or tuna roe)

SPAGHETTI WITH SHRIMP AND ZUCCHINI FLOWERS

SPAGHETTI CON GAMBERETTI E FIORI DI ZUCCA

Heat the oil in a skillet. Add the shallot and cook over low heat, stirring occasionally, for 5 minutes. Add the zucchini and cook, stirring and turning occasionally, for 5–7 minutes more, then pour in the vermouth. Meanwhile, bring the vegetable stock to a boil in a pan. Cook the spaghetti in plenty of salted boiling water until al dente. Drain, add to the skillet, and toss with the mixture. Add the shrimp to the boiling stock and cook for 2 minutes, then remove with a slotted spoon, and add to the spaghetti. Stir in the flower strips and season with salt and pepper. Cook for a few minutes more to let the flavors mingle, then serve.

Preparation time: 20 minutes

Cooking time: 25 minutes

Serves 4

2 tablespoons olive oil

1 shallot, finely chopped • 2 zucchini, sliced

1½ tablespoons dry white vermouth

1 cup vegetable stock • 12 ounces spaghetti

12 small shrimp, peeled and deveined

(see Spaghetti with Langoustines, page 63)

6 zucchini flowers, cut into strips • salt and pepper

SPAGHETTI WITH RAW TOMATO

SPAGHETTI AL POMODORO CRUDO

Preparation time: 30 minutes

Cooking time: 5 minutes

Serves 4

1 pound 2 ounces ripe vine tomatoes,
peeled, seeded, and chopped

4 tablespoons olive oil

10 fresh basil leaves, torn

2 garlic cloves

12 ounces spaghetti

salt and pepper

Put the tomatoes into a salad bowl, add the oil, basil, and garlic, and season with salt and pepper. Mix well, cover, and set aside in a cool place for 30 minutes to let the flavors mingle, then remove, and discard the garlic. Cook the spaghetti in a large pan of salted boiling water until al dente, then drain and toss with the raw tomato sauce, and serve.

SPAGHETTI WITH RICOTTA AND HERBS

SPAGHETTI ALLA RICOTTA CON LE ERBE

Preparation time: 10 minutes

Cooking time: 7 minutes

Serves 4

1⅓ cup ricotta cheese

6 fresh sage leaves

6 fresh basil leaves

1 tablespoon rosemary

1 tablespoon fresh marjoram

12 ounces spaghetti

salt and freshly ground white pepper

Process the ricotta and herbs in a food processor or blender. Cook the spaghetti in plenty of salted boiling water until al dente. Drain, reserving 2 tablespoons of the cooking water, and tip into a warmed serving dish. Dilute the sauce with the reserved cooking water and pour it over the spaghetti. Season with a little white pepper, toss well, and serve immediately.

SPAGHETTI WITH TUNA

SPAGHETTI CON IL TONNO

Preparation time: 15 minutes

Cooking time: 28 minutes

Serves 4

3 tablespoons olive oil

1 garlic clove

2½ ounces canned tuna in oil, drained and flaked

3 tablespoons concentrated tomato paste

1 tablespoon finely chopped fresh flat-leaf parsley

12 ounces spaghetti

salt and pepper

Heat the oil in a pan, add the garlic, cook until it has browned, then remove it from the pan and discard. Add the tuna and mix well. Stir the tomato paste with 1–2 tablespoons warm water in a bowl, then stir into the pan, and cook over low heat for 15 minutes. Remove the pan from the heat, stir in the parsley, and season with salt and pepper. Meanwhile, cook the spaghetti in a large pan of salted, boiling water until al dente, then drain, toss with the sauce, and serve.

SPAGHETTI WITH ARUGULA AND WALNUTS

SPAGHETTI CON RUCOLA E NOCI

Blanch the walnuts in boiling water for a few minutes, then drain, and rub off the skins. Chop the garlic with half the walnuts and put the mixture into a bowl. Add the arugula and oil, season with salt and pepper, and mix well. Chop the remaining walnuts. Cook the spaghetti in plenty of salted boiling water until al dente. Drain, tip into a serving dish, add the arugula mixture, and toss. Sprinkle with the remaining walnuts and Parmesan and serve immediately.

Preparation time: 10 minutes

Cooking time: 10 minutes

Serves 4

¾ cup walnuts

1 garlic clove

1 bunch of arugula, shredded

4 tablespoons olive oil

12 ounces spaghetti

grated Parmesan cheese, to serve

salt and pepper

SPAGHETTI WITH ROSEMARY

SPAGHETTI AL ROSMARINO

Heat the oil in a pan, add the rosemary, garlic, and chile and cook for about 2 minutes. Stir in the tomatoes with their juice and bring to a boil, then lower the heat, cover, and simmer for 30 minutes. Stir the flour with 1–2 tablespoons warm water. Season the rosemary sauce with salt, stir in the flour mixture and milk, and cook for another 5 minutes. Cook the spaghetti in a large pan of salted, boiling water until al dente, then drain, and transfer to a warmed serving dish. Sprinkle with the Parmesan and pour on the sauce.

Preparation time: 10 minutes

Cooking time: 40 minutes

Serves 4

2 tablespoons olive oil

2 tablespoons fresh rosemary needles,

finely chopped

1 garlic clove, finely chopped

½ fresh chile, seeded and finely chopped

9 ounces canned chopped tomatoes

1 tablespoon all-purpose flour

1 tablespoon milk

12 ounces spaghetti

½ cup grated Parmesan cheese

salt

SPAGHETTI WITH SARDINES

Preparation time: 30 minutes
Cooking time: 30 minutes
Serves 4
11 ounces fresh sardines
all-purpose flour, for dusting
3 tablespoons olive oil
2 garlic cloves
1 sprig fresh flat-leaf parsley, chopped,
plus extra to garnish
12 ounces spaghetti
salt and pepper

Rub off the fish scales with your fingers or the back of a knife and rinse under cold running water. Cut off the head of each fish. Gently squeeze the belly until the guts are visible then pull them out with a knife. Rinse well, then slit open the belly of each fish, and place, skin side uppermost, on a cutting board. Press firmly along the backbone with your fingers until the fish is flat. Turn it over and gently pull out the bones, snipping the backbone at the tail end with kitchen scissors. Rinse well, pat dry with paper towels and dust with flour. Heat the oil in a shallow pan. Add the garlic cloves and cook over low heat, stirring frequently, for a few minutes until lightly browned, then remove with a slotted spoon, and discard. Add the fish to the pan and brown on both sides, then mash with a fork. Cook over low heat for 15 minutes and, if necessary, drizzle with a little hot water. Season with salt and pepper and sprinkle with the parsley. Cook the spaghetti in plenty of salted boiling water until al dente. Drain, tip into the pan with the fish, and toss over the heat for a few minutes. Transfer to a warmed serving dish, garnish with parsley sprigs, and serve immediately.

6 tablespoons olive oil
2 garlic cloves
12 ounces sardines, scaled, cleaned
and boned (as above)
2 large tomatoes, peeled and chopped
1 tablespoon hot water
1 tablespoon chopped fresh flat-leaf parsley
12 ounces spaghetti
1 cup fresh bread crumbs
salt and pepper

Variation: Heat 4 tablespoons of the oil in a pan. Add the garlic cloves, and cook over low heat, stirring frequently, for a few minutes until lightly browned, then remove with a slotted spoon, and discard. Add the sardines, tomatoes, and hot water to the pan, and cook for 5 minutes. Season with salt and pepper, add the parsley, and cook for a further 5 minutes. Meanwhile, heat the remaining olive oil in a small skillet. Add the bread crumbs and cook, stirring constantly, for a few minutes until golden, then add to the sardines. Cook the spaghetti in plenty of salted boiling water until al dente. Drain, tip into a warm serving dish, pour the sardine sauce over it, and serve.

BASILICO

SPAGHETTI WITH VEGETABLES AND HERBS

SPAGHETTI CON SUGO BRILLANTE

Put the tomatoes, green bell pepper, onion, celery, zucchini, and garlic into a pan, season with salt, cover, and cook over low heat, stirring occasionally, for 25–30 minutes until the tomatoes have broken up and the vegetables are soft. Uncover the pan, increase the heat to medium, and cook, stirring frequently, until the liquid has reduced. Remove the pan from the heat and press the mixture through a strainer into a bowl with the back of a spoon. If necessary, return it to the pan and reduce the remaining liquid, stirring constantly. Heat the oil in a shallow pan. Add the tomato and vegetable sauce and mix well. Season to taste with salt and pepper and cook until the oil separates from the tomato mixture, creating a shiny effect. Cook the pasta in plenty of salted boiling water until al dente. Drain, tip into a warmed serving dish and pour the sauce over. Garnish with basil and serve immediately, handing the ricotta separately.

Preparation time: 30 minutes

Cooking time: 40 minutes

Serves 4

14 ounces tomatoes, chopped

1 green bell pepper, seeded and diced

1 onion, chopped

1 celery stalk, chopped

1 zucchini, diced

1 garlic clove, finely chopped

1 tablespoon chopped mixed fresh herbs, such as marjoram, savory, and oregano

3 tablespoons olive oil

12 ounces spaghetti

1 tablespoon grated ricotta salata cheese

salt and pepper • torn fresh basil leaves, to garnish

SPAGHETTI WITH WALNUT SAUCE

SPAGHETTI ALLA SALSA DI NOCI

Blanch the walnuts in boiling water for a few minutes, then drain, and rub off the skins. Chop finely and mix with the sugar and nutmeg in a bowl. Gradually stir in the oil and season with salt. Cook the spaghetti in plenty of salted boiling water until al dente. Meanwhile, melt the butter in a skillet. Add the bread crumbs and cook, stirring constantly, for a few minutes until golden brown. Drain the spaghetti, tip it into the skillet with the bread crumbs, and toss over the heat for 2 minutes. Pour the walnut sauce into the skillet and stir. Transfer to a warmed serving dish, sprinkle with Parmesan, and serve immediately. To ensure the ingredients are thoroughly mixed, put a few pats of butter on the pasta before adding the sauce and Parmesan.

Preparation time: 30 minutes

Cooking time: 15 minutes

Serves 4

¾ cup walnuts

pinch of sugar

pinch of freshly grated nutmeg

scant ½ cup olive oil

12 ounces spaghetti

1½ tablespoons butter

¾ cup fresh bread crumbs

salt

grated Parmesan cheese, to serve

Walnut sauce, usually served with pansotti (see Genoese Pansotti page 286), is also good with spaghetti. This sauce is one of the most traditional recipes of Liguria, a narrow coastal region between the sea and mountains in northwest Italy, where a limited amount of fresh produce grows in the wild. As a result, Ligurians must make the most of the crops that thrive, such as garlic and borage, olives, basil, walnuts, pine nuts, and onions.

SPAGHETTINI WITH CHEESE AND ARTICHOKES

Preparation time: 25 minutes
Cooking time: 50 minutes
Serves 4

2 tablespoons lemon juice
4 young globe artichokes, trimmed
2 tablespoons butter
4 tablespoons olive oil
1 onion, chopped
1 garlic clove, chopped
scant 1 cup dry white wine
scant ½ cup lukewarm water (optional)
1 sprig fresh marjoram, finely chopped
12 ounces spaghettini
2 ounces diced mild provolone cheese
3½ ounces diced white scamorza cheese
½ cup grated Parmesan cheese
salt and pepper

Half fill a bowl with water and stir in the lemon juice. Cut the artichokes into wedges and put them into the acidulated water to prevent discoloration. Melt the butter with half the oil in a shallow pan. Add the onion and garlic and cook over low heat, stirring occasionally, for 5 minutes. Drain the artichokes, add to the pan, and cook, stirring occasionally, for 10 minutes. Pour in the wine and cook until the alcohol has evaporated. Add a little lukewarm water if necessary. Stir in the marjoram, cover, and simmer gently for 20 minutes. Cook the spaghettini in plenty of salted boiling water until al dente. Drain, tip into a warmed serving dish, drizzle with the remaining oil, pour in the artichoke sauce, and add all the cheeses. Mix together thoroughly, season with pepper, and serve immediately.

SPAGHETTINI WITH EGG AND MOZZARELLA SAUCE

Preparation time: 15 minutes
Cooking time: 7 minutes
Serves 4

2 ounces salted anchovies
5 ounces mozzarella cheese, diced
2 egg yolks
12 ounces spaghettini
salt

Pinch the heads of the anchovies between your thumb and index finger and pull them off, taking the innards with them. Pinch along the top edge of each anchovy and pull out the backbones. Put them into a dish, pour in water to cover, and let soak for 10 minutes to remove some of the salt, then drain, and chop. Put them into a tureen and add the mozzarella. Beat the egg yolks with a pinch of salt in a bowl and add to the tureen. Cook the spaghettini in plenty of salted boiling water until al dente. Drain, transfer to the tureen, mix with the sauce, and serve immediately.

SPAGHETTINI WITH THREE FLAVORS

Put the anchovy fillets, capers, parsley, oregano, oil, and butter into a tureen. Beat the egg yolks with a pinch of salt in a bowl. Cook the spaghettini in plenty of salted boiling water until al dente. Drain, tip into the tureen, add the egg yolks, and stir. Season with pepper, sprinkle with the Parmesan, and serve immediately.

Preparation time: 10 minutes

Cooking time: 7 minutes

Serves 4

1 ounce canned anchovy fillets,
drained and chopped

2 ounces capers, drained

3 tablespoons fresh flat-leaf parsley, chopped

1 teaspoon dried oregano

2 tablespoons olive oil

2 tablespoons butter, diced

2 egg yolks

12 ounces spaghettini

½ cup grated Parmesan cheese

salt and pepper

SPAGHETTINI WITH TUNA AND OLIVES

Put the anchovies, tuna, olives, and capers into a tureen, season with salt and pepper, and mix well. Heat the oil in a pan. Add the garlic cloves and cook over low heat, stirring frequently, for a few minutes. Remove with a slotted spoon and discard. Add the tuna mixture and cook over medium heat, stirring occasionally, for 5 minutes. Cook the spaghettini in plenty of salted boiling until al dente. Drain and tip into a warmed serving dish. Add the sauce, toss, and serve immediately.

Tip: Capers are available preserved in salt or vinegar. The first option keeps the original flavor better. Once open, keep the capers preserved in vinegar refrigerated.

Preparation time: 15 minutes

Cooking time: 20 minutes

Serves 4

6 anchovy fillets in oil, drained

3½ ounces canned tuna in oil, drained and flaked

1¼ cups green olives, pitted

1 tablespoon capers, rinsed and drained

6 tablespoons olive oil

2 garlic cloves

12 ounces spaghettini

salt and pepper

VERMICELLI

Vermicelli is a type of dried pasta made from durum wheat semolina flour, like a thinner version of spaghetti. It is believed to be of Neapolitan origin, and in the south of Italy the two terms spaghetti and vermicelli are used interchangeably. The name means "little worms," and the first evidence of the existence of Vermicelli dates back to 1154. The twelfth-century Arab geographer al-Idrisi writes that, at Trabia in Sicily, "itriya" (vermicelli), was produced and exported throughout the island and into Muslim territories. This claim is confirmed by the survival of the Sicilian dialect word "tria", which means both modern spaghetti and the metal cutter that is used to produce it. Vermicelli is often served with fish-based sauces, but also works well in oven-baked dishes such as Vermicelli Pasticcio (see page 76).

FISHERMAN'S VERMICELLI

VERMICELLI DEL MARINAIO

Preparation time: 35 minutes

Cooking time: 30 minutes

Serves 4

2 tablespoons olive oil

1 garlic clove, crushed

½ dried chile, crumbled

11 ounces tomatoes, peeled and chopped

1 teaspoon sugar (optional)

3½ ounces live clams

7 ounces baby octopus, cleaned and cut into pieces

scant 1 cup dry white wine

12 ounces vermicelli

1 tablespoon chopped fresh flat-leaf parsley

salt

Heat the oil in a shallow pan. Add the garlic and chile and cook over low heat, stirring frequently, for 2–3 minutes. Add the tomatoes, season with salt, and simmer for 15 minutes. You can add 1 teaspoon sugar to remove any acidity. Meanwhile, scrub the clams under cold running water. Discard any with damaged shells or that do not shut immediately when sharply tapped. Put the clams into another pan, cover, and cook over high heat, shaking the pan occasionally, for 3–5 minutes until the shells open. Discard any that remain shut and remove the remainder from their shells. Add the octopus to the tomato sauce, pour in the wine, stir well, and simmer for 10 minutes. Add the clams and stir. Cook the vermicelli in plenty of salted boiling water until al dente. Drain, tip into a warmed serving dish, pour the sauce over, and sprinkle with the chopped parsley. Serve immediately.

VERMICELLI WITH CLAMS

VERMICELLI CON LE VONGOLE

Preparation time: 30 minutes
Cooking time: 30 minutes
Serves 4
2¼ pounds live clams, scrubbed
⅔ cup olive oil
2 garlic cloves
12 ounces vermicelli
1 tablespoon chopped fresh flat-leaf parsley
salt and pepper

Scrub the clams under cold running water. Discard any with broken shells or that do not shut immediately when sharply tapped. Heat the oil in a pan, add the garlic and clams, and cook for about 5 minutes until the shells open. Remove the pan from the heat and lift out the clams with a slotted spoon. Discard any that remain closed. Discard the garlic. Remove the clams from their shells. Strain the cooking liquid into a skillet and add the clams. Meanwhile, cook the vermicelli in a large pan of salted boiling water until al dente, then drain, and tip into the skillet. Cook for 2 minutes, tossing frequently, then season with salt and pepper to taste, and sprinkle with the parsley. Tip onto a warmed serving dish.

Tip: To create a perfect dish of pasta with clams, drain the pasta when half cooked, then add it to the pan with the clams to finish the cooking process. This way the pasta will absorb the liquid from the clams and enhance the flavor. For a variation to this dish, add some chopped tomatoes, peeled and seeded, or canned tomatoes. This recipe also works with the slightly thicker spaghettini.

VERMICELLI PASTICCIO

PASTICCIO DI VERMICELLI

Preparation time: 15 minutes
Cooking time: 25 minutes
Serves 6
2 tablespoons butter, plus extra for greasing
6 tablespoons bread crumbs
12 ounces vermicelli
9 ounces mozzarella cheese, diced
3½ ounces prosciutto, cut into strips
1 egg
⅓ cup grated Parmesan cheese
salt and pepper

Preheat the oven to 400°F. Grease an ovenproof dish with butter and sprinkle with 4 tablespoons of the bread crumbs. Cook the vermicelli in plenty of salted boiling water until al dente. Drain, return to the pan, and stir in half the butter. Tip half the vermicelli into the prepared dish and top with a layer of mozzarella and prosciutto, then cover with the remaining vermicelli. Beat the egg with the grated Parmesan in a bowl, season with salt and pepper, and pour over the pasta. Sprinkle with the remaining bread crumbs and dot with the remaining butter. Bake for 20 minutes. Remove from the oven, let stand for 5 minutes, and serve.

VERMICELLI
WITH HAKE SAUCE

VERMICELLI CON RAGÙ DI NASELLO

Preparation time: 30 minutes
Cooking time: 20 minutes
Serves 4
3 tablespoons olive oil
1¾ pounds hake, cleaned, boned, and
cut into pieces
1 onion, chopped
1 tablespoon concentrated tomato paste
1 tablespoon water
1 garlic clove, finely chopped
8 fresh basil leaves, torn
12 ounces vermicelli
1 tablespoon chopped fresh flat-leaf parsley
salt and pepper

Heat the oil in a shallow pan. Add the onion and cook over low heat, stirring occasionally, for 5 minutes. Add the pieces of hake and cook, stirring occasionally, until lightly browned all over. Mix the tomato paste with 1 tablespoon water in a bowl and add to the pan with the garlic and basil. Season with salt and pepper and simmer gently for 10 minutes until the sauce has thickened and the fish is cooked. Transfer the sauce to a food processor and process. Cook the vermicelli in plenty of salted boiling water until al dente. Drain, tip into a serving dish, and pour the hake sauce over. Sprinkle with the parsley and serve immediately.

VERMICELLI WITH EGGS
AND BUTTER

VERMICELLI ALLE UOVA E BURRO FUSO

Preparation time: 10 minutes
Cooking time: 15 minutes
Serves 4
2 eggs
⅔ cup grated Parmesan cheese
12 ounces vermicelli
4 tablespoons butter
salt and pepper

Break the eggs into a bowl, mix with half the Parmesan, and season with salt and pepper. Cook the vermicelli in plenty of salted boiling water until al dente. Meanwhile, put the butter into a heatproof bowl, set it over a pan of simmering water, and allow to melt. Drain the pasta, tip into the bowl with the eggs and cheese, and mix. Add the melted butter and the remaining Parmesan, mix together carefully, and serve immediately.

ZITE

Zite, or ziti, is a type of dried pasta originally from the city of Naples, and now widespread throughout southern Italy. Similar to spaghetti but thicker, tubular, and hollow, zite is made of durum wheat semolina flour and can be smooth or ridged. As zite strands are made very long, they are usually broken up before cooking. In Naples, zite is traditionally served as part of a wedding feast, and the name comes from the word "zita" in the Neapolitan dialect, which means "wife". Further south, in Puglia, it is typically served as Zite alla Sangiovanniello (Zite Sangiovanniello, see below), with a tomato, anchovy and caper sauce. Zite is also particularly suited to baked pasta dishes, such as the Sicilian Pasta con le Sarde (Pasta with Sardines, see page 80).

ZITE SANGIOVANNIELLO

ZITE ALLA SANGIOVANNIELLO

Preparation time: 10 minutes

Cooking time: 30 minutes

Serves 4

2 fresh anchovies

2 tablespoons olive oil

1 garlic clove

14 ounces fresh tomatoes, peeled and chopped, or canned chopped tomatoes

1 hot red chile, seeded and chopped

1 tablespoon capers, drained

1 sprig chopped fresh flat-leaf parsley

12 ounces zite

salt

Pinch the heads of the anchovies between your thumb and forefinger and pull them off, taking the innards with them. Pinch along the top edge of each anchovy and pull out the backbones. Heat the oil in a shallow pan. Add the garlic clove and cook over low heat, stirring frequently, for a few minutes until lightly browned. Remove the garlic with a slotted spoon and discard. Add the anchovies and cook, stirring constantly, until they have almost disintegrated. Add the tomatoes and chile and simmer for about 20 minutes until thickened. Stir in the capers and parsley. Cook the zite in plenty of salted boiling water until al dente. Drain, tip into a warmed serving dish, pour the sauce over, and serve immediately.

In Puglia there is a strong tradition of home-made pasta and many Puglian women are rightfully proud of their skill in making orecchiette and zite, both of which are still staples. This ancient art is still very much alive, and these varieties of pasta continue the legacy of the women who first made them, and whose lives were dedicated, with unfailing love and a spirit of sacrifice, to the family.

PASTA WITH SARDINES

Preparation time: 30 minutes

Cooking time: 1 hour

Serves 4

3 tablespoons golden raisins

4 salted anchovy fillets

7 ounces wild fennel

2 tablespoons olive oil, plus extra for brushing

1 onion, chopped

¼ cup pine nuts

pinch of saffron threads

12 ounces fresh sardines, scaled and cleaned

all-purpose flour, for dusting

vegetable oil, for deep-frying

11 ounces zite

salt

Place the golden raisins in a bowl, add hot water to cover, and let soak. In another bowl, cover the anchovies with water and soak for 10 minutes. Cook the fennel in lightly salted boiling water for 15–20 minutes, then drain, reserving the cooking liquid, and chop. Heat the oil in a pan, add the onion, and cook over low heat, stirring occasionally, for 5 minutes. Drain the anchovies, add to the pan and mash with a wooden spoon. Drain the raisins, squeezing out the excess liquid, and add to the pan with the fennel and pine nuts. Sprinkle with the saffron, cover, and cook over low heat for 15 minutes.

Open the sardines out like the pages of a book, leaving them attached along their backs. Rinse well, pat dry, and dust with flour, shaking off any excess. Heat the vegetable oil in a deep-fryer or large pan to 350–375°F or until a cube of day-old bread browns in 30 seconds. Add the sardines and deep-fry until golden brown, then remove, and drain on paper towels. Season with a little salt. Preheat the oven to 400°F and brush an ovenproof dish with oil.

Cook the zite in a large pan of salted boiling water mixed with the reserved fennel cooking water until al dente, then drain, return to the pan, and stir in half the sauce. Spoon a layer of pasta onto the base of the prepared dish and place a layer of sardines on top. Add a layer of the sauce and continue making layers until all the ingredients are used, ending with a layer of sauce. Bake for 10 minutes.

Tip: Wild fennel grows all over the coastal areas of the eastern Mediterranean, where it is widely used as an herb and a vegetable, eaten raw or cooked. The leaves are feathery and dill-like and bulbs have a more pronounced aniseed flavor than cultivated fennel. If not available, you can use regular fennel.

SHORT
PASTA

SHELLS

A popular type of dried short pasta, shells can be smooth or ridged and are so called because they resemble mollusk shells, "conchiglie" in Italian. The classic seashell shape has always been a feature of the decorative arts in Italy, and has been adopted by pasta makers too. The cavity of the shells is good for catching and holding sauces, and makes it ideal for light sauces of tomato, ricotta, pesto, peas, or pine nuts. Depending on the size, larger shells are called conchiglioni in Italian, smaller shells, conchigliette. Shells can also be colored with natural ingredients such as tomato or squid ink.

SHELLS WITH GORGONZOLA AND PISTACHIOS

CONCHIGLIE CON GORGONZOLA E PISTACCHI

Preparation time: 15 minutes
Cooking time: 10 minutes
Serves 4
½ cup pistachios
3½ ounces diced strong Gorgonzola
2 tablespoons heavy cream
11 ounces shell pasta
½ cup grated Parmesan cheese
salt

Put the pistachios into a heatproof bowl, pour over boiling water to cover, and let stand for 3 minutes. Drain well and when cool enough to handle, rub off the skins with your fingers. Chop the kernels and set aside. Put the Gorgonzola and cream into a pan and melt over low heat, stirring constantly until smooth, then remove from the heat. Cook the shells in plenty of salted boiling water until al dente. Drain, tip into a warmed serving dish, and toss with the melted Gorgonzola mixture, chopped pistachios, and Parmesan. Serve immediately.

SHELLS WITH HERBS

Preparation time: 20 minutes, plus marinating
Cooking time: 25 minutes
Serves 4
generous ½ cup olive oil
juice of ½ lemon, strained
1 bunch of chopped fresh mixed herbs, such as
thyme, sage, rue, and mint
½ onion, finely chopped
5–6 tomatoes, peeled and diced
12 ounces shell pasta • salt

Combine scant ½ cup of the oil and the lemon juice in a bowl with a fork. Add the herbs and let marinate for 2 hours. Heat the remaining oil in a small shallow pan. Add the onion and cook over low heat, stirring occasionally, for 5 minutes. Add the herbs and their marinade and cook, stirring occasionally, for another 5 minutes. Add the tomatoes and simmer, stirring occasionally, for about 15 minutes, until thickened. Season to taste with salt. Meanwhile, cook the shells in plenty of salted boiling water until al dente. Drain, tip into a warmed serving dish and pour the sauce over. Serve immediately.

SHELLS
WITH MOZZARELLA

Preparation time: 15 minutes
Cooking time: 8 minutes
Serves 4
11 ounces plum tomatoes, peeled and diced
7 ounces diced mozzarella cheese
10 torn fresh basil leaves
⅔ cup olive oil
12 ounces shell pasta
1 tablespoon capers in oil, drained
salt

Put the tomatoes, mozzarella, basil, and olive oil into a tureen. Cook the pasta in plenty of salted boiling water until al dente. Drain and immediately tip on top of the mixture in the tureen so that the mozzarella melts slightly. Add the capers, toss well, and serve immediately.

Tip: You can use this sauce to make a cold pasta salad. Proceed as above but slightly undercook the pasta and cool it down under running water. For a tastier result, leave the seasoned pasta refrigerated for at least an hour before serving.

SHELLS WITH SPINACH

Preparation time: 20 minutes
Cooking time: 20 minutes
Serves 4
4 tablespoons butter
1 shallot, chopped
4⅔ cup frozen chopped spinach
12 ounces shell pasta
1 egg • scant ½ cup ricotta cheese
salt and pepper

Melt the butter in a pan. Add the shallot and cook over low heat, stirring occasionally, for 5 minutes. Add the spinach and stir well, then season with salt, cover, and cook for a few minutes until heated through. Be careful to remove the pan from the heat before the mixture dries out. Put the egg and ricotta into a tureen, season lightly with pepper, and beat until smooth and combined. Alternatively, you can replace the eggs with 2 ounces light cream. Cook the shells in plenty of salted boiling water until al dente. Drain and stir into ricotta mixture. Add the spinach mixture, toss lightly, and serve immediately.

SHELLS WITH
SARDINIAN ARTICHOKES

CONCHIGLIE CON I CARCIOFI SARDI

Quarter the artichokes, remove, and discard the chokes, and slice very thinly. Heat the oil in a shallow pan. Add the garlic and parsley and cook over low heat, stirring frequently, for 2 minutes. Stir in the artichokes, cover, and cook over low heat, stirring occasionally and adding a little hot water if necessary, for 20 minutes. Season to taste with salt and finish cooking. Meanwhile, cook the shells in plenty of salted boiling water until al dente. Drain and toss with the artichoke sauce. Transfer to a warmed serving dish, season generously with pepper, and serve immediately.

Preparation time: 20 minutes

Cooking time: 30 minutes

Serves 4

4 Sardinian globe artichokes, trimmed

2 tablespoons olive oil

1 garlic clove, finely chopped

2 tablespoons chopped fresh flat-leaf parsley

12 ounces shell pasta

salt and pepper

TIMBALE OF FILLED
LARGE SHELLS

TIMBALLO DI CONCHIGLIONI FARCITI

Melt half the butter in a shallow pan. Add the onion, veal, and chicken and cook over medium heat, stirring frequently, for 8–10 minutes until the meat is lightly browned. Pour in the wine and cook until the alcohol has evaporated. Lower the heat and simmer for 10 minutes. Stir in the truffle, ham, and chicken livers and cook, stirring occasionally, for another 5 minutes. Stir in the cream and season with salt and pepper. Remove the pan from the heat. Preheat the oven to 350°F and grease an ovenproof dish with butter. Cook the shells in plenty of salted boiling water until al dente. Drain and fill each shell with a teaspoon of the mixture. Put the filled shells into the prepared dish. Dot with the remaining butter and sprinkle with the Emmenthal. Bake for 40 minutes, then serve.

Preparation time: 40 minutes

Cooking time: 1 hour 5 minutes

Serves 4

4 tablespoons butter, plus extra for greasing

½ onion, finely chopped

3 ounces ground veal

3 ounces ground chicken

scant ½ cup dry white wine

1 black truffle, chopped

½ cup diced ham

2 ounces chicken livers, trimmed and cut into pieces

scant ½ cup heavy cream

9 ounces large shell pasta

½ cup grated Emmenthal cheese

salt and pepper

DITALINI

Ditalini, meaning "small thimbles" in Italian, is a cylindrical type of dried short pasta, which can be smooth or ridged. Variations of the same type include the larger ditali, which is about ⅔ inch long and ⅓ inch in diameter. In the regions of Lazio, in central Italy, and Calabria in the south, ditalini is traditionally combined with broccoli. Ditalini is also commonly used in soups, paired with beans and peas and in timbales (see Eggplant and Ditalini Timbale, page 92). It can be substituted with other types of short pasta, such as small macaroni.

DITALINI WITH ZUCCHINI

DITALINI CON ZUCCHINE

Preparation time: 20 minutes
Cooking time: 30 minutes
Serves 4

4 tablespoons butter
2 tablespoons olive oil
½ small onion, chopped
3 ounces mild smoked bacon, cut into strips
1¾ cups shelled peas
6 young zucchini, sliced
11 ounces ditalini or ditali
grated Parmesan cheese, to serve
salt

Melt the butter with the oil in a skillet. Add the onion and cook over low heat, stirring occasionally, for 5 minutes. Add the bacon and cook for 4–6 minutes, then add the peas. Cover and cook gently for 20 minutes. Add the zucchini and stir, then re-cover the pan, and cook for another 15 minutes. Season to taste with salt and pepper. Meanwhile, cook the ditalini in plenty of salted boiling water until al dente. Drain, tip into the skillet and toss. Serve immediately, handing the Parmesan separately.

EGGPLANT AND DITALINI TIMBALE

Preparation time: 1 hour

Cooking time: 50 minutes

Serves 6

3 tablespoons butter, plus extra for greasing

4 tablespoons very fine fresh bread crumbs

2 eggplants, thinly sliced into long strips

all-purpose flour, for dusting

olive oil or vegetable oil, for deep-frying

12 ounces ditalini

7 ounces diced mozzarella cheese

3½ ounces shaved provolone cheese

⅓ cup grated Parmesan cheese

7 ounces luganega sausage, cut into pieces

salt and pepper

Preheat the oven to 350°F. Grease a 1½-inch deep round ovenproof dish or cake tin with butter and sprinkle with the bread crumbs. Dust the eggplants with flour, shaking off any excess. Heat the oil in a deep-fryer to 350–375°F or until a cube of day-old bread browns in 30 seconds. Add the eggplant slices, in batches if necessary, and deep-fry for 5–10 minutes until golden brown on both sides. Remove with a slotted spoon and drain on paper towels. Line the base and sides of the prepared dish with the eggplant slices, slightly overlapping the edges. Cook the ditalini in plenty of salted boiling water until al dente. Drain, return to the pan, and add the mozzarella, provolone, and Parmesan. Toss, season with salt and pepper, and stir in the sausage pieces. Spoon the mixture evenly into the prepared dish and fold the overlapping pieces of eggplant over the filling. Dot with the butter and bake for about 30 minutes. Serve immediately.

BOW TIES

A type of short, dried pasta made of durum wheat semolina flour, bow-tie pasta is called farfalle in Italian, which literally means "butterflies". They are made from tightly scalloped 2-inch squares of pasta pinched in at the center. The shape dates back to the sixteenth century, originating in the Lombardy and Emilia-Romagna regions of northern Italy. Known as gassa in the city of Genoa in the northwest, strichetto and galani in the cities of Bologna and Parma in Emilia-Romagna, other variations include the larger farfallone and the smaller farfalline. Bow ties are ideal for holding tomato sauce and other light sauces with butter, peas and cream, and is also good in cold pasta salads.

BOW TIES WITH CHEESE

FARFALLE AI FORMAGGI

Preparation time: 5 minutes

Cooking time: 10 minutes

Serves 4

Put the Gorgonzola, crescenza, and butter into a small pan, add the milk, and melt over low heat, stirring until smooth. Add the nutmeg and season to taste with salt. Cook the bow ties in plenty of salted boiling water until al dente. Drain and tip into a warmed serving dish. Pour the sauce on top, toss well, and sprinkle with the Parmesan. Serve immediately.

Gorgonzola is one of the best-known Italian cheeses. The name comes from the village of Gorgonzola, near Milan, where it seems that the cheese was invented by chance when a herdsman inadvertently left some milk in a bucket for a few days. The milk coagulated and became a very tasty cheese marbled with green veins of the mold Penicillium glaucum: the first Gorgonzola.

3½ ounces Gorgonzola cheese

3½ ounces crescenza or other stracchino cheese

1 teaspoon butter

2–3 tablespoons milk

pinch of grated nutmeg

12 ounces bow-tie pasta

scant 1 cup grated Parmesan cheese

salt

BOW TIES WITH SHRIMP

FARFALLE CON I GAMBERI

Preparation time: 20 minutes
Cooking time: 30 minutes
Serves 4
1 cup shelled peas
2 tablespoons olive oil
1 shallot, chopped
12 raw shrimp, peeled and deveined
(see Spaghetti with Langoustines, page 63)
scant ½ cup dry white wine
12 ounces bow-tie pasta
2 tablespoons chopped fresh flat-leaf parsley
salt and pepper

Blanch the peas in salted boiling water for 5 minutes, then drain. Heat the oil in a pan. Add the shallot and cook over low heat, stirring occasionally, for 5 minutes. Add the peas and cook, stirring occasionally, for 10 minutes. Add the shrimp, pour in the wine, and cook until the alcohol has evaporated. Stir and cook for 3 minutes more. Meanwhile, cook the bow ties in plenty of salted boiling water until al dente. Drain, tip into the pan with the sauce, and toss over the heat for 2 minutes. Season with pepper and transfer to a warmed serving dish. Sprinkle with the parsley and serve immediately.

BOW TIES WITH PROSCIUTTO AND PESTO

FARFALLE AL PROSCIUTTO E PESTO

Preparation time: 30 minutes
Cooking time: 20 minutes
Serves 6
3½ ounces prosciutto, thinly sliced
4 tablespoons butter
½ cup pine nuts
scant ½ cup white wine
1 tablespoon pesto (see Trenette with Pesto, page 238)
15 ounces bow-tie pasta
salt
grated Parmesan cheese, to serve

Spread out the slices of prosciutto on a tray and put into the freezer for 30 minutes, then cut into julienne strips. Melt the butter in a shallow pan. Add the prosciutto and cook, stirring occasionally, for 3–5 minutes, then stir in the pine nuts. Pour in the wine and cook until the alcohol has evaporated, then simmer gently for another 10 minutes. Remove from the heat and stir in the pesto. Meanwhile, cook the bow ties in plenty of salted boiling water until al dente. Drain, tip into a warmed serving dish, and pour the sauce over. Sprinkle with plenty of Parmesan and serve immediately.

The only way of sampling a true Genoese pesto sauce is to go to Liguria, a region in northwest Italy famous for a type of basil with small leaves and a delicate aroma. Common basil with large leaves has a more aggressive fragrance.

BOW TIES WITH CRAB

Melt the butter with the oil in a shallow pan. Add the shallots and cook over low heat, stirring occasionally, for 5 minutes. Pour in the lukewarm water, add the quartered artichoke hearts and crab meat, stir, and cook for 15 minutes. Pour in the cream, season with salt and pepper, cover, and simmer for a few minutes more. Cook the bow ties in plenty of salted boiling water until al dente. Drain and tip into the pan with the sauce. Increase the heat and toss well. Transfer to a warmed serving dish and serve immediately.

Preparation time: 30 minutes

Cooking time: 35 minutes

Serves 4

2 tablespoons butter

2 tablespoons olive oil

2 shallots, thinly sliced

scant ½ cup lukewarm water

8 globe artichoke hearts, trimmed and cut into quarters

7 ounces crab meat, drained if canned

scant ½ cup heavy cream

12 ounces bow-tie pasta

salt and pepper

BOW TIES WITH RICOTTA

Put the ricotta into a bowl and break it up with a fork. Add the diced and grated cheeses and stir in the egg yolks—the mixture should be fairly thick. Cook the bow ties in plenty of salted boiling water until al dente. Drain, tip into the ricotta mixture, and toss well so that everything has a nice golden yellow color. Serve immediately.

Ricotta is the whey produced during the first phase of cheese making, which is then re-cooked ("ricotta") to evaporate the liquid.

Preparation time: 10 minutes

Cooking time: 5 minutes

Serves 4

9 ounces ricotta cheese

2 ounces finely diced smoked scamorza or provolone cheese

2 tablespoons grated Parmesan cheese

2 egg yolks

12 ounces bow-tie pasta

salt

YELLOW BOW TIES

Cook the bow ties in plenty of salted boiling water until al dente. Meanwhile, melt the butter in a heatproof bowl set over a pan of simmering water. Remove the butter from the heat and stir in the saffron. Drain the bow ties, transfer to a warmed serving dish, and pour the saffron butter over. Sprinkle with the Parmesan, toss, and serve immediately.

Preparation time: 25 minutes

Cooking time: 18 minutes

Serves 4

12 ounces bow-tie pasta

4 tablespoons butter

pinch of saffron threads

⅔ cup grated Parmesan cheese

BOW TIES WITH RADICCHIO

Melt the butter in a shallow pan. Add the onion and cook over low heat, stirring occasionally, for 5 minutes. Add the radicchio and cook, stirring occasionally, for a few minutes until wilted. Add the sausage and cook, stirring occasionally, for about 10 minutes. Stir in the cream and cook, stirring frequently, until thickened. Season to taste with salt. Cook the bow ties in plenty of salted boiling water until al dente. Drain, tip into a warmed serving dish and pour the sauce over. Sprinkle with the Parmesan and serve immediately.

Tip: For a lower calorie content, substitute the cream with ¼ cup ricotta cheese mixed with 1–2 tablespoons of the pasta cooking water.

Preparation time: 20 minutes

Cooking time: 30 minutes

Serves 4

1½ tablespoons butter

1 small white onion, chopped

1 head of Treviso radicchio, coarsely chopped

8-inch length of luganega or other Italian

sausage, cut into pieces

scant ½ cup heavy cream

12 ounces bow-tie pasta

½ cup grated Parmesan cheese

salt

BOW TIES WITH MASCARPONE

Put the tomatoes, butter, oil, onion, basil, and a pinch of salt into a pan and cook over low heat, stirring occasionally for 20 minutes. Remove the pan from the heat and transfer the mixture to a food processor. Process to a purée and scrape into a bowl, then stir in the mascarpone. Cook the bow ties in plenty of salted boiling water until al dente. Drain, transfer to a warmed serving dish, and toss with the sauce. Sprinkle with Parmesan and serve immediately.

Made from cream skimmed off the milk and treated with heat and acidity, mascarpone is a typical cheese of Lodi and Abbiategrasso in Lombardy, northern Italy. The name comes from "mascherpa," which in certain areas of Lombardy means "cream." It is a white cheese with a delicate flavor and soft consistency suitable for use in both sweet and savory dishes.

Preparation time: 20 minutes

Cooking time: 25 minutes

Serves 4

9 ounces tomatoes, peeled

2 tablespoons butter

2 tablespoons olive oil

1 small onion, chopped

10 torn fresh basil leaves

⅓ cup mascarpone cheese

11 ounces bow-tie pasta

salt

grated Parmesan cheese, to serve

BOW TIES WITH SMOKED PANCETTA

Preparation time: 20 minutes
Cooking time: 40 minutes
Serves 4
1 tablespoon olive oil
generous ½ cup diced smoked pancetta
1 fresh chile, seeded and chopped
9 ounces tomatoes, peeled and chopped
scant 1 cup heavy cream
12 ounces bow-tie pasta
⅓ cup grated Parmesan cheese
salt

Heat the oil in a pan, add the pancetta and chile, and cook over medium heat for 5 minutes until lightly browned. Add the tomatoes, season with salt, and cook over low heat for 25 minutes. Stir in the cream and cook over very low heat for 5 minutes until thickened. Meanwhile, cook the bow ties in a large pan of salted boiling water until al dente. Drain, tip into the sauce, and cook, stirring constantly, for 30 seconds. Sprinkle with the Parmesan and serve.

SUMMER BOW TIES

Preparation time: 20 minutes
Cooking time: 30 minutes
Serves 4
2 tablespoons olive oil
1 scallion, finely chopped
1 garlic clove, finely chopped
6 torn fresh basil leaves
1 tablespoon chopped fresh marjoram
2 young zucchini, cut into julienne strips
1 yellow bell pepper, seeded and cut into julienne strips
1 eggplant, cut into julienne strips
scant 1 cup dry white wine
12 ounces bow-tie pasta
salt and pepper

Heat the oil in a large pan. Add the scallion, garlic, basil, and marjoram and cook over low heat, stirring occasionally, for 5 minutes. Stir in the zucchini, yellow bell pepper, and eggplant, pour in the wine, and cook until the alcohol has evaporated. Season with salt and pepper and simmer for 20–25 minutes until the vegetables are tender. Cook the pasta in plenty of salted boiling water until al dente. Drain, tip into the pan with the vegetables, and toss over the heat for a few minutes. Transfer to a warmed serving dish and serve immediately.

BOW TIES WITH SARDINES

Preparation time: 40 minutes
Cooking time: 30 minutes
Serves 4

1¾ pounds fresh sardines
2 tablespoons olive oil
1 small onion, chopped
1 celery stalk, chopped
1 garlic clove, chopped
1 bunch of chopped fresh flat-leaf parsley
scant 1 cup white wine
12 ounces bow-tie pasta
1 potato, diced
salt and pepper

Rub off the scales of the fish with your fingers or the back of a knife and rinse under cold running water. Cut off the head of each fish. Gently squeeze the belly until the guts protrude, trap them with the knife, and pull them out. Rinse well, then slit open the belly of each fish, and place, skin side uppermost, on a cutting board. Press firmly along the backbone with your fingers until the fish is flat. Turn it over and gently pull out the bones, snipping the backbone at the tail end with kitchen scissors. Heat the oil in a pan. Add the onion, celery, and garlic, and cook over low heat, stirring occasionally, for 5 minutes. Stir in the parsley, add the sardines, and season lightly with salt and pepper. Increase the heat, pour in the wine, and cook until the alcohol has evaporated. Lower the heat and simmer, adding a little hot water if necessary, for 15 minutes. Cook the bow ties and potato in plenty of salted boiling water until al dente. Drain, tip into a serving dish, and pour the sardine sauce over. Serve immediately.

This is a simplified version of the well-known Sicilian dish Pasta con le Sarde (Pasta with Sardines, see page 80), which includes wild fennel, pine nuts and golden raisins.

BOW TIES WITH SAUSAGE

Preparation time: 15 minutes
Cooking time: 35 minutes
Serves 4

2 tablespoons butter
4 tablespoons olive oil
1 onion, chopped • 1 celery stalk, chopped
1 carrot, chopped • 1 garlic clove
1 pound 2 ounces tomatoes, peeled and diced
10 torn fresh basil leaves
2 small sausages, skinned and diced
scant 1 cup dry white wine
12 ounces bow-tie pasta
salt and pepper

Melt the butter with the oil in a pan. Add the onion, celery, and carrot and cook over low heat, stirring occasionally, for 5 minutes. Add the garlic clove and cook, stirring frequently, for a few minutes until golden brown. Remove the garlic with a slotted spoon and discard. Add the tomatoes, basil, and sausages, pour in the wine, increase the heat, and cook until the alcohol has evaporated. Lower the heat, stir, and season to taste with salt and pepper, then simmer for 20–25 minutes until thickened. Meanwhile, cook the bow-ties in plenty of salted boiling water until al dente. Drain, tip into the pan with the sauce, and toss well. Serve immediately.

FUSILLI

Fusilli, meaning "little spindles" in Italian, is a corkscrew-shaped type of dried pasta made of durum wheat semolina flour, water, and salt. It is made using a special, thin utensil like a knitting needle with a rounded end, so that the pieces slide easily off. Fusilli can be long or short, hollow or solid. This flexible pasta shape, springy and with bite, originated in the regions of Molise and Basilicata in southern Italy, but has since spread throughout the country. Best suited to strong flavors, fusilli is perfect with vegetables sauces that stick to its coils, or with shellfish.

FUSILLI IN PUMPKIN CREAM

FUSILLI ALLA CREMA DI ZUCCA

Preheat the oven to 350°F. Cut off the top of the pumpkin and scoop out the flesh, reserving the "shell." Discard the seeds and membranes and slice the flesh. Put the slices into an ovenproof dish in a single layer and bake, turning once, for 40 minutes. Meanwhile, cook the turnip greens in just enough boiling water to cover for 5–10 minutes until tender. Drain and let cool. Remove the pumpkin from the oven and mash with a potato masher. Heat the oil in a large pan. Add the onion and garlic and cook over low heat, stirring occasionally, for 5 minutes. Meanwhile, cook the fusilli in plenty of salted boiling water until al dente. Drain, tip into the pan, and add the turnip greens, mashed pumpkin, cream, and Parmesan. Season to taste with salt and pepper, mix gently, and heat through for a few minutes. Spoon the mixture into the reserved pumpkin shell and serve immediately.

Preparation time: 30 minutes

Cooking time: 1 hour

Serves 4

1 pumpkin, weighing about 1½ pounds

1 pound 2 ounces turnip greens

3 tablespoons olive oil

1 onion, chopped

1 garlic clove, finely chopped

12 ounces fusilli

⅔ cup heavy cream

½ cup grated Parmesan cheese

salt and pepper

FUSILLI IN CUTTLEFISH INK

FUSILLI AL NERO DI SEPPIA

Cut the cuttlefish into strips. Heat the oil in a pan, add the onion, and cook over low heat, stirring occasionally, until softened. Add the cuttlefish and cook over medium heat, stirring occasionally, until lightly browned. Add the wine and cook until it has evaporated. Stir in the tomato paste, season with salt and pepper, lower the heat, cover, and cook for 1 hour. Cook the fusilli in a large pan of salted boiling water until al dente. Pour the cuttlefish ink into the sauce and stir in the parsley. Drain the pasta, tip it into the sauce, mix well, and transfer to a warmed serving dish.

Preparation time: 20 minutes

Cooking time: 1 hour 15 minutes

Serves 4

1½ pounds prepared cuttlefish, ink sacs reserved (see Fusilli with Cuttlefish, page 106)

2 tablespoons olive oil

1 onion, very thinly sliced

scant 1 cup dry white wine

2 tablespoons tomato paste

12 ounces fusilli

1 tablespoon chopped fresh flat-leaf parsley

salt and pepper

WHOLE WHEAT FUSILLI WITH SEITAN, MUSHROOMS, AND TOFU

FUSILLI INTEGRALI CON SEITAN, FUNGHI E TOFU

Put the onion into a shallow pan, pour in 5 tablespoons of the vegetable stock, the olive oil, and soy sauce, cover, and simmer for 10 minutes. Increase the heat to medium-high, add the mushrooms, seitan, and tofu, and cook, adding stock if necessary, for another 10 minutes. Cook the fusilli in plenty of salted boiling water until al dente. Drain, tip it into the pan of sauce, and toss. Add the herbs and chile and serve immediately.

Seitan consists mainly of wheat gluten and has a pleasant flavor, a soft consistency, and is easy to digest. It can be used as a substitute for meat, but has a lower nutritional value.

Preparation time: 20 minutes

Cooking time: 30 minutes

Serves 4

1 onion, cut into julienne strips

5–7 tablespoons vegetable stock

3 tablespoons olive oil

2 tablespoons soy sauce

scant 1½ cups sliced porcini mushrooms

7 ounces seitan (see note), sliced

3½ ounces firm tofu, sliced

12 ounces whole wheat fusilli

1 sprig chopped fresh marjoram

1 sprig chopped fresh basil

1 sprig chopped fresh flat-leaf parsley

1 fresh chile, seeded and shredded

salt

FUSILLI PIZZA

FUSILLI PIZZA

Preparation time: 20 minutes
Cooking time: 30 minutes
Serves 4

butter, for greasing
14 ounces tomatoes, peeled and chopped
1 tablespoon olive oil, plus extra for drizzling
pinch of dried oregano
1 tablespoon chopped fresh basil
12 ounces fusilli or other short pasta
½ cup grated Parmesan cheese
3½ ounces diced mozzarella cheese
salt

Preheat the oven to 350°F and grease an ovenproof dish with butter. Process the tomatoes to a purée in a food processor or blender. Heat the oil in a pan. Add the puréed tomatoes and cook over low heat, stirring occasionally, for 10–15 minutes until thickened. Stir in the oregano and basil and remove from the heat. Cook the pasta in plenty of salted boiling water until al dente. Drain, return to the pan, and pour the sauce over. Sprinkle with the Parmesan and toss well to mix. Spoon the mixture into the prepared dish, top with the diced mozzarella, and drizzle with oil. Bake for about 10 minutes until the mozzarella starts to melt. Serve immediately straight from the dish.

FUSILLI WITH ARTICHOKES

FUSILLI AI CARCIOFI

Preparation time: 25 minutes
Cooking time: 30 minutes
Serves 4

⅓ cup dried mushrooms
2 tablespoons olive oil
½ onion, chopped
1 garlic clove
1 tablespoon chopped fresh flat-leaf parsley
3 young globe artichokes, trimmed and thinly sliced
1 teaspoon concentrated tomato paste
scant ½ cup dry white wine
1½ teaspoons butter
12 ounces fusilli
salt and pepper

Put the mushrooms into a heatproof bowl, pour in lukewarm water to cover, and let soak for 30 minutes. Drain, squeeze out the excess liquid, and chop. Heat the oil in a pan. Add the onion, garlic, parsley, and mushrooms and cook over low heat, stirring occasionally, for 8–10 minutes until lightly browned. Meanwhile, cut the artichokes into strips. Add the artichokes to the pan, season with salt and pepper, and cook, stirring occasionally, for 10 minutes. Mix the tomato paste with 1 tablespoon water in a small bowl and add to the pan. Pour in the wine and cook until the alcohol has evaporated. Stir in the butter and simmer for 10 minutes, then remove the pan from the heat. Cook the pasta in plenty of salted boiling water until al dente. Drain, return to the pan, and pour the artichoke sauce over it. Transfer to a warmed serving dish and serve immediately.

FUSILLI WITH ZUCCHINI

FUSILLI ALLE ZUCCHINE

Preparation time: 20 minutes
Cooking time: 30 minutes
Serves 4
2 tablespoons butter
2 tablespoons olive oil
1 onion, chopped
6 young zucchini, sliced
12 ounces fusilli
1 egg yolk
½ cup grated pecorino cheese
salt and pepper

Melt the butter with the oil in a pan. Add the onion and cook over low heat, stirring occasionally, for 8–10 minutes until lightly browned. Add the zucchini, season with salt, and cook for 20 minutes until tender. Meanwhile, cook the fusilli in plenty of salted boiling water until al dente. Drain and tip into a warmed serving dish. Remove the zucchini from the heat and stir in the egg yolk, until the zucchini are coated. Pour the zucchini sauce over the pasta, sprinkle with the pecorino, season with pepper, and serve immediately.

FUSILLI WITH CUTTLEFISH

FUSILLI CON LE SEPPIOLINE

Preparation time: 45 minutes
Cooking time: 40 minutes
Serves 4
1 pound 2 ounces baby cuttlefish
2 tablespoons butter
2 tablespoons olive oil
2 shallots, chopped
1 garlic clove, chopped
1 celery heart, finely chopped
scant ½ cup dry white wine
1 cup fish stock
12 ounces fusilli
scant ½ cup heavy cream
1 tablespoon chopped fresh flat-leaf parsley
grated rind of ½ lemon
salt and pepper

To clean the cuttlefish, cut off the tentacles just in front of the eyes, squeeze out the beak from the center, and discard. Separate and skin the tentacles and pull off the skin from the body. Cut along the back and remove and discard the cuttlebone. Remove and discard the innards and head. Cut the body sacs into strips and the tentacles into pieces. Melt the butter with the oil in a pan. Add the shallots and garlic and cook over low heat, stirring occasionally, for 5 minutes. Increase the heat to medium, stir in the celery, and cook for 3 minutes, then add the cuttlefish, and season with salt and pepper. Pour in the wine and cook until the alcohol has evaporated. Pour in the fish stock, cover, and simmer for 20 minutes. Cook the fusilli in plenty of salted boiling water until al dente. Drain, tip into the cuttlefish sauce, and add the cream, parsley, and lemon rind. Season with pepper, toss well, and serve immediately.

FUSILLI WITH MUSHROOMS

FUSILLI AI FUNGHI

Heat the oil in a pan, add the onion and mushrooms, and cook over low heat, stirring occasionally, for 10 minutes. Season with salt and pepper and add the tomatoes with their juice. Simmer for 45 minutes, then remove the pan from the heat, and add the parsley. Meanwhile, cook the fusilli in a large pan of salted boiling water until al dente, drain, and tip onto a warmed serving dish. Sprinkle with the Parmesan, add the butter, and toss. Spoon the mushroom sauce on top and serve.

Preparation time: 20 minutes

Cooking time: 1 hour

Serves 4

3 tablespoons olive oil

1 onion, chopped

1¾ pounds chanterelle mushrooms or honey fungus, chopped

9 ounces canned tomatoes

1 tablespoon chopped fresh flat-leaf parsley

12 ounces fusilli

⅓ cup grated Parmesan cheese

2 tablespoons butter

salt and pepper

FUSILLI WITH ARUGULA AND PECORINO

FUSILLI ALLA RUCOLA CON PECORINO

Heat the oil in a shallow pan. Add the onion and garlic and cook over low heat, stirring occasionally, for 5 minutes. Add the tomatoes, season with salt, and simmer for 25 minutes until thickened. Cook the fusilli in plenty of salted boiling water until almost al dente, then about 3 minutes from the end of cooking add the arugula to the pan. When the pasta is al dente, drain the pasta and arugula and tip into the pan with the sauce. Toss, transfer to a warmed serving dish, and serve with the pecorino and pepper.

Preparation time: 20 minutes

Cooking time: 30 minutes

Serves 4

2 tablespoons olive oil

1 onion, chopped

3 garlic cloves, chopped

2¼ pounds ripe tomatoes, coarsely chopped

12 ounces fusilli

3 bunches of arugula

½ cup grated pecorino cheese

salt and pepper

107

FUSILLI WITH VEGETABLES

Preparation time: 20 minutes

Cooking time: 25 minutes

Serves 4

2 tablespoons olive oil

1 garlic clove, finely chopped

1 tomato, peeled and diced

1 zucchini, diced • 1 celery heart, diced

2 carrots, diced

1 yellow bell pepper, seeded and diced

12 ounces fusilli

½ cup grated Parmesan cheese

1 tablespoon chopped fresh flat-leaf parsley

salt and pepper

Heat the oil in a pan. Add the garlic and cook over low heat, stirring frequently, for 2–3 minutes. Season with salt and pepper, add the tomato, zucchini, celery heart, carrots, and yellow bell pepper and cook over low heat, stirring occasionally, for 20 minutes. Meanwhile, cook the fusilli in plenty of salted boiling water until al dente. Drain, tip into a tureen, sprinkle with the Parmesan, add the vegetables, and stir carefully. Garnish with the parsley and serve immediately.

FUSILLI TIMBALE

Preparation time: 1 hour

Cooking time: 1 hour and 10 minutes

Serves 6

4 tablespoons butter, plus extra for greasing

4 leeks, white parts only, thinly sliced

¾ cup dry white wine

5 tablespoons milk

12 ounces fusilli

1 cup grated Parmesan cheese

2 eggs

6 fresh sage leaves

salt and pepper

Preheat the oven to 350°F. Grease an ovenproof dish with butter. Melt half the butter in a pan, add the leeks, pour in water to a depth of ¾ inch, and cook over low heat for 10 minutes until softened. Add the wine, increase the heat to medium, and cook until it has evaporated. Pour in the milk and cook until it has evaporated, then season with salt and pepper to taste. Cook the fusilli in a large pan of salted boiling water until al dente, then drain. Cover the base of the prepared dish with a thick layer of fusilli, spoon a little of the leek mixture on top, sprinkle with some of the Parmesan, and dot with some of the remaining butter. Repeat these layers until all the ingredients are used, ending with a layer of fusilli. Beat the eggs with a pinch of salt and pepper, pour over the fusilli, and dot with butter. Garnish with the sage and bake for 40 minutes. Remove the timbale from the oven and let stand for 10 minutes before serving.

ELBOW MACARONI

Elbow macaroni is a short, curved variety of dried pasta called gomiti in Italian, which literally means "elbows." It can be either "lisce" (smooth) or "rigate" (ridged) and is about ½ inch in diameter and 1½ inches long. Elbow macaroni is typically combined with sauces made with sausage, cheese and vegetables.

RIDGED ELBOW MACARONI WITH TURNIPS

GOMITI RIGATI ALLE RAPE

Blanch the turnips in lightly salted boiling water for about 5 minutes. Drain and let cool, then dice. Chop together the shallot, rosemary, and garlic. Heat the oil in a shallow pan. Add the shallot mixture and cook over low heat, stirring occasionally, for 5 minutes. Add the ham and turnip, season with salt and pepper, and cook over low heat, stirring occasionally, for 10 minutes. Mash together the butter and cornstarch in a bowl until combined, then stir into the pan. Pour in the milk, and simmer, stirring constantly, until the mixture has the consistency of thick cream. Cook the elbow macaroni in plenty of salted boiling water until al dente. Drain, tip into a warmed serving dish, pour the sauce over and sprinkle with the Parmesan. Serve immediately.

Preparation time: 25 minutes

Cooking time: 40 minutes

Serves 4

7 ounces white turnips, thickly sliced

1 shallot

1 sprig fresh rosemary

1 garlic clove

2 tablespoons olive oil

generous ½ cup diced lean ham

1 tablespoon butter, softened

1 teaspoon cornstarch

scant 1 cup skimmed milk

12 ounces ridged elbow macaroni

½ cup grated Parmesan cheese

salt and pepper

ELBOW MACARONI WITH PUMPKIN AND RADICCHIO

GOMITI CON ZUCCA E RADICCHIO

Preparation time: 30 minutes

Cooking time: 30 minutes

Serves 4

2 tablespoons olive oil

1 small onion, chopped

11 ounces pumpkin or butternut squash, peeled, seeded and cut into strips

⅔ cup lukewarm water

1 head of Treviso or Chioggia radicchio, cut into thin strips

1 bunch of finely chopped fresh flat-leaf parsley

12 ounces ridged elbow macaroni

salt and pepper

Heat the oil in a shallow pan. Add the onion and cook over low heat, stirring occasionally, for 5 minutes. Increase the heat to medium, add the pumpkin, and cook, stirring occasionally, for 5 minutes until evenly browned. Add the lukewarm water, season with salt and pepper, cover, and simmer for 15 minutes. Stir in the radicchio and three-quarters of the parsley and cook for another 5 minutes. Cook the pasta in plenty of salted boiling water until al dente. Drain, tip into a warmed serving dish, and pour the sauce over. Sprinkle with the remaining parsley and serve immediately.

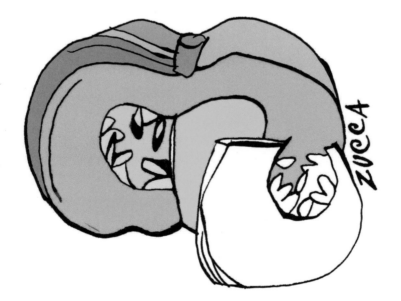

ZUCCA

MACARONI

Maccheroni was the name given to pasta when it first appeared in the noble courts of southern Italy. Even today, in the south of Italy, the term can refer to all types of durum wheat pasta or to home-made pasta. In northern Italy however, the term generally covers several types of dried, short pasta, which are hollow, cylindrical and more or less straight, some ridged with closely packed grooves and some with none at all, and with hundreds of names. In the English-speaking world this type of tubular pasta is more often called macaroni. Maccheroncini, or small macaroni, is a variation on the basic type. Given the variety within the family, macaroni can be matched with virtually any type of sauce and is ideal for oven-baked recipes. It is perhaps most often associated outside Italy with cheese sauces, as in the case of Maccheroni ai Quattro Formaggi (Macaroni with Four Cheeses, see opposite).

MACARONI FROM MOLISE

MACCHERONI ALLA MOLISANA

Preparation time: 15 minutes
Cooking time: 15 minutes
Serves 6
2 tablespoons olive oil
1 garlic clove, finely chopped
1 onion, finely chopped
3½ ounces diced pancetta or bacon
1 sprig finely chopped fresh flat-leaf parsley
4 fresh basil leaves, torn
1 fresh red chile, seeded and chopped
15 ounces macaroni
½ cup grated pecorino cheese
salt

Heat the oil in a shallow pan. Add the garlic and onion and cook over low heat, stirring occasionally, for 5 minutes. Add the pancetta or bacon, parsley, basil, and chile and cook for a few minutes. Meanwhile, cook the macaroni in plenty of salted boiling water until al dente. Drain and return to the pan. Pour the sauce over, sprinkle with the pecorino, and mix well. Transfer to a warmed serving dish and serve immediately.

The cuisine of Molise in southern Italy has retained its traditional style based on local produce and hard work. Wheat, meat, fish, pulses and vegetables are all found in the region's kitchens, but it is wheat that produces the characteristic specialities: delicious pasta, cooked strictly al dente with an abundant sprinkling of "diavolino"—red chile—and grated pecorino, alone or mixed with Parmesan.

MACARONI WITH CUTTLEFISH

Put the cuttlefish, tomatoes with their juice, onion, garlic, potato, pea, parsley, and oil in a large pan and cook over medium heat, stirring frequently, for 10 minutes. Lower the heat, cover, and cook for another 30 minutes. Season with salt and pepper to taste. Cook the macaroni in a large pan of salted, boiling water until al dente, then drain, and tip into the sauce. Mix well, transfer to a warmed serving dish, and serve.

Preparation time: 20 minutes

Cooking time: 50 minutes

Serves 4

1 pound 5 ounces cleaned baby cuttlefish (see Fusilli with Cuttlefish, page 106)

9 ounces canned chopped tomatoes

1 onion, finely chopped

2 garlic cloves, chopped

1 large potato, sliced

1¾ cups shelled baby peas

2 tablespoons chopped fresh flat-leaf parsley

4 tablespoons olive oil

12 ounces macaroni • salt and pepper

MACARONI WITH FOUR CHEESES

Melt the butter in a heatproof bowl set over a pan of simmering water. Add the mozzarella, caciotta, and Emmenthal and mix but do not melt completely. Season lightly with salt and remove from the heat. Cook the macaroni in plenty of salted boiling water until al dente. Drain, tip into a warmed serving dish, and pour the butter and cheese mixture over it. Sprinkle with the Parmesan and serve immediately.

Preparation time: 15 minutes

Cooking time: 15 minutes

Serves 4

3 tablespoons butter

5 ounces mixed diced mozzarella, caciotta, and Emmenthal cheese

12 ounces macaroni

½ cup grated Parmesan cheese • salt

MACARONI WITH OLIVES AND MUSHROOMS

Put the olives, mushrooms, garlic, and parsley into a bowl. Season with salt and pepper, and drizzle with olive oil. Let marinate for about 1 hour. Cook the macaroni in plenty of salted boiling water until al dente. Drain, tip into a serving dish, pour the sauce over and serve.

Preparation time: 20 minutes, plus 1 hour marinating

Cooking time: 10 minutes

Serves 4

1¾ cups green olives, pitted and chopped

5 ounces porcini mushrooms in olive oil, drained and sliced • 2 garlic cloves, chopped

1 sprig chopped fresh flat-leaf parsley

olive oil, for drizzling

12 ounces macaroni • salt and pepper

MACARONI WITH MUSHROOMS

MACCHERONI AI FUNGHI PORCINI

Preparation time: 10 minutes
Cooking time: 30 minutes
Serves 4

2 tablespoons butter
3 tablespoons olive oil
1 garlic clove
3⅓ cups sliced porcini mushrooms
5 ounces canned chopped tomatoes, drained
1 tablespoon chopped fresh flat-leaf parsley
12 ounces macaroni • salt and pepper

Heat the butter and oil in a pan, add the garlic clove and porcini, and cook, stirring occasionally, for 5 minutes. Add the tomatoes, season with salt and pepper to taste, cover, and cook over low heat for about 20 minutes. Remove and discard the garlic and stir in the parsley. Cook the macaroni in a large pan of salted boiling water until al dente, then drain, toss with the porcini sauce, and serve.

Tip: This sauce can also be made without tomatoes, in which case use 3 tablespoons butter.

NEAPOLITAN MACARONI TIMBALE

TIMBALLO DI MACCHERONI NAPOLETANO

Preparation time: 1 hour 30 minutes
Cooking time: 1 hour 20 minutes
Serves 6

½ cup dried mushrooms
4 tablespoons butter, plus extra for greasing
1 garlic clove, chopped
½ onion, chopped
7 ounces chicken hearts and livers, trimmed and cut into pieces
3½ ounces luganega sausage, skinned and cut into pieces
14 ounces ripe tomatoes, peeled, seeded and chopped
12 ounces macaroni
4 tablespoons fresh bread crumbs
5 ounces mozzarella cheese, diced
½ cup grated Parmesan cheese
salt

Put the mushrooms into a heatproof bowl and pour in warm water to cover. Let soak for 20 minutes, then drain, squeeze out the excess liquid, and chop. Melt the butter in a pan. Add the garlic and onion and cook over low heat, stirring occasionally, for 8 minutes until light golden brown. Increase the heat to medium, add the chicken hearts and livers, the sausage, and the mushrooms, season with salt, stir, and cook for a few minutes. Add the tomatoes, cover, and simmer, stirring occasionally, for 30 minutes.

Cook the macaroni in plenty of salted boiling water until al dente. Drain, return to the pan, pour the sauce over, and let cool. Preheat the oven to 350°F. Grease a deep cake pan with butter and sprinkle with half the bread crumbs. Stir the mozzarella and Parmesan into the cooled pasta. Spoon the mixture into the prepared pan, smooth the surface, and sprinkle with the remaining bread crumbs. Bake for about 40 minutes until well browned. Remove the pan from the oven and let stand for a few minutes, then turn out the timbale onto a warmed dish, and serve immediately.

MACARONI WITH PANCETTA

MACCHERONI ALLA PANCETTA

Heat the oil in a skillet. Add the pancetta or bacon and sage leaves and cook over medium-low heat for 8–10 minutes until browned. Beat the egg with the cream in a bowl and season with salt and pepper. Cook the macaroni in plenty of salted boiling water until al dente. Drain, tip into a serving dish, and immediately pour over the egg and cream mixture, mixing thoroughly. Remove and discard the sage leaves, add the pancetta to the pasta, sprinkle with the Parmesan, and serve.

Preparation time: 15 minutes

Cooking time: 20 minutes

Serves 4

2 tablespoons olive oil

scant 1 cup diced smoked pancetta or bacon

4 fresh sage leaves • 1 egg

2 tablespoons light cream

12 ounces macaroni

⅔ cup grated Parmesan cheese

salt and pepper

PASTICCIO FROM FERRARA

PASTICCIO ALLA FERRARESE

Put the squab into a pan, season with salt, drizzle with olive oil, dot with the butter, cover, and cook over medium-low heat, turning occasionally, for 45 minutes. Lift out the birds from the pan and remove and discard the skin. Cut the meat off the bones and cut into strips. Combine the strips of meat, eggs, Parmesan, and béchamel sauce in a bowl. Cook the macaroni in plenty of salted boiling water until al dente. Drain, tip into the bowl and mix well. Preheat the oven to 350°F. Cut the pastry dough into two pieces, one slightly larger than the other. Roll out the larger piece on a lightly floured surface and use to line the base of a pie dish. Brush the rim with water. Spoon in the macaroni mixture. Roll out the remaining dough on a lightly floured surface and use to cover the pie, pressing the edges together to seal. Knock up the edges with the back of a knife blade. Bake for about 20 minutes until the pastry is golden brown. Serve immediately.

The dish that unites Emilia-Romagna in northern Italy, an area of two combined regions, is pasta with filling. While tortelli (see page 310), served in the various provinces with imaginative fillings, symbolises this area, Pasticcio is a close and popular relation.

Preparation time: 30 minutes

Cooking time: 1 hour 15 minutes

Serves 4

2 squab, cleaned and trussed

olive oil, for drizzling

4 tablespoons butter

2 eggs, lightly beaten

3 cups grated Parmesan cheese

4 tablespoons béchamel sauce (see Baked Pumpkin Pasta, page 272)

10 ounces macaroni

9 ounces ready-made pie dough, thawed if frozen

all-purpose flour, for dusting

salt

MACARONI WITH BELL PEPPERS

Heat the oil in a skillet. Add the garlic clove and cook over low heat, stirring frequently, for a few minutes until browned. Remove the garlic with a slotted spoon and discard. Add the anchovies and cook, mashing with a wooden spoon until they have disintegrated. Add the bell pepper strips, season with salt and pepper and cook, stirring occasionally, for 12–15 minutes until the bell peppers are soft but not mushy. Cook the pasta in plenty of salted boiling water until al dente. Drain, tip into the skillet, toss well, and cook for a few minutes more to allow the flavors to mingle. Serve sprinkled with a little oregano if you like.

Preparation time: 20 minutes

Cooking time: 30 minutes

Serves 4

2 tablespoons olive oil

1 garlic clove

4 canned anchovy fillets, drained

2 yellow bell peppers, seeded and cut into strips

12 ounces macaroni

salt and pepper

chopped fresh oregano, to garnish (optional)

WHOLE WHEAT MACARONI WITH CHICORY

Cook the chicory in boiling water for 10 minutes, then drain, reserving the cooking water, and squeeze out the excess liquid. Chop finely. Put the tomatoes into a food processor and process. Heat the oil in a shallow pan. Add the garlic cloves and chile and cook over low heat, stirring frequently, for 2–3 minutes. Add the chicory, increase the heat to high, and cook, stirring constantly, for 3 minutes. Add the tomatoes, season with salt, lower the heat, and simmer for 15 minutes. Pour the reserved cooking water into a pan, top up with fresh water, and bring to a boil. Add a pinch of salt and the macaroni and cook until the pasta is al dente. Drain and tip into a warmed serving dish. Remove and discard the garlic cloves and chile from the sauce and pour it over the pasta. Toss well, sprinkle with the basil and Parmesan, and serve immediately.

Preparation time: 30 minutes

Cooking time: 35 minutes

Serves 4

3 heads of green chicory

11 ounces fresh plum tomatoes, peeled and coarsely chopped, or canned chopped tomatoes

2 tablespoons olive oil

2 garlic cloves

1 fresh chile

12 ounces whole wheat macaroni

6 torn fresh basil leaves

½ cup grated Parmesan cheese

salt

PASTA 'NCASCIATA

PASTA 'NCASCIATA

Put the eggplant slices into a colander, sprinkling each layer with salt, and let drain for 30 minutes, then rinse, and pat dry. Heat 4 tablespoons of the oil in a skillet. Add the eggplant slices in batches, and cook over medium-low heat for 5–10 minutes on each side until golden brown. Remove with a spatula and drain on paper towels. Heat the remaining oil in a shallow pan. Add the garlic clove and cook over low heat, stirring frequently, for a few minutes until lightly browned. Remove the garlic with a slotted spoon and discard. Add the tomatoes, basil leaves, beef, ham, and chicken livers to the pan, season with salt and pepper, cover, and cook over medium heat for 20 minutes. Cook the macaroni in plenty of salted boiling water until al dente. Meanwhile, preheat the oven to 350°F. Grease a springform cake pan with butter and sprinkle with the bread crumbs. Drain the pasta, return to the pan, and pour the sauce over. Add the mozzarella, egg wedges, and eggplants, and stir. Transfer the mixture to the prepared pan, sprinkle with the pecorino and bake for about 20 minutes. Remove the dish from the oven and let stand for 5 minutes, then turn out onto a warmed serving dish and serve.

Traditions are strong in Sicily. It is a place with a baroque heart not only in the churches and the customs, but also in the kitchen. Pasta 'Ncasciata, which means "compressed pasta" and includes meat, chicken livers, tomatoes, mozzarella, pecorino, eggplants and ham, is a fine example of an age-old dish.

Preparation time: 1 hour

Cooking time: 1 hour 15 minutes

Serves 6

3 eggplants, sliced

½ cup olive oil

1 garlic clove

1 pound 5 ounces ripe tomatoes,

peeled and diced

4 fresh basil leaves

⅔ cup diced lean beef

½ cup diced ham

3 ounces chicken livers, trimmed and chopped

15 ounces macaroni

butter, for greasing

4 tablespoons fresh bread crumbs

3 ounces diced mozzarella cheese

2 hard-cooked eggs, cut into wedges

⅓ cup grated pecorino cheese

salt and pepper

MACARONI AU GRATIN

MACCHERONI GRATINATI

Preheat the oven to 475°F. Grease an ovenproof dish with butter. Combine the béchamel sauce, Parmesan, butter, and egg yolks. Cook the macaroni in a large pan of salted boiling water until just al dente, then drain, and tip into a bowl. Gently stir in half the béchamel sauce mixture and put in the prepared dish, then spoon the remaining béchamel sauce mixture on top. Bake for 15–20 minutes until golden brown.

Preparation time: 10 minutes

Cooking time: 30 minutes

Serves 4

2 tablespoons butter, plus extra for greasing

1 quantity béchamel sauce (see Baked Pumpkin Pasta, page 272)

⅔ cup grated Parmesan cheese

2 egg yolks • 12 ounces macaroni • salt

PIQUANT MACARONI WITH BELL PEPPERS

MACCHERONI PICCANTI AI PEPERONI

Preparation time: 30 minutes

Cooking time: 1 hour 30 minutes

Serves 4

2 red bell peppers

7 ounces diced mozzarella cheese

8 black olives, pitted and sliced

8 green olives, pitted and sliced

4 torn fresh basil leaves

olive oil, for drizzling

9 ounces macaroni

butter, for greasing • salt and pepper

Preheat the oven to 350°F. Put the bell peppers onto a cookie sheet and roast, turning twice, for 1 hour. Remove them from the oven, wrap in aluminum foil while still hot, and let cool. When cold, unwrap the bell peppers, peel, seed, and cut the flesh into thin strips. Combine the bell pepper strips, mozzarella, olives, and basil in a bowl, drizzle with olive oil, and season lightly with salt and pepper. Cook the macaroni in plenty of salted boiling water until al dente. Drain the pasta, return to the pan, and add the bell pepper mixture. Mix well, pour into the prepared dish, and bake for 20 minutes.

SMALL MACARONI IN MEAT SAUCE

MACCHERONCINI AL RAGÙ

Preparation time: 20 minutes

Cooking time: 35 minutes

Serves 4

⅓ cup dried mushrooms

3 tablespoons olive oil

½ onion, chopped

1 carrot, chopped

2 tablespoons fresh flat-leaf parsley

7 ounces ground beef

scant ½ cup white wine

scant ½ cup warm milk • 10 ounces small macaroni

½ cup grated Parmesan cheese • salt and pepper

Put the mushrooms into a heatproof bowl, pour in warm water to cover, and let soak for 20 minutes. Drain and squeeze out the excess liquid, then chop. Heat the oil in a pan. Add the onion, carrot, parsley, ground meat, and mushrooms and cook over medium heat, stirring frequently, until the meat is lightly browned. Pour in the wine and cook until the alcohol has evaporated. Pour in the warm milk and cook, stirring occasionally, for another 15–20 minutes more until the meat is cooked through and tender. Season to taste with salt and pepper. Cook the pasta in plenty of salted boiling water until al dente. Drain and tip into a warmed serving dish. Pour the sauce on top and sprinkle with the Parmesan. Serve immediately.

SMALL MACARONI WITH MASCARPONE

MACCHERONCINI AL MASCARPONE

Preparation time: 10 minutes

Cooking time: 10 minutes • Serves 4

1 egg yolk • scant 1 cup mascarpone cheese

pinch of freshly grated nutmeg

½ cup grated Parmesan cheese

12 ounces small macaroni • salt and pepper

Combine the egg yolk, mascarpone, nutmeg, Parmesan and a pinch of pepper in a tureen. Cook the pasta in plenty of salted boiling water until al dente, reserving a few tablespoons of the cooking water. Drain, tip into the tureen, and toss, adding the reserved cooking water if necessary. Taste and adjust the seasoning, if necessary, and serve immediately.

SMALL MACARONI WITH FRANKFURTERS, CREAM AND EGG

MACCHERONCINI AI WURSTEL, PANNA E UOVO

Poach the frankfurters in barely simmering water according to the instructions on the packet. Remove from the pan, chop, and let cool. Beat the cream with the egg yolk in a bowl, add the frankfurters, and season with salt and pepper. Cook the macaroni in plenty of salted boiling water until al dente. Drain, return to the pan, add the butter, season with salt, and pour the frankfurter mixture over it. Mix thoroughly and serve immediately, handing the Parmesan separately.

Preparation time: 10 minutes

Cooking time: 18 minutes

Serves 4

3 frankfurters, each 4–6 inches long

scant 1 cup heavy cream

1 egg yolk

12 ounces small macaroni

3 tablespoons butter • salt and pepper

grated Parmesan cheese, to serve

SMALL MACARONI WITH GORGONZOLA

MACCHERONCINI AL GORGONZOLA

Mash the Gorgonzola in a heatproof bowl with a fork, then work in the butter until the mixture is smooth and creamy. Gradually mix in the cream and season with salt and pepper. Set the bowl over a pan of simmering water and heat through, stirring frequently. Cook the macaroni in plenty of salted boiling water until al dente. Drain, tip into a warmed serving dish, pour the cheese sauce over, and serve immediately.

Preparation time: 15 minutes

Cooking time: 20 minutes

Serves 4

5 ounces Gorgonzola cheese

2 tablespoons butter, softened

scant 1 cup heavy cream

12 ounces small macaroni

salt and pepper

SMALL MACARONI WITH SAUSAGE

MACCHERONCINI ALLA SALSICCIA

Melt the butter in a shallow pan. Add the onion and cook over low heat, stirring occasionally, for 5 minutes. Pour in the wine and cook until the alcohol has evaporated. Add the sausage pieces and basil and cook for a few minutes, then pour in the cream and milk, and season with salt. Simmer for about 15 minutes. Meanwhile, cook the pasta in plenty of salted boiling water until al dente. Drain, tip into the pan with the sauce, and toss for a few seconds. Season with white pepper, sprinkle with the Parmesan, and serve immediately.

Preparation time: 20 minutes

Cooking time: 30 minutes

Serves 4

2 tablespoons butter

1 onion, chopped

scant ½ cup dry white wine

12 ounces small macaroni rigati

7 ounces luganega sausage, skinned and cut into pieces

4 torn fresh basil leaves

scant ½ cup heavy cream • scant ½ cup milk

½ cup grated Parmesan cheese

salt and freshly ground white pepper

MEZZE MANICHE

Mezze maniche, meaning "half sleeves" in Italian, is a type of dried pasta originating in central and southern Italy. Hollow and very similar to macaroni and rigatoni, but shorter, it is sometimes called "maniche di frate" ("monk's sleeves"). The surface of mezze maniche is ridged, which makes it suitable for all kind of sauces. It is also good in cold pasta salads.

MEZZE MANICHE WITH CREAMY GARBANZO BEAN SAUCE

MEZZE MANICHE CON CREMA DI CECI

Preparation time: 15 minutes
Cooking time: 25 minutes
Serves 4

1½ cups cooked or canned garbanzo beans, drained
2 tablespoons olive oil
1 garlic clove
1 sprig finely chopped fresh rosemary, plus extra to garnish
12 ounces mezze maniche
salt and pepper

Put half the garbanzo beans into a food processor or blender and process to a purée. Heat the oil in a pan. Add the garlic clove and cook over low heat, stirring frequently, for a few minutes until lightly browned. Remove the garlic with a slotted spoon and discard. Add the puréed garbanzo beans and the whole garbanzo beans to the pan, sprinkle with the rosemary, and season with salt and pepper. Cook over low heat, stirring frequently, for 10 minutes. Cook the mezze maniche in plenty of salted boiling water until al dente. Drain, tip into a warmed serving dish, and pour the garbanzo bean sauce over. Garnish with rosemary sprigs and serve immediately.

PENNE

These short, diagonally-cut tubes have a streamlined shape similar to a quill pen (penne means "quills" in Italian). Typical of the region of Calabria in southern Italy, but probably one of the most commonly used of all short pasta types, penne is chewy and substantial and can be "lisce" (smooth) or "rigate" (ridged) on the surface. If not specified in the recipe, you can use both types. Penne can also vary in size, and although it is typically ½ inch in diameter and about 2 inches long, it can also be mezze penne, which is half the size, or pennette, which is even smaller. Penne can be used with almost any ingredient and goes well with meat, fish, and vegetables. It also suits a variety of cooking methods, including frying and baking in oven-baked dishes such as Pasticcio (see page 137).

PENNE NORMA

PASTA ALLA NORMA

Preparation time: 1 hour
Cooking time: 35–40 minutes
Serves 4

2 small eggplants, thinly sliced
⅔ cup olive oil
1 garlic clove, crushed
12 ounces canned chopped tomatoes or
2¼ cups bottle strained tomatoes
6 fresh basil leaves, torn
12 ounces penne
scant ½ cup grated ricotta salata cheese
salt and pepper

Put the eggplant slices into a colander, sprinkle each layer with salt, and let drain for 30 minutes, then rinse, and pat dry with paper towels. Heat 6 tablespoons of the oil in a large skillet. Add the eggplant slices and cook in batches over medium heat for 5–10 minutes on each side until golden brown. Remove with a spatula and drain on paper towels. Meanwhile, heat the remaining oil in a pan. Add the garlic, tomatoes, and basil, season with salt and pepper, and cook over low heat, stirring occasionally, for 30 minutes. Remove the pan from the heat and transfer the mixture to a food processor or blender. Process to a purée. Cook the penne in plenty of salted boiling water until al dente. Drain and tip into a warmed serving dish. Sprinkle with half the ricotta, spoon the tomato sauce over it, and arrange the eggplant slices on top. Sprinkle with remaining ricotta and serve without tossing.

This dish from the city of Catania in Sicily was named in honor of the famous composer Vincenzo Bellini, author of the opera "Norma".

FRIED PENNE

PENNE IN TEGAME

Preparation time: 5 minutes
Cooking time: 10 minutes
Serves 4
4 tablespoons butter
1 onion, thinly sliced • 12 ounces penne
½ cup grated Parmesan cheese
salt and pepper

Melt the butter in a pan, add the onion, then add the penne. Mix well to coat the pasta with butter, then pour in enough boiling water to cover. Add salt and cook until the penne is al dente, adding more boiling water if necessary. Season with pepper, transfer to a warm serving dish, and sprinkle with the Parmesan. Serve immediately.

PENNE ARRABBIATA

PENNE ALL'ARRABBIATA

Preparation time: 10 minutes
Cooking time: 30 minutes
Serves 4
6 tablespoons oil
2 garlic cloves
½ fresh chile, seeded and chopped
1 pound 2 ounces canned chopped tomatoes, drained
12 ounces penne lisce
1 tablespoon chopped fresh flat-leaf parsley
salt

Heat the oil in a skillet, add the garlic cloves and chile, and cook until the garlic browns. Remove the cloves from the pan and discard. Add the tomatoes to the pan, season with salt, and cook for about 15 minutes. Cook the penne in a large pan of salted boiling water until al dente, then drain, and tip into the skillet. Toss over high heat for a few minutes, then transfer to a warm serving dish. Sprinkle with the parsley and serve immediately.

PENNE WITH OLIVES AND TOMATOES

PENNE CON OLIVE E POMODORI

Preparation time: 20 minutes
Cooking time: 5 minutes
Serves 4
4 ripe tomatoes, peeled and diced
4 tablespoons plain yogurt
olive oil, for drizzling
12 ounces penne
½ cup black olives, pitted and sliced
1 tablespoon chopped fresh flat-leaf parsley
1 tablespoon chopped fresh chervil
salt and pepper

Put the tomatoes into a large bowl and season with salt and pepper. Gently stir in the yogurt and drizzle with olive oil. Cook the penne in plenty of salted boiling water until al dente. Drain, tip into the bowl, add the olives and chopped herbs, and toss lightly. Serve immediately.

PENNE WITH HAM AND MUSHROOMS

PENNE AL PROSCIUTTO E FUNGHI

Put the mushrooms into a bowl, pour in lukewarm water to cover, and let soak for 20 minutes. Drain, squeeze out the excess liquid, and slice. Melt the butter with the oil in a pan. Add the onion and cook over low heat, stirring occasionally, for 8–10 minutes until lightly browned. Add the mushrooms and ham and cook, stirring occasionally, for a few minutes, then pour in the wine, and cook until the alcohol has evaporated. Season with salt and pepper and simmer for 20 minutes, adding enough hot stock to prevent the mixture from sticking. Stir in the cream and heat through for a few minutes more. Meanwhile, cook the pasta in plenty of salted boiling water until al dente. Drain, tip into a warmed serving dish, and pour the sauce over. Sprinkle with the Parmesan and serve immediately.

Preparation time: 10 minutes

Cooking time: 40 minutes

Serves 4

1 cup dried mushrooms

2 tablespoons butter

2 tablespoons olive oil

1 onion

⅓ cup diced ham

scant ½ cup dry white wine

12 ounces penne

4–5 tablespoons hot vegetable stock

3 tablespoons heavy cream

½ cup grated Parmesan cheese

salt and pepper

PENNE WITH BLACK OLIVES

PENNE ALLE OLIVE NERE

Put the olives and cream in a pan and cook over low heat for about 15 minutes. Cook the penne in a large pan of salted boiling water until al dente, then drain. Spoon half the olive sauce onto the base of a warm serving dish and top with the pasta. Sprinkle with the Parmesan, then spoon the remaining sauce on top. Mix well and serve.

Preparation time: 15 minutes

Cooking time: 20 minutes

Serves 4

1¼ cups black olives, pitted and sliced

¾ cup heavy cream

12 ounces penne lisce

⅓ cup grated Parmesan cheese

salt

PENNE WITH PEAS AND ARTICHOKES

PENNE AI PISELLI E CARCIOFI

Preparation time: 20 minutes
Cooking time: 30 minutes
Serves 4
2 tablespoons butter
2 tablespoons olive oil
3 cups shelled peas
3 young globe artichokes, trimmed and thinly sliced
⅔ cup water • 12 ounces penne
½ cup grated Parmesan cheese • salt

Melt the butter with the oil in a pan. Add the peas and artichokes and cook over low heat, stirring frequently, for 5 minutes. Season with salt, pour in the water, cover, and simmer for 20–25 minutes until tender. Cook the penne in plenty of salted boiling water until al dente. Drain, tip into a warmed serving dish, and pour the sauce over. Sprinkle with the Parmesan and serve immediately.

PENNE WITH PUMPKIN

PENNE CON LA ZUCCA

Preparation time: 30 minutes
Cooking time: 30–35 minutes
Serves 4
2 tablespoons olive oil • 1 shallot, chopped
⅓ cup finely diced pancetta or bacon
1 pound 2 ounces pumpkin, peeled, seeded, and diced
scant 1 cup dry white wine
1 tablespoon butter
12 ounces penne rigate
1 tablespoon chopped fresh flat-leaf parsley
½ cup grated Parmesan cheese

Heat the oil in a pan. Add the shallot and cook over low heat, stirring occasionally, for 5–8 minutes until lightly browned. Add the pancetta or bacon, increase the heat to medium and cook, stirring frequently, for 4–5 minutes. Add the pumpkin, season with salt and pepper, lower the heat and simmer, gradually stirring in the wine, for about 20 minutes until the pumpkin is pulpy. Remove the pan from the heat and stir in the butter. The sauce should be creamy and moist. Cook the penne in plenty of salted boiling water until al dente. Drain, return to the pan and pour the pumpkin sauce over. Transfer to a warmed serving dish, sprinkle with the parsley and Parmesan and serve immediately.

PENNE WITH TURNIP GREENS

PENNE CON CIME DI RAPA

Preparation time: 12 minutes
Cooking time: 18 minutes
Serves 4
1 pound 2 ounces turnip tops
4 anchovy fillets
3 tablespoons olive oil, plus extra for drizzling
12 ounces penne • salt and pepper

Cook the turnip greens in salted, boiling water for 10 minutes, then drain, and chop. Put the anchovy fillets and the oil in a food processor and process to a purée. Cook the penne in a large pan of salted boiling water until al dente, then drain and tip into a fairly deep warmed serving dish. Add the turnip greens, drizzle with oil, season with pepper, and stir. Pour in the anchovy purée, mix again, and serve.

PENNE WITH RICOTTA AND PESTO

PENNE AL PESTO E RICOTTA

Chop the basil with the garlic and put into a bowl. Season with salt, add the oil, ricotta, olives, and pecorino, and mix well. The sauce should be runny so, if necessary, add more olive oil. Cook the penne in plenty of salted boiling water until al dente, then drain, and toss with the sauce. Serve immediately.

Preparation time: 5 minutes

Cooking time: 5 minutes

Serves 4

10 fresh basil leaves

1 garlic clove

½ cup extra virgin olive oil

scant ¼ cup ricotta cheese

8 green olives, pitted and chopped

4 tablespoons grated pecorino cheese

12 ounces penne

salt

PENNE WITH SAFFRON

PENNE GIALLE

Bring the stock to a boil. Heat the butter and oil in another large pan, add the onion, and cook over low heat, stirring occasionally, for 5 minutes until softened. Add the penne and stir until it is shiny and coated with fat. Add a ladleful of hot stock and stir until it has been absorbed. Continue adding stock, a ladleful at a time, as if making risotto, until the pasta is completely cooked. Stir the saffron into the last ladleful of stock before adding it to the pan. Mix well until the dish is an even yellow color. Remove the pan from the heat, sprinkle with the Parmesan, mix well, and stir in a pat of butter if you like. Transfer to a warmed serving dish and serve.

Preparation time: 15 minutes

Cooking time: 30 minutes

Serves 4

1 quantity meat or vegetable stock

3 tablespoons butter, plus extra for serving (optional)

1 tablespoon olive oil

1 onion, thinly sliced

12 ounces penne lisce

pinch of saffron threads

½ cup grated Parmesan cheese

ROYAL PENNE

PENNE REALI

Preparation time: 15 minutes
Cooking time: 20 minutes
Serves 4
3 tablespoons butter, plus extra for greasing
scant ½ cup golden raisins
3 hard-cooked eggs, chopped
1 cup heavy cream
pinch of ground cinnamon
6 tablespoons grated Parmesan cheese
12 ounces penne
salt and pepper

Preheat the oven to 350°F and grease an ovenproof dish with butter. Put the golden raisins into a heatproof bowl, pour in warm water to cover, and let soak for 10 minutes, then drain, and squeeze out the excess liquid. Melt 3 tablespoons of the butter in a skillet. Add the chopped eggs and cook over low heat, stirring gently, for a few minutes. Pour in the cream and add the cinnamon, raisins and half the Parmesan. Cook the penne in plenty of salted boiling water until al dente. Drain, tip into the skillet, and toss with the sauce. Transfer the mixture to the prepared dish, sprinkle with the remaining Parmesan, and dot with the remaining butter. Bake for 5–10 minutes, until the top is golden brown. Serve immediately.

TASTY PENNE

PENNE SAPORITE

Preparation time: 10 minutes
Cooking time: 10 minutes
Serves 4
12 ounces penne lisce
7 ounces ricotta cheese
3 ounces mortadella, coarsely chopped
grated Parmesan cheese, to serve
salt

Cook the penne in plenty of salted boiling water until al dente. Meanwhile, put the ricotta and mortadella into a food processor or blender and process to a smooth purée. Spoon the purée into the base of a tureen. If it seems too thick, stir in 1–2 tablespoons of the pasta cooking water. Drain the penne, tip into the tureen, and stir well to mix. Sprinkle with the Parmesan and serve immediately.

GREEN PENNE

PENNE AL VERDE

Melt the butter with the oil in a pan. Add the onion and carrot and cook over low heat, stirring occasionally, for 5 minutes. Add the green bell pepper, olives, cream, and hot water and simmer over low heat for about 20 minutes. Cook the pasta in plenty of salted boiling water until al dente. Drain carefully, tip into the pan, and toss with the sauce. Transfer to a warmed serving dish and serve immediately.

The best quality olive oil is extra virgin, made from the first, cold pressing. It has a lower degree of acidity then regular olive oil.

Preparation time: 15 minutes

Cooking time: 30 minutes

Serves 4

3 tablespoons butter

2 tablespoons extra virgin olive oil

1 small onion, chopped

1 carrot, chopped

1 green bell pepper, seeded and diced

scant 1 cup green olives, pitted

3 tablespoons heavy cream

$\frac{2}{3}$ cup hot water

12 ounces penne rigate

salt

PENNETTE WITH MOZZARELLA, EGG, AND ANCHOVIES

PENNETTE ALLA MOZZARELLA, UOVA E ACCIUGHE

Combine the anchovy fillets, egg yolks, and mozzarella in a bowl and season with salt and pepper. Cook the pennette in plenty of salted boiling water until al dente. Drain, return to the pan, and pour the sauce over. Serve immediately.

Tip: Buy canned anchovy fillets preserved in olive oil. Once opened, transfer any unused anchovies to a small dish, cover, and store in the refrigerator.

Preparation time: 10 minutes

Cooking time: 15 minutes

Serves 4

4 canned anchovy fillets, drained and chopped

3 egg yolks

7 ounces diced mozzarella cheese

12 ounces pennette

salt and pepper

PENNE RIGATE IN VODKA

Melt the butter in a pan, add the ham, tomato paste, and parsley, season with salt and pepper, and cook, stirring occasionally, for about 10 minutes. Stir in the cream and vodka and cook until the vodka has evaporated. Cook the penne in a large pan of salted boiling water until al dente, then drain, and tip into a warmed serving dish. Pour the sauce over the pasta.

Preparation time: 10 minutes

Cooking time: 20 minutes

Serves 4

4 tablespoons butter

1 thick slice cooked ham, diced

2 tablespoons tomato paste

1 tablespoon chopped fresh flat-leaf parsley

5 tablespoons heavy cream

3 tablespoons vodka

12 ounces penne rigate

salt and pepper

PENNE RIGATE WITH HERBS

Pinch the heads of the anchovies between your thumb and index finger and pull them off, taking the innards with them. Pinch along the top edge of each anchovy and pull out the backbones. Rinse the fish and pat dry, then chop. Heat the oil in a pan. Add the anchovies, olives, garlic, and herbs and cook over low heat, stirring occasionally, for 5 minutes. Add the tomatoes, season with salt and pepper, cover, and simmer, stirring occasionally, for 15 minutes. Stir in the capers. Cook the penne in plenty of salted boiling water until al dente. Drain, tip into the pan with the sauce, and toss for 1 minute. Transfer to a warmed serving dish and serve immediately, handing the pecorino separately.

Preparation time: 25 minutes

Cooking time: 30 minutes

Serves 4

3 fresh anchovies

3 tablespoons olive oil

½ cup green olives, pitted and chopped

2 garlic cloves, chopped

1 bay leaf

1 leaf chopped fresh sage

1 leaf chopped fresh pennyroyal or mint

1 sprig chopped fresh rosemary

1 sprig chopped fresh flat-leaf parsley

9 ounces canned chopped tomatoes

½ tablespoon capers, rinsed

12 ounces penne rigate

grated pecorino cheese, to serve

salt and pepper

PENNE WITH RICOTTA AND MASCARPONE CREAM

PENNE ALLA CREMA DI RICOTTA E MASCARPONE

Preparation time: 15 minutes

Cooking time: 10 minutes

Serves 4

4 tablespoons butter, softened

scant ½ cup ricotta cheese

¼ cup mascarpone cheese • ½ diced ham

12 ounces penne rigate • salt and pepper

Put the butter into a tureen, beat in the ricotta and mascarpone with a whisk, and season with salt and pepper. Stir in the ham. Cook the pasta in plenty of salted boiling water until al dente. Drain and tip into the tureen. Mix well and serve immediately

Tip: For additional flavor, add a pinch of saffron and ¼ cup of blanched baby peas to the cheese mixture.

PENNE RIGATE WITH ARTICHOKES

PENNE RIGATE AI CARCIOFI

Preparation time: 20 minutes

Cooking time: 30 minutes

Serves 4

juice of ½ lemon, strained

4 globe artichokes

4 tablespoons olive oil

1 garlic clove, chopped

1 tablespoon chopped fresh flat-leaf parsley

12 ounces penne rigate

salt and pepper

Half-fill a bowl with water and stir in the lemon juice. Working on one artichoke at a time, break off the stem, remove the coarse, outer leaves and choke, if necessary. Cut into quarters, then slice thinly, and drop into the acidulated water to prevent discoloration. Heat the oil in a pan, add the garlic and parsley, and cook over low heat for 2 minutes. Drain the artichokes, add to the pan, and mix well. Cover and cook over low heat for a few minutes, then add 2–3 tablespoons water, season with salt, and re-cover the pan so that the artichokes cook in their own steam. Meanwhile, cook the penne in a large pan of salted, boiling water until al dente, then drain, and tip into a serving dish. Pour the artichoke sauce, which should not be too runny, over the pasta, season with pepper, and serve.

PENNETTE AND MOZZARELLA GRATIN

GRATIN DI PENNETTE ALLA MOZZARELLA

Preparation time: 20 minutes

Cooking time: 20–25 minutes

Serves 4

butter, for greasing

scant 1 cup grated Gruyère cheese

3 eggs

7 ounces diced mozzarella cheese

12 ounces pennette

salt and pepper

Preheat the oven to 350°F and grease an ovenproof dish with butter. Reserve 1 tablespoon of the Gruyère. Beat the eggs in a bowl, gradually adding the mozzarella and remaining Gruyère. Season with salt and pepper. Cook the pasta in plenty of salted boiling water until al dente. Drain, tip into the egg mixture, and stir. Transfer to the prepared dish and sprinkle with the reserved Gruyère. Bake for 20 minutes or until the top is golden brown. Remove from the oven and let stand for 5 minutes, then serve.

PENNETTE WITH BACON AND GREEN OLIVES

PENNETTE ALLA PANCETTA E OLIVE VERDI

Preparation time: 15 minutes

Cooking time: 30 minutes

Serves 4

4 tablespoons olive oil • 1 small onion, chopped

2 ounces pancetta or bacon, cut into strips

scant 1 cup green olives, pitted and halved

14 ounces canned chopped tomatoes

½ chile, seeded (optional) and chopped

12 ounces pennette rigate

⅓ cup grated pecorino cheese

⅓ cup grated Parmesan cheese • salt

Heat the oil in a skillet. Add the onion, pancetta or bacon, and olives cook over low heat, stirring occasionally, for 5 minutes. Add the tomatoes and chile and simmer gently, stirring occasionally, for 20 minutes. Cook the penne in plenty of salted boiling water until al dente. Drain, tip into the skillet, and toss with the sauce. If the sauce seems too thick, add a little of the pasta cooking water. Transfer to a warmed serving dish, sprinkle with the cheeses, and serve immediately.

PASTICCIO OF PENNE WITH MUSHROOMS

PASTICCIO DI PENNE AI FUNGHI

Preparation time: 50 minutes

Cooking time: 50 minutes

Serves 6

3 tablespoons butter, plus extra for greasing

1 tablespoon olive oil

1 garlic clove

1 pound 5 ounces porcini mushrooms, thinly sliced

¾–1 cup lukewarm vegetable stock

scant 1 cup heavy cream

1 tablespoon chopped fresh flat-leaf parsley

1 egg yolk

11 ounces pennette lisce

½ cup grated Parmesan cheese

9 ounces ready-made pie pastry dough,

thawed if frozen

all-purpose flour, for dusting

salt and pepper

Heat 1 tablespoon of the butter with the oil in a shallow pan. Add the garlic clove and cook over low heat, stirring frequently, for a few minutes until golden brown. Remove the garlic with a slotted spoon and discard. Add the mushrooms, pour in ⅔ cup of the stock, cover and cook over medium heat for 10 minutes until softened (if necessary, add a little more warm stock.) Season to taste with salt and pepper, pour in the cream, mix gently, and cook for a few minutes until thickened. Remove the pan from the heat and stir in the parsley. Beat the egg yolk with 2 tablespoons of the remaining stock and gradually stir into the mixture to coat the mushrooms with the sauce. Cook the pennette in plenty of salted boiling water until al dente, then drain. Preheat the oven to 350°F and grease an ovenproof dish with butter. Spoon half the pasta over the base of the prepared dish. Sprinkle with half the Parmesan and dot with half the remaining butter. Spoon half the mushroom sauce on top, then repeat the layers, finishing with mushroom sauce. Roll out the dough on a lightly floured surface to ⅛ inch thick. Lift the dough onto the dish and tuck in the edges. Bake for 20 minutes until the pastry is golden brown. Remove from the oven and serve immediately.

137

PENNE WITH A GRATIN OF CHERRY TOMATOES

PENNE CON POMODORINI GRATINATI

Preparation time: 25 minutes

Cooking time: 25 minutes

Serves 6

2 salted anchovies

olive oil, for brushing and drizzling

60 cherry tomatoes, halved

1 cup fresh bread crumbs

¼ cup grated Gruyère or ⅔ cup grated Parmesan cheese

2 garlic cloves, finely chopped

1 sprig finely chopped fresh thyme

1 sprig finely chopped fresh marjoram

1 ounce salted capers, rinsed and chopped

15 ounces penne • 10 torn fresh basil leaves

salt and pepper

Pinch the heads of the anchovies between your thumb and index finger and pull them off, taking the innards with them. Pinch along the top edge of each anchovy and pull out the backbones. Put the anchovies into a dish, pour in water to cover, and let soak to remove some of the salt, then drain, pat dry, and chop finely. Preheat the oven to 400°F and brush an ovenproof dish with oil. Put the tomatoes into the dish. Combine the bread crumbs, cheese, garlic, thyme, marjoram, capers, and anchovies in a bowl and season with salt and pepper. Spread the mixture over the tomatoes, drizzle with oil, and bake for about 15 minutes until the topping is golden brown. Meanwhile, cook the pasta in plenty of salted boiling water until al dente. Drain and tip into a warmed serving dish. Add the tomato gratin, garnish with the basil, and serve immediately.

PENNE WITH LETTUCE

PENNE ALLA LATTUGA

Preparation time: 30 minutes

Cooking time: 25 minutes

Serves 4

2 tablespoons butter, plus extra for greasing

14 cups shredded lettuce

3 tablespoons olive oil

12 ounces penne or sedani (see page 151)

scant 1 cup grated Gruyère cheese

salt and pepper

Preheat the oven to 350°F and grease an ovenproof dish with butter. Place the lettuce in a bowl, add the oil, and season with salt and pepper. Cook the penne in a large pan of salted boiling water until al dente, then drain, and tip into the prepared dish. Cover with the lettuce, sprinkle with the Gruyère, and dot with the butter. Bake for about 20 minutes.

PENNETTE WITH GORGONZOLA AND GREEN BELL PEPPERS

*PENNETTE AL GORGONZOLA
E PEPERONI VERDI*

Preheat the oven to 400°F. Put the bell peppers on a cookie sheet and roast, turning occasionally, for about 20 minutes until charred. Using tongs, transfer to a plastic bag and tie the top. When they are cool enough to handle, peel off the skins, halve, and seed. Cut the flesh into thin strips. Melt the Gorgonzola in a small skillet over very low heat, stir in the milk, and season with salt and a little pepper. Cook the pennette in plenty of salted boiling water until al dente. Drain and toss with the cheese mixture and bell pepper strips. Serve immediately.

Preparation time: 20 minutes

Cooking time: 30 minutes

Serves 4

2 green bell peppers

5 ounces diced mild Gorgonzola cheese

2 tablespoons milk

12 ounces pennette rigate

salt and pepper

PENNETTE WITH ZUCCHINI

PENNETTE ALLE ZUCCHINE

Melt the butter with the oil in a large skillet on low heat. Add the shallot and cook over low heat, stirring occasionally, for 5 minutes. Add the zucchini and cook, stirring and turning frequently, for 15 minutes. Add the marjoram and season to taste with salt. Cook the pennette in plenty of salted boiling water until al dente. Drain, tip into the skillet, and toss with the zucchini. Serve immediately, handing the Parmesan separately.

Preparation time: 20 minutes

Cooking time: 30 minutes

Serves 4

2 tablespoons butter

3 tablespoons olive oil

1 shallot, chopped

scant 2½ thickly sliced zucchini

1 tablespoon chopped fresh marjoram

12 ounces pennette

½ cup grated Parmesan cheese

salt

139

PENNETTE WITH CREAMY ARTICHOKE SAUCE

Preparation time: 25 minutes

Cooking time: 30 minutes

Serves 4

juice of ½ lemon, strained

4 globe artichokes

2 tablespoons olive oil

1 garlic clove, crushed

12 ounces pennette

⅔ cup grated Parmesan cheese

3–4 tablespoons milk

salt and pepper

Half fill a bowl with water and stir in the lemon juice. Trim the artichokes and remove the tough leaves and the chokes, if necessary. Cut into slices and immediately put into the acidulated water to prevent discoloration. Heat the oil in a shallow pan. Add the garlic and cook over low heat, stirring occasionally, for a few minutes until lightly browned. Drain the artichokes, add to the pan, and season with salt. Cover and cook over medium heat for about 20 minutes until tender. Cook the pennette in plenty of salted boiling water until al dente. Meanwhile, transfer half the artichokes to a food processor or blender, add the Parmesan, and process, adding the milk if necessary to obtain a creamy consistency. Drain the pasta, tip it into a warmed serving dish, pour the processed artichokes over and add the remaining sliced artichokes. Season with pepper and serve immediately.

PENNETTE WITH CHERRY TOMATOES AND GREEN BEANS

Preparation time: 40 minutes

Cooking time: 35 minutes

Serves 4

4 canned anchovy fillets, drained

3½ ounces bread, crusts removed

1 bunch of fresh basil

2 tablespoons olive oil, plus extra for brushing

1⅓ cups green beans, trimmed

2 garlic cloves

7 ounces cherry tomatoes, halved

pinch of chile powder

12 ounces whole wheat pennette

salt and pepper

Put the anchovy fillets into a small bowl, add water to cover, and let soak for 10 minutes to remove some of the salt. Meanwhile, tear the bread into pieces and put into a food processor blender with the basil. Process until thoroughly combined. Brush a small, shallow nonstick skillet with oil and heat gently. Add the bread mixture, flatten, and cook, turning once, until golden brown on both sides. Remove the skillet from the heat. Cook the beans in salted boiling water for 10–15 minutes until tender. Drain, reserving the cooking water, and cut into short lengths. Meanwhile, drain the anchovies, pat dry, and chop. Chop the toasted bread. Heat the oil in a large pan. Add the garlic cloves and cook over low heat, stirring frequently, for a few minutes until lightly browned. Remove the garlic with a slotted spoon and discard. Add the anchovies, tomatoes, beans, and chile powder to the pan, season with salt and pepper, and cook, stirring occasionally, for 10 minutes. Pour the reserved cooking water into a large pan and top up with fresh water if necessary. Stir in salt, add the pennette, and cook until al dente. Drain, tip into the pan with the vegetables, and toss over the heat for a minute. Add the toasted bread, stir, transfer to a warmed serving dish, and serve immediately.

PENNETTE
WITH ONION SAUCE

PENNETTE ALLA SALSA DI CIPOLLE

Heat the oil in a pan. Add the onions and cook over low heat, stirring occasionally, for 5 minutes. Pour in the stock, cover, and simmer, stirring occasionally, for 20 minutes until the onions have almost disintegrated. Meanwhile, cook the pennette in plenty of salted boiling water until al dente. Drain, tip into the pan of onions, increase the heat to high, and toss for a few minutes. Beat the eggs with a pinch of salt and pepper in a tureen, add the pasta, sprinkle with the Parmesan, toss again, and serve immediately.

Preparation time: 10 minutes

Cooking time: 25 minutes

Serves 4

2 tablespoons olive oil

11 ounces onions, thinly sliced

⅔ cup vegetable stock

12 ounces pennette lisce

3 eggs

½ cup grated Parmesan cheese

salt and pepper

PENNETTE WITH
BELL PEPPER SAUCE

PENNETTE ALLA SALSA DI PEPERONI

Preheat the oven to 350°F. Put the red bell pepper on a cookie sheet and roast, turning occasionally, for 1 hour. Remove from the oven and when cool enough to handle peel, seed, and dice the flesh. Heat 2 tablespoons of the oil in a pan. Add the shallot and red bell pepper, season with salt, and cook over low heat, stirring occasionally, for 5 minutes, then remove the pan from the heat.

Heat the remaining oil in another pan. Add the garlic cloves and cook over low heat, stirring frequently, for a few minutes until lightly browned. Remove the garlic with a slotted spoon and discard. Reserve 2 tablespoons of the green and yellow bell peppers, add the remainder to the pan, and cook, stirring occasionally, for 10 minutes. Beat the robiola into the red bell pepper mixture, adding enough of the water to obtain a creamy mixture. Stir the mixture into the pan with the other bell peppers and cook, stirring constantly, for a few minutes.

Cook the penne in plenty of salted boiling water until al dente. Drain, tip into the pan with the sauce, and toss over the heat for a minute. Transfer to a warmed serving dish, sprinkle with Parmesan, and garnish with the reserved bell peppers and basil leaves.

Preparation time: 25 minutes

Cooking time: 1 hour 20 minutes

Serves 4

1 red bell pepper

4 tablespoons olive oil

1 shallot, chopped

2 garlic cloves

1 green bell pepper, peeled, seeded and diced

1 yellow bell pepper, peeled, seeded and diced

9 ounces robiola cheese

2–3 tablespoons hot water

12 ounces mezze penne

½ cup grated Parmesan cheese

6 fresh basil leaves

salt and pepper

PIPE

Pipe, which means "pipes" in Italian, is a type of dried pasta made of durum wheat semolina flour. Like the smaller pipette, its shape is similar to a short, hollow cylinder with a ridged surface, which has been curled into a half-moon shape. The internal cavity is ideal to catch and retain the sauce, and pipe is also good in soups and pasta salads.

PIPE WITH ARUGULA

PIPE ALLA RUCOLA

Heat the oil in a skillet. Add the tomatoes and cook over medium heat, stirring occasionally, for 4–5 minutes. Add the arugula and season with salt. Lower the heat, cover, and cook for 5 minutes. Cook the pasta in plenty of salted boiling water until al dente. Drain, tip into the skillet, and toss well. Add the mozzarella, toss again, and remove from the heat as soon as the cheese starts to become stringy. Transfer to a warm serving dish and serve immediately.

Preparation time: 20 minutes

Cooking time: 20–25 minutes

Serves 4

4 tablespoons olive oil

9 ounces tomatoes, peeled and diced

1 bunch of arugula, chopped • 12 ounces pipe

2 small diced mozzarella cheeses, about 5 ounces each

salt and pepper

PIPETTE WITH PUMPKIN FLOWERS AND PANCETTA

PIPETTE AI FIORI DI ZUCCA E PANCETTA

Remove and discard the pistils from the pumpkin flowers and cut into thin strips. Stir the saffron in the lukewarm water in a small bowl and set aside. Melt the butter in a shallow pan. Add the pancetta or bacon and cook over medium heat, stirring occasionally, for 4–5 minutes until lightly browned. Pour in the cream, lower the heat, add the saffron with its soaking water, and mix well. Cook the pipette in plenty of salted boiling water until al dente. Drain, return to the pan, and add the saffron sauce and the strips of pumpkin flowers. Transfer the pasta to a warmed serving dish and serve immediately.

Preparation time: 20 minutes

Cooking time: 20 minutes

Serves 4

5 ounces pumpkin flowers

pinch of saffron threads, lightly crushed

1 tablespoon lukewarm water

2 tablespoons butter

⅔ cup diced smoked pancetta or bacon

2 tablespoons heavy cream

12 ounces pipette • salt

RIGATONI

Rigatoni is a type of dried pasta made of durum wheat semolina flour that is long, wide and tubular, similar to macaroni but slightly bigger, varying in length from 1¾–3¼ inches. The name rigatoni means "ridged" or "those with lines," after the Italian word for "line," "riga." Of uncertain origin, rigatoni is suitable for virtually any kind of sauce thanks to its length and cavity, but particularly complements those containing meat because of its ridges. In southern Italy, in the regions of Campania and Puglia, it is also commonly used in baked pasta dishes.

RIGATONI WITH CREAM, PESTO, AND TOMATOES

RIGATONI PANNA, PESTO E POMODORO

Preparation time: 10 minutes
Cooking time: 20 minutes
Serves 4
scant 1 cup heavy cream
11 ounces fresh tomatoes, thinly sliced, or canned chopped tomatoes, drained
2 tablespoons pesto (see Trenette with Pesto, page 238)
12 ounces rigatoni
½ cup grated Parmesan cheese • salt

Pour the cream into a pan, add the tomatoes, and cook over low heat for 10 minutes. Remove the pan from the heat and stir in the pesto. Meanwhile, cook the rigatoni in a large pan of salted boiling water until al dente, then drain, and tip into a warm serving dish. Sprinkle the pasta with the Parmesan, spoon the sauce over and serve immediately.

BAKED RIGATONI

RIGATONI AL FORNO

Preparation time: 40 minutes
Cooking time: 45 minutes
Serves 4
For the béchamel sauce
3 tablespoons butter
⅓ cup all-purpose flour
2¼ cups lukewarm milk
12 ounces plain or wholewheat rigatoni
7 ounces diced fontina or other semi-soft cheese
½ cup grated Gruyère cheese
salt and pepper

First make the béchamel sauce. Melt the butter in a pan. Stir in the flour and cook over medium heat, stirring constantly, for 2–3 minutes until golden brown. Gradually stir in the milk, a little at a time. Bring to a boil, stirring constantly, lower the heat, and simmer gently, stirring constantly, for 20 minutes until thickened and smooth. Remove the pan from the heat and stir in the fontina. Season lightly with salt and pepper. Cook the rigatoni in plenty of salted boiling water until al dente. Meanwhile, preheat the oven to 350°F. Drain the pasta and mix with the béchamel sauce. Tip into an ovenproof dish, sprinkle with the Gruyère, and bake for about 20 minutes until golden brown. Serve immediately.

RIGATONI WITH MARJORAM

RIGATONI ALLA MAGGIORANA

Heat the oil in a pan. Add the onion and carrot and cook over low heat, stirring occasionally, for 5 minutes. Add the sausage and tomatoes, season with salt and pepper, and simmer, stirring occasionally, for about 15 minutes, adding enough of the stock to prevent the mixture sticking to the pan. Stir the marjoram into the sauce and remove the pan from the heat. Cook the rigatoni in plenty of salted boiling water until al dente. Drain, tip into a warmed serving dish, and pour the sauce over it. Sprinkle with the Parmesan and serve immediately.

Preparation time: 30 minutes

Cooking time: 25 minutes

Serves 4

2 tablespoons olive oil

1 onion, chopped

1 carrot, chopped

3½ ounces Italian sausage, skinned and cut into pieces

11 ounces tomatoes, diced

3–4 tablespoons vegetable stock

2 tablespoons chopped fresh marjoram

12 ounces rigatoni

½ cup grated Parmesan cheese

salt and pepper

RIGATONI WITH PEAS

RIGATONI CON PISELLI

Put the mushrooms into a bowl, pour in hot water to cover, and let soak for 30 minutes. Meanwhile, melt the butter with the oil in a shallow pan. Add the onion and cook over low heat, stirring occasionally, for 5 minutes. Add the tomatoes, crush with a fork, season with salt and pepper, and cook for 10 minutes. Drain the mushrooms, squeeze out the excess liquid, add to the pan, and simmer for 15 minutes. Stir in the anchovies and cook for a few minutes, then add the peas, and heat through. Cook the rigatoni in plenty of salted boiling water until al dente. Drain, tip into a warmed serving dish, and pour the sauce over. Serve immediately.

Preparation time: 20 minutes

Cooking time: 45 minutes

Serves 4

½ cup dried mushrooms

2 tablespoons butter

2 tablespoons olive oil

1 onion, chopped

9 ounces canned tomatoes

4 canned anchovy fillets, drained and chopped

9 ounces canned peas, drained

12 ounces rigatoni

salt and pepper

RIGATONI WITH MEATBALLS

Combine the ground meat, parsley, and garlic in a bowl, then stir in the egg, and season with salt and pepper. Shape the mixture into small meatballs, dust with flour, and set aside. Heat the oil in a pan, add the onion, celery, carrot, and rosemary and cook over low heat, stirring occasionally, for 5 minutes. Then add the meatballs, and increase the heat to medium. Cook until the meatballs are lightly browned all over, add the bottle strained tomatoes and season with salt. Lower the heat, cover, and simmer, stirring occasionally, for about 40 minutes. Cook the rigatoni in a large pan of salted boiling water until al dente, then drain, and tip into the pan with the meatballs. Mix well and heat through for 2 minutes. Transfer to a warm serving dish and sprinkle with the Parmesan.

Preparation time: 30 minutes

Cooking time: 1 hour

Serves 4

11 ounces ground meat

1 sprig chopped fresh flat-leaf parsley

½ garlic clove, chopped

1 egg, lightly beaten

all-purpose flour, for dusting

3 tablespoons olive oil

1 onion, thinly sliced

1 celery stalk, chopped

1 carrot, chopped

1 sprig chopped small fresh rosemary

1¾ cups bottle strained tomatoes

12 ounces rigatoni

⅓ cup grated Parmesan cheese

salt and pepper

SILVER RIGATONI

Heat the olive oil in a pan. Add the tomatoes and cook over medium heat, stirring occasionally, for 5 minutes. Meanwhile mix the olive paste with 3 tablespoons water in a bowl. Add the pecorino and diluted olive paste to the pan and season to taste with salt and pepper. Cook the pasta in plenty of salted boiling water until al dente. Drain and toss with the sauce. Garnish with the basil and serve immediately.

Tip: Instead of washing the basil leaves, clean them with a wet cloth. It is also better to tear them by hand than to chop them with a knife.

Preparation time: 15 minutes

Cooking time: 20 minutes

Serves 4

2 tablespoons olive oil

4 tomatoes, peeled and diced

scant ¼ cup black olive paste

3 tablespoons water

12 ounces rigatoni

½ cup grated pecorino cheese

torn fresh basil, to garnish

salt and pepper

WAGON WHEELS

Wagon wheels are a type of dried pasta made from durum wheat semolina flour. They are called ruote in Italian, which literally means "wheels." Wagon wheels are ridged all along their external circumference, which makes them suitable for most sauces, but mainly those with vegetables. Wagon wheels also work for cold pasta salads.

WAGON WHEELS WITH SAFFRON AND PEAS

RUOTE ALLO ZAFFERANO E PISELLI

Put the saffron into a heatproof bowl, add 3 tablespoons warm water, and let steep. Melt the butter in a skillet. Add the onion and cook over low heat, stirring occasionally, for 5 minutes. Stir in the saffron and its soaking water. Blanch the peas in salted boiling water for 3 minutes, then drain, add to the skillet, and cook, stirring occasionally, for another 10 minutes. Cook the wagon wheels in plenty of salted boiling water until al dente. Drain, tip into the skillet, and toss well. Serve immediately.

Preparation time: 20 minutes

Cooking time: 30 minutes

Serves 4

pinch of saffron threads

3 tablespoons warm water

3 tablespoons butter

1 small onion, thinly sliced

4½ cups shelled baby peas

12 ounces wagon-wheel pasta

salt

WAGON WHEELS WITH FRANKFURTERS

RUOTE CON WURSTEL

Preparation time: 15 minutes

Cooking time: 10 minutes

Serves 4

4 frankfurters, each 4–6 inches long

3 tablespoons butter

2 tablespoons chopped fresh flat-leaf parsley

12 ounces wagon-wheel pasta

½ cup grated Parmesan cheese

salt

Briefly blanch the frankfurters in boiling water, then drain. Remove and discard the casings and chop the flesh. Melt the butter in a small skillet. Add the chopped frankfurters, parsley, and a pinch of salt and cook over low heat for a few minutes. Meanwhile, cook the wagon wheels in plenty of salted boiling water until al dente. Drain and toss with the remaining butter and the frankfurter mixture. Serve immediately, handing the Parmesan separately.

WAGON WHEELS WITH ZUCCHINI AND TOMATOES

RUOTE ALLE ZUCCHINE E POMODORI

Preparation time: 20 minutes

Cooking time: 30 minutes

Serves 4

4 tablespoons olive oil

10 fresh basil leaves, torn, plus extra to garnish

2 garlic cloves, finely chopped

1 pound 5 ounces zucchini, diced

11 ounces tomatoes, peeled, seeded, and coarsely chopped

12 ounces wagon-wheel pasta

salt and pepper

Heat half the oil with half the basil and half the garlic in a shallow pan. Add the zucchini and cook, stirring occasionally, for 10 minutes until lightly browned. Meanwhile, heat the remaining oil in a another shallow pan. Add the remaining garlic and the tomatoes, season with salt and pepper, and cook over medium-high heat, stirring occasionally, for 5 minutes. Tip the zucchini into the pan of tomatoes, add the remaining basil, and cook for another 2–3 minutes more. Cook the wagon wheels in plenty of salted boiling water until al dente. Drain, return to the pan, and pour the sauce over. Transfer to a warmed serving dish, garnish with extra basil leaves, and serve immediately.

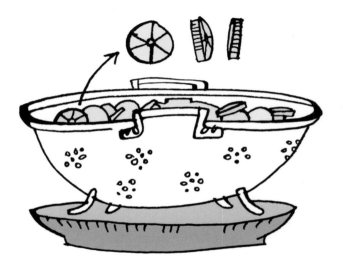

SEDANI

A type of short, dried pasta from the macaroni family, sedani is made of durum wheat semolina flour. It has a cylindrical, hollow, and slightly bent shape, with a ridged surface. The name comes from the Italian word for "celery," "sedano," which it resembles. Sedani is also sometimes called maccheroncini, or small macaroni. Its versatile shape combines well with simple sauces made with tomatoes, cream, or vegetables. Sedani also works well in baked dishes.

PASTA WITH CAULIFLOWER

PASTA E CAVOLFIORE

Cook the cauliflower in lightly salted boiling water for 10–12 minutes until just tender but still firm. Drain and let cool, then cut into florets. Melt 3 tablespoons of the butter in a skillet. Add the cauliflower florets and cook over medium-low heat, stirring occasionally, for 5–8 minutes until lightly colored. Add the scamorza, fontina and Parmesan, stir well, and turn off the heat. Cover the pan until all the cheese has melted.

Cook the sedani in plenty of salted boiling water until al dente. Meanwhile, preheat the oven to 350°F. Drain the pasta, return to the pan, and drizzle with oil. Dice the remaining butter, add to the pasta with the cauliflower florets, and stir to mix. Transfer the mixture to an ovenproof dish, pour the béchamel over to cover, and bake for about 20 minutes until golden brown. Serve immediately.

Preparation time: 50 minutes
Cooking time: 1 hour 25 minutes
Serves 4

1 cauliflower
5 tablespoons butter
1 diced smoked scamorza cheese
3 ounces diced fontina cheese
½ cup grated Parmesan cheese
salt
12 ounces sedani or other short pasta
olive oil, for drizzling
1 quantity béchamel sauce (see Baked Rigatoni, page 144)

TORTIGLIONI

A type of dried pasta from the macaroni family, tortiglioni is tubular and similar to rigatoni, but slightly longer. Originating in Naples in southern Italy, it has a slightly curved shape and unmistakable spiral grooving. A particularly versatile and original shape, tortiglioni is best combined with full-bodied sauces such as those with meat, cream, and mushrooms, and is also good for making baked pasta dishes.

TORTIGLIONI WITH MUSHROOM AND EGGPLANT

TORTIGLIONI CON FUNGHI E MELANZANE

Preparation time: 15 minutes

Cooking time: 20 minutes

Serves 4

2 tablespoons olive oil

1 onion, thinly sliced

1 garlic clove

7 ounces mushrooms, chopped

1 eggplant, diced

scant ½ cup heavy cream

12 ounces tortiglioni

½ cup grated Parmesan cheese

salt and pepper

Heat the oil in a pan, add the onion and garlic, and cook over low heat until the garlic has browned. Remove and discard the garlic, add the mushrooms and eggplant to the pan, and cook, stirring frequently, until light golden brown. Stir in the cream, season with salt and pepper, cover, and cook over low heat for another 10 minutes. Meanwhile, cook the tortiglioni in a large pan of salted boiling water until al dente, then drain, tip into the pan of sauce, and cook for 1 minute. Transfer to a warm serving dish and sprinkle with the Parmesan.

FRESH PASTA
PASTA FRESCA

FRESH PASTA

Fresh pasta is the type that was once called home-made pasta, a doug
made from soft wheat flour, unlike dried pasta, which requires hard durur
wheat semolina flour. The queen of fresh pasta is egg pasta, used for makin
tagliatelle, maltagliati, and pasta with fillings, such as lasagna, cannellon
tortellini and ravioli. Until a few decades ago egg pasta was eaten only o
special occasions and at wealthy tables. For everyday pasta, it was mor
usual just to mix flour and water, as still seen today in some regional dishe
such as Orecchiette (see page 182).

AN IMPORTANT DIFFERENCE

With the exception of a few types of pasta from southern Italy, the so
wheat flour is the key to the difference in taste, nutritional value, an
texture between fresh and dried pasta. "Triticum vulgare," a soft whea
with opaque grains and a starchy texture, has very different chemica
properties from those of hard wheat, "Triticum durum," and contains les
starch, more proteins and fats, more mineral salts, and more vitamins
There are also major differences in the gluten, which in soft wheat flou
is supple and elastic and does not retain the starches released in wate
so offering lower resistance to cooking. Dough made with this flour an
water tends to become sticky, so eggs are added because they contai
animal proteins with characteristics similar to those of gluten and whic
coagulate when heated. Eggs improve the consistency of the pasta
the proteins are increased in proportion to the starches, there are mor
vitamins fats, and mineral salts, and above all the cooking improves

EACH TO THEIR OWN TASTE

Every city, town, region and village in Italy has its own method of making pasta: The shape, sauce, filling, and even the dough varies. On the Po river plain in the north, where the climate favors the cultivation of soft wheat, they tend to use more eggs, whereas in central Italy, where the wheat becomes semihard, fewer eggs are used, and eggs disappear completely in the southern regions such as Puglia, Basilicata, and Calabria, where durum wheat semolina flour is used for fresh pasta such as orecchiette and cavatelli. As well as the quality of the ingredients, good results depend on a number of factors, ranging from the way in which the dough is handled to the warmth of the cook's hands, which can affect the drying of the pasta. The best way to keep alive the tradition of home-made fresh pasta and the next best thing to having an expert in the kitchen are the recipes of the north and northwest regions of Tuscany, Liguria and Emilia-Romagna, such as Pumpkin Tortelli (see page 313).

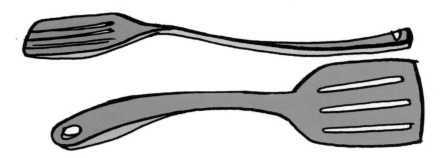

LASAGNA AS BASIC PASTA

Lasagna can rightly be considered the basis for all fresh pasta. It was really only when the ancient "laganum," the ancestor of modern pasta, had been cut into regular shapes—squares, strips, ribbons or strands—that it acquired an independent status as a pasta dish, and more than just an all-purpose pasta dough. Lasagna is among the first known pasta dishes and was held in high esteem by medieval cooks. They cooked it in water and stock and served it sprinkled with plenty of cheese and spices. In the Middle Ages, Italian cooks paid considerable attention to the shape of the pasta, and many new types of pasta made an appearance in addition to the classics: Croseti, a kind of orecchiette, and formentine, thin ribbons similar to tagliatelle. Towards the end of The Middle Ages, various types of tagliatelle and taglierini became widespread. Around the sixteenth century fresh pasta became very sweet, when sugar was added to the basic mixture, and eggs were used more frequently and in larger quantities.

FILLED PASTA

Fresh pasta is also very often used to make filled pasta. The pasta encloses a fine filling or purée and is a worthy heir to the Latin "laganum," whose overlapping layers separated layers of ground meat. In the Middle Ages until the fifteenth century, filled pasta meant a miniature pie, a tortello, also known as "raviolo," which was fried in a pan, and resembled larger pies that were cooked in the dry heat of the oven. The pasta that wrapped the raviolo was delicate and at times so thin as to become invisible. This led to "naked ravioli," in which the filling was covered only in a coating of flour, resembling some modern gnocchi. In this way the original pasta dough was sacrificed on the altar of gastronomy in parts of northern Italy. However, the repertoire of filled pasta was rich and various, depending on the region, including ravioli, tortelli, cappelletti, anolini, and agnolotti. Pasta's culinary traditions, with or without fillings, developed in regional cuisines and was

nriched with personal touches. The variety of fillings using more or less
ophisticated ingredients can be roughly divided into two groups: Those
vithout and those with meat. The first type was documented in works from
ne early Middle Ages. A cookbook by an anonymous Venetian describes
ne of the first examples of ravioli di magro based on vegetables and
esh cheese. The composition of pasta with fillings was perfected from
ne fifteenth century onward and the range of ingredients was extended
 include meat. In his *Libro de Arte Coquinaria*, Maestro Martino includes
ne recipe Ravioli in Tempo di Carne, which has a filling of pork or veal,
easoned cheese, aromatic herbs, spices and capon breast. Martino points
ut that it is also excellent made with pheasant, partridge and other game.

FROM THE ROLLING PIN
TO THE MACHINE

rom the two large families of ravioli and tortellini, filled pasta gradually
eveloped to acquire many shapes and flavors. Nor did it escape the
nanges in the industrial world where everything bowed to mechanization.
he rolling pin gradually made way for small machines, first turned with a
andle and later powered by electricity. It was discovered that pasteurized
asta kept longer and so could be sold further afield. Evolution in production
echnology and the science of preservation, facilitated the spread of fresh
asta beyond Italy's regions and, indeed, throughout Italy itself.

COOKING INSTRUCTIONS

QUANTITY

The recommended quantity to serve 4 is 1¾ cups flour and 2 eggs plus a pinch of salt, which produces 10 ounces fresh pasta, about 2¾ ounces per serving.

OLIVE OIL

When boiling sheets of pasta for lasagna, add 1 tablespoon olive oil to the cooking water to prevent them sticking together.

COOKING AND PREPARATION TIME

Fresh pasta cooks faster than dried pasta. When boiling filled pasta remember that the filling adds flavor so the quantity of salt in the water should be reduced. The times indicated for the recipes have been calculated as an average as they vary according to the type heat, quality of the ingredients, and the skill of the cook.

SAUCE AND CHEESE

Fresh pasta absorbs more sauce than dried pasta, although the same rules still apply– the grated cheese should be sprinkled on the pasta before adding the sauce and the serving dish must be very warm. If you require cheese, always use fresh and grate it just before sprinkling it on the pasta. Do not overdo the quantity. Those who wish may add more at the table from the cheese dish. It is worth pointing out that metal spoons may rust on contact with fatty particles, so it is better to serve the cheese with a spoon made from another material, such as wood.

STORAGE

You can keep home-made fresh pasta for about 15 days and up to a month in the freezer provided it has been fully air-dried, laid out on a board covered with lightly floured white cloths, for about 24 hours.

SAMMARZANO

AGLIO

€ 3,49

BASIC RECIPES FOR FRESH PASTA

FRESH PASTA DOUGH

PASTA ALL'UOVO

Sift the flour and a pinch of salt into a mound on a counter. Make a well in the center and add the eggs. Using your fingers, gradually incorporate the flour, then knead for about 10 minutes. If the mixture is too soft, add a little extra flour; if it is too firm, add a little water. Shape the dough into a ball and let rest for 15 minutes. Roll out on a lightly floured counter or use a pasta machine to make a thin sheet, and cut out shapes such as fettuccine, lasagna, maltagliati, orecchiette, pappardelle, stracci, tagliatelle, taglierini, trenette, and trofie.

Preparation time: 30 minutes,
plus 20 minutes resting
Serves 4

1¾ cups all-purpose flour, preferably Italian type 00, plus extra for dusting
2 eggs, lightly beaten
salt

GREEN PASTA DOUGH

PASTA VERDE

Sift the flour and a pinch of salt into a mound on a counter. Make a well in the center and add the eggs and spinach. Using your fingers, gradually incorporate the flour, then knead for a 10 minutes. If the spinach is very damp, add more flour, a little at a time. Shape the dough into a ball and let rest for 15 minutes, then roll out on a lightly floured counter or use a pasta machine to make a fairly thick sheet. This pasta may be used for lasagna, tagliatelle, tortellini, and ravioli.

Preparation time: 30 minutes,
plus 20 minutes resting
Serves 4

1¾ cups all-purpose flour, preferably Italian type 00, plus extra for dusting
2 eggs, lightly beaten
generous 1 cup cooked spinach, chopped • salt

RED PASTA DOUGH

PASTA ROSSA

Sift the flour into a mound on a counter and make a well in the center. Break the eggs into the well and add a pinch of salt and the beet juice. Knead for 10 minutes, adding more flour, a little at a time, if the beet juice makes the dough too wet. Let the pasta rest for 15 minutes, then roll out on a lightly floured counter into a fairly thick sheet or use a pasta machine. This pasta can be used for lasagna, tagliatelle, and ravioli with a spinach and ricotta filling. The sauces most suitable are the classic ones: Meat, melted butter, and cheese.

Preparation time: 30 minutes,
plus 20 minutes resting
Serves 4

1¾ cups all-purpose flour, preferably Italian type 00, plus extra for dusting
2 eggs
scant 1 cup beet juice
salt

CUT
PASTA

BIGOLI

Bigoli is a hand-made version of spaghetti that is thick, with a tubular shape and an uneven surface. It comes from the city of Mantua in Lombardy and from the Veneto region, in northern Italy. It is produced using a press fitted with a special mold, known as the "bigolaro," said to have been imported from China by Marco Polo. The original dough is made with soft wheat flour, butter and eggs, which can be duck eggs. The pasta name itself could derive from the local dialect word "bigàt" (grub), which may refer to the manner in which the bigoli comes out of the mold. In Venice, bigoli is known as "mori" (Moors), and is prepared using whole wheat flour. Bigoli is particularly well suited to strong sauces, and in the traditional Venetian recipe it is cooked in duck broth and seasoned with the juice of duck giblets. In Padua, near Venice, it is served with chicken livers. A common Lent recipe is Bigoli in Salsa d'Acciughe (Bigoli with Anchovies, see page 168).

BIGOLI WITH SEA URCHINS

BIGOLI AI RICCI DI MARE

Wrap your hand in a dish towel to protect it from the spikes and hold a sea urchin firmly with the soft central part uppermost. Using kitchen scissors, cut around the soft part and remove a 3-inch disk of shell. Discard the disk and drain off any liquid from inside the shell. Remove and discard the black parts from inside the shell, then scoop out the orange roe with a teaspoon, keeping the clusters of roe as whole as possible. Discard the shell. Repeat with the remaining sea urchins. Heat the oil in a pan. Add the garlic cloves and chile and cook over low heat, stirring frequently, for a few minutes until the garlic is lightly browned. Remove the garlic with a slotted spoon and discard. Add the sea urchin roes and cook over low heat for a few minutes, then remove from the heat, and keep warm. Cook the bigoli in plenty of salted boiling water for 2–3 minutes until al dente. Drain, transfer to a warmed serving dish, and pour the sea urchin sauce over. Sprinkle with the parsley and serve immediately.

Preparation time: 25 minutes

Cooking time: 20 minutes

Serves 4

20 very fresh sea urchins

2 tablespoons olive oil

2 garlic cloves, lightly crushed

½ dried red chile, crumbled

14 ounces fresh bigoli (see Bigoli with Anchovies, page 168)

1 tablespoon chopped fresh flat-leaf parsley

salt

BIGOLI WITH ANCHOVIES

BIGOLI ALLE ACCIUGHE

Preparation time: 30 minutes,
plus 1 hour resting
Cooking time: 40 minutes
Serves 4–6

3½ cups all-purpose flour, preferably Italian type 00

3 eggs, lightly beaten

4 tablespoons olive oil • 2 onions, chopped

1 tablespoon chopped fresh flat-leaf parsley

3 canned anchovy fillets, drained • salt

Sift the flour with a pinch of salt into a mound on a counter and make a well in the center. Add the eggs and enough water to make an elastic dough. Make the bigoli by pressing the dough through the bigolaro (see page 167), a little at a time. Heat the oil in a pan, add the onions and parsley, and cook over low heat, stirring occasionally, for 5 minutes until the onions are softened. Add the anchovies and cook, mashing with a wooden spoon until they disintegrate. Cook the bigoli in salted, boiling water for 2–3 minutes until al dente. Drain and toss with the onion mixture.

BIGOLI WITH BRANDY

BIGOLI AL BRANDY

Preparation time: 20 minutes
Cooking time: 30 minutes
Serves 4

2 tablespoons butter

14 ounces tomatoes, peeled, seeded, and diced

pinch of sugar • ¾ cup brandy

2 tablespoons olive oil • 1 onion, finely chopped

1 celery stalk, finely chopped • 1 carrot, finely chopped

14 ounces fresh bigoli (see Bigoli
with Anchovies, above)

salt and pepper

Melt the butter in a pan over low heat. Add the tomatoes and sugar, stir, drizzle with the brandy, and cook until the alcohol has evaporated. Season with salt and simmer, stirring occasionally, for 10 minutes. Heat the oil in a skillet. Add the onion, celery, and carrot and cook over low heat, stirring occasionally, for 5 minutes, then stir into the tomato sauce. Cook the bigoli in plenty of salted boiling water for 2–3 minutes until al dente. Drain, tip into a warmed serving dish, and pour the sauce over. Season with pepper and serve immediately.

BIGOLI WITH ONIONS

BIGOLI ALLE CIPOLLE

Preparation time: 15 minutes
Cooking time: 20 minutes
Serves 4

6 tablespoons butter • 4 onions, thinly sliced

½ teaspoon dried thyme

14 ounces fresh bigoli (see Bigoli
with Anchovies, above)

¼ cup grated Gruyère cheese

salt and pepper

Melt the butter in a shallow pan. Add the onions and cook over low heat, stirring occasionally, for about 20 minutes until very soft and golden brown. Add the thyme and season with salt and pepper. Remove from the heat and keep warm. Cook the bigoli in plenty of salted boiling water for 2–3 minutes until al dente. Drain, tip into the pan with the sauce, toss, sprinkle with the Gruyère, and season with pepper. Serve immediately.

FETTUCCINE

A type of fresh egg pasta meaning "small ribbons" in Italian, fettuccine is similar to tagliatelle, but a little wider (1/2 inch) and a little thicker (1/8 inch). The names are often used interchangeably, however, particularly in the south of Italy where tagliatelle is sometimes known as fettuccine. The flat, elongated shape of fettuccine is best suited to sauces based on meat, sausage, mushrooms and tomatoes. Fettuccine is frequently served in central and southern Italy, and is also used in soufflés (see Fettuccine Soufflé, page 175).

FETTUCCINE FROM ALBA

FETTUCCINE D'ALBA

Roll out the pasta dough on a lightly floured counter into a sheet. Cut into strips about 1/2-inch wide and let dry on floured dish towels. Combine the Parmesan, nutmeg, and a pinch each of salt and pepper in a tureen and put in a warm place. Cook the fettuccine in plenty of salted boiling water for 2–3 minutes until al dente. Drain, tip into the tureen, add the butter, and toss gently. Sprinkle with the truffle shavings and serve immediately.

The Piedmont region of northern Italy is famous for its tasty first courses where the palate is indulged at the start of the meal with unforgettable flavors. The abundant use of truffles, a celebrated local product, gives a special touch and aroma to even the simplest dishes. The Bianco d'Alba truffle is the most precious of the ten species harvested in Italy, with large examples commanding record prices.

Preparation time: 1 hour,

plus 1 hour resting

Cooking time: 8 minutes

Serves 4

1 quantity Fresh Pasta Dough (see page 163)

1 cup grated Parmesan cheese

pinch of freshly grated nutmeg

4 tablespoons butter

1 Bianco d'Alba truffle, shaved

salt and pepper

169

FETTUCCINE FLAVORED WITH BASIL

FETTUCCINE PROFUMATE AL BASILICO

Put the mushrooms into a heatproof bowl, pour in warm water to cover, and let soak for 15 minutes, then drain, squeeze out the excess liquid, and chop. Melt the butter in a shallow pan. Add the ham, mushrooms, and basil and cook over low heat, stirring occasionally for 5 minutes. Season with salt and pepper and simmer for 30 minutes. Cook the fettuccine in plenty of salted boiling water for 2–3 minutes until al dente. Drain, tip into a warmed serving dish, and pour the basil sauce over. Sprinkle with the Parmesan and serve immediately.

Preparation time: 15 minutes

Cooking time: 40 minutes

Serves 4

¼ cup dried mushrooms

2 tablespoons butter

generous ½ cup chopped prosciutto

20 fresh basil leaves

10 ounces fresh fettuccine (see Fettuccine from Alba, page 169)

½ cup grated Parmesan cheese

salt and pepper

ASPARAGUS NESTS

NIDI AGLI ASPARAGI

Melt the butter in a shallow pan. Add the shallot and cook over low heat, stirring occasionally, for 5 minutes. Add the asparagus tips, cover, and cook over low heat for about 10 minutes until tender. Season with salt and white pepper. Cook the fettuccine in plenty of salted boiling water for 2–3 minutes until al dente. Drain, tip into a warmed serving dish, and add the asparagus mixture. Sprinkle with the Gruyère and chopped ham and serve immediately.

Preparation time: 15 minutes

Cooking time: 20 minutes

Serves 4

3 tablespoons butter

1 small shallot, chopped • 40 asparagus tips

10 ounces fresh fettuccine (see Fettuccine from Alba, page 169)

⅓ cup grated Gruyère cheese

½ cup chopped ham

salt and freshly ground white pepper

FETTUCCINE IN BROWN BUTTER

FETTUCCINE AL BURRO BRUNO

Cook the fettuccine in a large pan of salted boiling water for 2–3 minutes until al dente. Meanwhile, melt the butter in a skillet over low heat and stir in the meat juices, which should be fairly concentrated. Drain the pasta, add to the skillet, toss well, and transfer to a warmed serving dish. Sprinkle with the Parmesan and serve.

Traditionally, this dish is prepared using the leftover juices from a dish of roast meat, such as veal, cooked the day before.

Preparation time: 10 minutes

Cooking time: 7 minutes

Serves 4

10 ounces fresh fettuccine (see Fettuccine from Alba, page 169)

4 tablespoons butter

4–5 tablespoons meat juices

⅔ grated Parmesan cheese • salt

FETTUCCINE IN CREAM SAUCE

Preparation time: 12 minutes
Cooking time: 15 minutes
Serves 4
4 tablespoons butter
10 ounces fresh fettuccine
(see Fettuccine from Alba, page 169)
4 tablespoons heavy cream
½ cup grated Parmesan cheese
salt and pepper

Melt the butter in a heatproof bowl set over a pan of simmering water. Cook the fettuccine in plenty of salted boiling water for 2–3 minutes until al dente. Drain, return to the pan, and add the cream and half the Parmesan. Toss gently without breaking up the pasta. Pour in the hot melted butter. Transfer to warmed plates and season with pepper. Serve immediately.

FETTUCCINE WITH CHICKEN AND ALMONDS

Preparation time: 20 minutes
Cooking time: 30 minutes
Serves 4
2 tablespoons butter
1 shallot, chopped
5 ounces skinless boneless chicken
breast portion, chopped
scant ½ cup dry white wine
⅓ cup almonds, chopped
scant 1 cup heavy cream
10 ounces fresh fettuccine
(see Fettuccine from Alba, page 169)
⅓ cup grated Parmesan cheese
salt and pepper

Melt the butter in a small pan. Add the shallot and cook over low heat, stirring occasionally, for 5 minutes. Add the chicken, stir well, and cook for a few minutes. Pour in the wine and cook until the alcohol has evaporated, then add the almonds and stir in the cream. Simmer over low heat, stirring occasionally, for about 10 minutes, then season with salt and pepper. Cook the fettuccine in plenty of salted boiling water for 2–3 minutes until al dente. Drain, tip into a warmed serving dish, pour the chicken sauce over it and sprinkle with the Parmesan. Serve immediately.

FETTUCCINE WITH HAM

FETTUCCINE AL PROSCIUTTO COTTO

Preparation time: 15 minutes

Cooking time: 20 minutes

Serves 4

4 tablespoons butter

1 onion, very thinly sliced

5 ounces ham in a single piece, diced

3 eggs

3 tablespoons grated Parmesan cheese, plus extra to serve

pinch of freshly grated nutmeg

2 tablespoons heavy cream

10 ounces fresh fettuccine (see Fettuccine from Alba, page 169)

salt and pepper

Melt half the butter in a pan. Add the onion and ham and cook over low heat, stirring occasionally, for 10 minutes. Meanwhile, beat the eggs with the Parmesan, nutmeg, and cream in a large tureen and season with salt and pepper. Cook the fettuccine in plenty of salted boiling water for 2–3 minutes until al dente. Drain, but not completely, tip into the tureen, and stir. Add the ham mixture and remaining butter if the pasta is a little dry. Sprinkle with Parmesan, season with pepper, and serve immediately.

FETTUCCINE WITH ORANGE BLOSSOM

FETTUCCINE CON FIORI D'ARANCIA

Preparation time: 15 minutes

Cooking time: 30 minutes

Serves 4

4 tablespoons olive oil

7 ounces ground meat

2½ ounces Italian sausages, chopped

1 garlic clove

½ onion, chopped

4 fresh tomatoes, peeled and chopped, or canned peeled tomatoes

10 fresh basil leaves, torn

2 ounces orange blossom, plus extra to garnish

14 ounces fresh fettuccine (see Fettuccine from Alba, page 169)

salt and pepper

Heat the oil in a skillet. Add the ground meat, sausages, garlic clove, and chopped onion and cook over medium-low heat, stirring occasionally, for 6–8 minutes until the meat is lightly browned. Remove and discard the garlic as soon as it browns. Meanwhile, if using canned tomatoes, process them with a little water in a food processor or blender. Add the fresh tomatoes or puréed canned tomatoes and the basil to the skillet and cook over low heat, stirring occasionally, for 10–15 minutes until the meat is cooked through and the sauce has thickened. Gently stir in the orange blossom. Cook the pasta in plenty of salted boiling water for 2–3 minutes until al dente. Drain, tip into a warmed serving dish, top with the sauce, and garnish with a little orange blossom. Serve immediately.

FETTUCCINE WITH SAUSAGE IN BALSAMIC VINEGAR

FETTUCCINE CON SALSICCIA ALL'ACETO BALSAMICO

Melt the butter in a pan. Add the onion and sausage and cook over low heat, stirring frequently, for 10 minutes. Add the tomatoes, season with salt and pepper, stir well, and simmer for 10 minutes. Cook the fettuccine in plenty of salted boiling water for 2–3 minutes until al dente. Drain, tip into the pan with the sauce, and toss over the heat for 30 seconds. Drizzle with the balsamic vinegar, garnish with the marjoram, and serve immediately.

Tip: There are many surprising ways of using balsamic vinegar. The most traditional include sprinkled on flakes of Parmesan, risotto, escalopes or a fresh salad. It can also be served "in spoonfuls" as an unusual aperitif or, for a more sophisticated palate, with strawberries and ice cream.

Preparation time: 15 minutes

Cooking time: 30 minutes

Serves 4

2 tablespoons butter

1 onion, chopped

3 ounces Italian sausage, skinned and chopped

7 ounces canned chopped tomatoes

10 ounces fresh fettuccine

(see Fettuccine from Alba, page 169)

1 tablespoon balsamic vinegar

chopped fresh marjoram, to garnish

salt and pepper

FETTUCCINE SOUFFLÉ

SOUFFLÉ DI FETTUCCINE

Preheat the oven to 350°F and grease a soufflé dish with butter. Reserve 2 tablespoons of the milk, pour the remainder into a pan and bring just to a boil, then remove from the heat. Cook the fettuccine in plenty of salted boiling water for 2–3 minutes until al dente. Drain, leaving it slightly moist, and tip into a large bowl. Add the butter and toss gently. Sprinkle with Gruyère and Parmesan, add the spinach, season with pepper and gradually pour in the hot milk. Let stand for a few minutes. Meanwhile, beat the egg yolks with the remaining milk in a bowl. Stiffly whisk the egg whites in another grease-free bowl. Stir the egg yolk mixture into the pasta, then fold in the egg whites. Pour the mixture into the prepared dish and bake for 30 minutes. Increase the oven temperature to 400°F and bake for another 5 minutes. Serve immediately.

Preparation time: 40 minutes

Cooking time: 40 minutes

Serves 6

6 tablespoons butter, plus extra for greasing

1¾ cups milk

8 ounces fresh fettuccine (see Fettuccine from Alba, page 169)

scant 1 cup grated Gruyère cheese

generous 1 cup grated Parmesan cheese

11 ounces spinach, chopped

6 eggs, separated

salt and pepper

MACCHERONI ALLA CHITARRA

A specialty of the Abruzzo region in central Italy, maccheroni alla chitarra is a type of fresh pasta that gains its name from the method of production. Invented during the second half of the nineteenth century, the "chitarra," or "guitar," is a device consisting of a wooden frame with metal threads, spaced approximately ⅛–⅕ inch apart. Sheets of fresh pasta about ¼ inch thick are placed on top of the grille, and then pushed through using a rolling pin. This produces long pasta similar to spaghetti but with a square section. Maccheroni alla chitarra is commonly combined with meat sauces, such as chicken livers (see opposite).

MACCHERONI ALLA CHITARRA WITH PANCETTA AND ASPARAGUS

MACCHERONI ALLA CHITARRA CON PANCETTA E ASPARAGI

Preparation time: 25 minutes
Cooking time: 40 minutes
Serves 4

14 ounces asparagus, trimmed
3 tablespoons olive oil
1½ ounces pancetta or bacon, cut into strips
1 shallot, chopped
scant 1 cup dry white wine
10 ounces fresh maccheroni alla chitarra (see Maccheroni alla Chitarra with Tomato Sauce, opposite)
2 tomatoes, diced
½ cup grated Parmesan cheese
salt and pepper

Tie the asparagus into a bundle and put into a tall pan or asparagus pan. Pour in boiling water to reach to just below the tips, add a pinch of salt, cover, and cook for 10 minutes until tender. Remove from the pan, and cut into short lengths. Heat the oil in a pan. Add the pancetta or bacon and cook over medium-low heat, stirring occasionally, for 4–5 minutes. Add the shallot and cook, stirring occasionally, for 5 minutes. Pour in the wine and cook until the alcohol has evaporated. Add the asparagus, season with salt and pepper, and simmer for 10 minutes. Cook the pasta in plenty of salted boiling water for 2–3 minutes until al dente. Drain, tip into the pan with the sauce, and toss. Add the tomatoes and toss over the heat for 1 minute. Sprinkle with the Parmesan and serve immediately.

MACCHERONI ALLA CHITARRA WITH MEAT JUICES

Preheat the oven to 350°F. Melt the butter with the oil in a roasting pan. Season the piece of veal with salt, sprinkle with the rosemary, and add to the pan. Cook over low heat, turning frequently, for 10 minutes. Pour in the wine and cook until the alcohol has evaporated. Transfer the pan to the oven and roast for 1 hour until tender. Cook the pasta in plenty of salted boiling water for 2–3 minutes until al dente. Drain and tip into a warmed serving dish. Remove the pan from the oven and transfer the meat to a dish (keep warm and serve as the second course). Pour the roasting juices over the pasta, sprinkle with Parmesan, and serve immediately.

Preparation time: 45 minutes

Cooking time: 1 hour 20 minutes

Serves 4

5 tablespoons butter

2 tablespoons olive oil

1¾ pounds boneless rump roast

2 teaspoons chopped fresh rosemary

scant 1 cup dry white wine

12 ounces fresh maccheroni alla chitarra (see Maccheroni alla Chitarra with Tomato Sauce, below)

½ cup grated Parmesan cheese • salt

MACCHERONI ALLA CHITARRA WITH CHICKEN LIVERS

Heat the butter and oil in a skillet, add the onion, and cook over low heat, stirring occasionally, for 5 minutes. Add the chicken livers and cook, stirring occasionally, until browned. Add the stock and cook until it has evaporated, then season with salt. Cook the maccheroni in a large pan of salted boiling water for 2–3 minutes until al dente, drain, and toss with the sauce. Sprinkle with the Parmesan and serve.

Preparation time: 15 minutes

Cooking time: 30 minutes

Serves 6

6 tablespoons butter • 3 tablespoons olive oil

1 onion, chopped • 12 ounces chicken livers, trimmed and chopped • 4 tablespoons meat stock

14 ounces fresh maccheroni alla chitarra

(see Maccheroni alla Chitarra with Tomato Sauce, below)

3 tablespoons grated Parmesan cheese • salt

MACCHERONI ALLA CHITARRA WITH TOMATO SAUCE

Roll out the pasta dough on a lightly floured counter into a sheet ⅛ inch thick. Place on the chitarra and roll over it with a rolling pin so that the wires cut the pasta into long square-section ribbons. For the sauce, heat the olive oil in a skillet, add the tomatoes, and cook, stirring occasionally, for 10 minutes. Season with salt and chile powder. Cook the maccheroni in a large pan of salted boiling water for 2–3 minutes until al dente, drain, toss with the tomato sauce, and serve immediately.

Preparation time: 40 minutes, plus 1 hour resting

Cooking time: 15 minutes

Serves 6

3½ cups all-purpose flour, preferably Italian type 00, plus extra for dusting

4 eggs, lightly beaten • salt

For the sauce

6 tablespoons olive oil • pinch of chile powder • salt

1 pound 2 ounces plum tomatoes, peeled and diced

MALTAGLIATI

Meaning "badly cut" in Italian, maltagliati is a type of fresh pasta made from the trimmings of lasagna and other home-made pasta. It originated in the Emilia-Romagna region in northern Italy and has since spread throughout the country. Further north, in the city of Mantua in Lombardy, the dough is often cut into long narrow triangles, while in Emilia-Romagna and the Veneto region in the northeast, it is cut into small diamond shapes. It is commonly served in broth or as an ingredient of bean soups. It also goes well with vegetable sauces. Another type of pasta, made from durum wheat semolina flour and cut into short penne-like shapes, also goes by the name maltagliati, and is served with meat, tomato and chunky vegetable sauces.

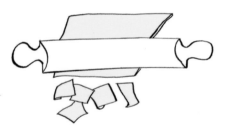

MALTAGLIATI WITH BELL PEPPERS
MALTAGLIATI AI PEPERONI

Preheat the oven to 400°F. Put the bell peppers onto a cookie sheet and roast for 1 hour. Remove from the oven, wrap in aluminum foil, and let cool for 1 hour. Unwrap the bell peppers, peel, and seed them, then cut the flesh into large strips. Put the bell pepper strips, oil, and a pinch of salt into a food processor or blender and process to a purée. Transfer the purée to a pan and heat gently. Cook the maltagliati in plenty of salted boiling water for 2–3 minutes until al dente. Drain, tip into a warmed serving dish, and pour the hot sauce over. Serve immediately.

Preparation time: 40 minutes, plus 1 hour cooling
Cooking time: 1 hour 5 minutes
Serves 4
2 red bell pepper
5 tablespoons olive oil
14 ounces fresh maltagliati (see Maltagliati with Pumpkin, overleaf)
salt

MALTAGLIATI WITH PUMPKIN

Preparation time: 1 hour 10 minutes,
plus 1 hour resting
Cooking time: 35 minutes
Serves 6
1½ quantity Fresh Pasta Dough (see page 163)
3 tablespoons olive oil • scant ½ cup butter
1 pound 2 ounces pumpkin, peeled, seeded and diced
pinch of freshly grated nutmeg
⅔ cup grated Parmesan cheese
salt and pepper

Roll out the pasta dough on a lightly floured counter into a sheet. Cut into wide, irregular pieces and let dry on floured dish towels. Heat the oil and 6 tablespoons of the butter in a pan, add the pumpkin, and cook over low heat, stirring occasionally, for 5 minutes. Add a little water, season with salt, and simmer, stirring frequently, until the pumpkin is tender. Meanwhile, cook the pasta in a large pan of salted boiling water for 2–3 minutes until just al dente. Drain, stir into the pumpkin, and add the remaining butter, the nutmeg, and a little pepper. Mix well, sprinkle with the Parmesan, and serve.

OAT PASTA WITH VEGETABLE AND PURÉE SAUCE

Preparation time: 1 hour, plus 1 hour resting
Cooking time: 55 minutes
Serves 6
2¼ cups fine oatmeal
½ cup durum wheat semolina flour
1¾ cups all-purpose flour, preferably Italian type 00, plus extra for dusting
3 eggs • 3 egg yolks
salt
For the vegetable sauce
3 tablespoons butter
2 small shallots, sliced
3½ ounces leek, cut into julienne strips
7 ounces eggplants, cut into julienne strips
5 ounces fennel, cut into julienne strips
5 ounces vine tomatoes, cut into julienne strips
scant 1½ cups sliced white mushrooms
For the purée sauce
2 tablespoons olive oil
1 shallot, chopped • 7 ounces zucchini, diced
5 tablespoons vegetable stock or water
¼ cup heavy cream • salt and pepper

Make the pasta dough. Combine the oatmeal and both types of flour into a mound on a counter and make a well in the center. Break the eggs into the well and add the egg yolks and a pinch of salt. Knead thoroughly, shape into a ball, cover with a clean dish towel and let rest for 1 hour. Meanwhile, make the vegetable sauce. Melt the butter in a pan. Add the shallots and cook over low heat, stirring occasionally, for 5 minutes. Add all the remaining vegetables and simmer, stirring occasionally, for 15 minutes. Make the purée sauce. Heat the oil in a shallow pan. Add the shallot and cook over low heat, stirring occasionally, for 5 minutes. Add the zucchini and stock or water, season with salt and pepper, cover, and simmer, stirring occasionally, for 15 minutes. Stir in the cream and cook for another 5 minutes. Remove from the heat, transfer to a food processor or blender, and process to a purée. Roll out the dough on a lightly floured counter into a sheet and cut into wide, irregular pieces. Cook in plenty of salted boiling water for 2–3 minutes until al dente. Drain, tip into the pan with the vegetable sauce, and toss for 2 minutes. Stir in the purée and transfer to a warmed serving dish. Serve immediately.

ORECCHIETTE

Orecchiete, meaning "small ears," is a signature dish from the Puglia region in southern Italy. It is made with a very firm dough made of durum wheat semolina flour, either by hand or commercially produced. These small shapes have a rough exterior and a smooth interior, which is created by pressing down lightly with the thumb on small balls of pasta. Locals in Puglia assert that it is modeled on "trulli," cylindrical houses with coned roofs that are found in the region. Orecchiette varies slightly in consistency and shape from one area to another, according to the type of flour used, and has various regional names: ricchietelle in Foggia, strascinati in Bari, chiangarelle in Taranto, and stacchiodde in Brindisi. The rough exterior makes it perfect for holding sauce, and the most traditional recipe is Orecchiette con Cime di Rapa (Orecchiette with Turnip Greens, see opposite).

ORECCHIETTE (basic recipe)

ORECCHIETTE (ricetta base)

Preparation time: 40 minutes, plus 1 hour resting

Serves 4

1¾ cups all-purpose flour, preferably Italian type 00

generous ½ cup durum wheat semolina flour

warm water

salt

Combine the flour, semolina flour and a pinch of salt and heap into a mound on the counter. Make a well in the center, add a little warm water, and mix to a firm, elastic dough. Knead well, then shape into long rolls 1 inch in diameter. Cut into sections and drag them slowly over the counter, one at a time, using the tip of a knife to form small shells. Put each shell upside down on the tip of your thumb and press it down on the counter to accentuate its curvature.

ORECCHIETTE WITH EGGPLANTS AND BASIL

ORECCHIETTE ALLE MELANZANE E BASILICO

Heat the oil with the garlic clove in a skillet. Add the eggplants and cook over medium-low heat, stirring frequently, for 5–8 minutes, until lightly browned. Add the chopped basil and season to taste with salt. Lower the heat, cover, and cook for 20 minutes, then remove, and discard the garlic clove. Cook the orecchiette in plenty of salted boiling water for 2–3 minutes until al dente. Drain, tip into the skillet, and toss well. Serve immediately.

Preparation time: 15 minutes

Cooking time: 35 minutes

Serves 4

4 tablespoons olive oil

1 garlic clove • 2 eggplants, diced

20 fresh basil leaves, chopped

10 ounces Orecchiette (see opposite) • salt

ORECCHIETTE WITH MEAT SAUCE

ORECCHIETTE AL RAGÙ

Heat the oil in a large shallow pan. Add the onion and cook over low heat, stirring occasionally, for 5 minutes. Add the meat and cook, stirring frequently, for 5–8 minutes until lightly colored. Pour in the wine and cook until the alcohol has evaporated. Stir in the tomatoes, chile, and lemon rind, season with salt and pepper, cover, and simmer for 20 minutes. Cook the orecchiette in plenty of salted boiling water for 2–3 minutes until al dente. Drain, tip into the pan with the sauce, and toss over the heat for 2 minutes. Transfer to a warmed serving dish, sprinkle with the pecorino, and serve immediately.

Tip: Earthenware pans, lined with enamel and with a tight-fitting lid, are the ideal choice for cooking a meat sauce. By maintaining even heat they allow prolonged cooking of the food and enhance its flavor.

Preparation time: 18 minutes

Cooking time: 35 minutes

Serves 4–6

3 tablespoons olive oil

1 onion, finely chopped

14 ounces ground veal

scant 1 cup dry white wine

14 ounces tomatoes, peeled and diced

1 dried red chile, crumbled • grated rind of ½ lemon

14 ounces Orecchiette (see opposite)

½ cup grated pecorino cheese

salt and pepper

ORECCHIETTE WITH TURNIP GREENS

ORECCHIETTE CON CIME DI RAPA

Cook the orecchiette in a large pan of salted boiling water for 10 minutes, then add the turnip greens and cook for another 5 minutes until tender. Drain, transfer to a warm serving dish, drizzle with plenty of olive oil, and season with pepper. Alternatively, heat 4 tablespoons olive oil with 2 garlic cloves, add the drained orecchiette mixture, cook for a few minutes, then discard the garlic, and serve immediately.

Preparation time: 12 minutes

Cooking time: 18 minutes

Serves 4

12½ ounces Orecchiette (see opposite)

14 ounces turnip greens

olive oil, for drizzling

salt and pepper

ORECCHIETTE WITH BROCCOLI

ORECCHIETTE CON BROCCOLI

Cook the broccoli in salted boiling water for 8 minutes, then drain. Heat the olive oil in a pan, add the garlic and chile, and cook for 3 minutes, then add the broccoli, and cook over low heat, stirring occasionally, for 5 minutes until tender. Meanwhile, cook the orecchiette in a large pan of salted boiling water for 2–3 minutes until al dente, then drain, and toss with the broccoli. Serve with Parmesan or pecorino.

Tip: Alternatively, the broccoli may be cooked with the orecchiette. In this case, drain everything, then drizzle with olive oil, and sprinkle with grated pecorino. This recipe works well with other types of short dried pasta, such as rigatoni.

Preparation time: 12 minutes

Cooking time: 20 minutes

Serves 4

1¾ pounds broccoli, cut into florets

2 tablespoons olive oil

1 garlic clove, chopped

1 fresh chile, seeded and chopped

10 ounces Orecchiette (see page 182)

grated Parmesan or pecorino cheese, to serve

salt

ORECCHIETTE WITH CHICKEN

ORECCHIETTE AL PETTO DI POLLO

Heat the oil in a shallow pan. Add the garlic cloves and cook over low heat, stirring frequently, for a few minutes until lightly browned. Remove the garlic with a slotted spoon and discard. Increase the heat to medium, add the artichokes and chicken and cook, stirring occasionally, for 10 minutes. Pour in the wine and cook until the alcohol has evaporated. Crumble in the bouillon cube, season with salt and pepper, stir, and simmer for another 5 minutes. Cook the orecchiette in plenty of salted boiling water for 2–3 minutes until al dente. Drain, tip into the pan with the sauce, and sprinkle with the parsley and Parmesan. Add the butter, toss, transfer to a warmed serving dish, and serve.

Preparation time: 20 minutes

Cooking time: 30 minutes

Serves 4

3 tablespoons olive oil

2 garlic cloves

2 young globe artichokes, trimmed and thinly sliced

9 ounces skinless boneless chicken breast, diced

scant 1 cup dry white wine

1 vegetable bouillon cube

10 ounces Orecchiette (see page 182)

1 sprig chopped fresh flat-leaf parsley

½ cup grated Parmesan cheese

1 tablespoon butter

salt and pepper

ORECCHIETTE WITH OVEN-ROASTED TOMATOES

ORECCHIETTE CON POMODORI AL FORNO

Preparation time: 15 minutes
Cooking time: 50 minutes
Serves 4
1 pound 5 ounces vine tomatoes, halved and seeded
1 sprig fresh flat-leaf parsley
1 garlic clove
pinch of dried oregano
olive oil, for drizzling
10 ounces Orecchiette (see page 182)
½ cup grated pecorino cheese
salt and pepper

Preheat the oven to 350°F. Put the tomatoes into an ovenproof dish, cut sides uppermost. Chop the parsley and garlic clove together and sprinkle them over the tomatoes with the oregano. Season with salt and pepper and drizzle with olive oil. Roast for 30–40 minutes. Cook the orecchiette in plenty of salted boiling water for 2–3 minutes until al dente. Drain, tip into the dish of tomatoes, and stir well. Sprinkle with the grated pecorino, season with pepper, and transfer to a warmed serving dish. Serve immediately.

ORECCHIETTE WITH SPECK

ORECCHIETTE ALLO SPECK

Preparation time: 18 minutes
Cooking time: 25 minutes
Serves 4
2 tablespoons olive oil
1 onion, finely chopped
4 zucchini, thickly sliced
3½ ounces speck or smoked bacon, cut into strips
¼ cup heavy cream
10 ounces Orecchiette (see page 182)
salt and pepper

Heat the oil in a shallow pan. Add the onion and cook over low heat, stirring occasionally, for 5 minutes. Add the zucchini, season with salt and pepper, and cook, stirring occasionally, for 15 minutes. Add the speck or bacon, stir in the cream, and cook for a few minutes more until the speck is tender. Taste and adjust the seasoning if necessary, remove from the heat, and keep warm. Cook the orecchiette in plenty of salted boiling water for 2–3 minutes until al dente. Drain, tip into a warmed serving dish, and pour the sauce over. Serve immediately.

ORECCHIETTE WITH TOMATO AND RICOTTA

ORECCHIETTE CON POMODORO E RICOTTA

Preparation time: 45 minutes
Cooking time: 40 minutes
Serves 4
4 tablespoons olive oil
9 ounces canned tomatoes
6 fresh basil leaves
12½ ounces Orecchiette (see page 182)
½ cup grated firm ricotta cheese • salt

Heat the oil in a small pan, add the tomatoes and a pinch of salt, and simmer for about 30 minutes. Mash the tomatoes with a fork, add the basil, turn off the heat, and cover. Cook the orecchiette in a large pan of salted, boiling water for 2–3 minutes until al dente, drain well, and transfer to a warmed serving dish. Pour the tomato sauce over the pasta and sprinkle with the ricotta.

PAPPARDELLE

Wide ribbons of fresh pasta similar to large tagliatelle, pappardelle ranges in width from 1 inch up to 2¼ inches. Traditionally, pappardelle is made from large sheets of dough and cut into strips using a pasta wheel. It has its origins in central and northern Italy, and the name itself is of Tuscan origin. In Bologna, in northern Italy, pappardelle is often called larghissime, "very wide". Available both dried and fresh, it sometimes has serrated edges and is typically served with rich meat, mushroom, and organ meat sauces. In Tuscany, it is mainly served with hare, duck, or wild boar sauces, while in the Veneto region in northern Italy it is generally accompanied by a veal sauce.

PAPPARDELLE (basic recipe)

PAPPARDELLE (ricetta base)

Preparation time: 40 minutes, plus 1 hour resting

Serves 4–6

3½ cups all-purpose flour, plus extra for dusting

4 eggs

salt

Sift the flour into a mound on a counter and make a well in the center. Break the eggs into the well and add a pinch of salt. Knead thoroughly, shape into a ball, cover with a clean dish towel and let rest for 1 hour. Roll out the dough on a lightly floured counter into a fairly thick sheet. Cut into strips about 1¼ inches wide.

PAPPARDELLE IN WALNUT SAUCE

PAPPARDELLE ALLE NOCI

Preparation time: 10 minutes

Cooking time: 15 minutes

Serves 4

3 tablespoons butter

¾ cup coarsely chopped walnuts

1 tablespoon pink peppercorns, crushed

1 tablespoon chopped fresh flat-leaf parsley

10 ounces Pappardelle (see above) • salt

Melt the butter in a skillet. Add the walnuts and peppercorns and cook over low heat, stirring constantly, for a few minutes. Remove the skillet from the heat and stir in the parsley. Cook the pasta in plenty of salted boiling water for 2–3 minutes until al dente. Drain, tip into the skillet, and toss well. Transfer to a warmed serving dish and serve immediately.

PAPPARDELLE WITH CAULIFLOWER AND GORGONZOLA

Parboil the cauliflower in salted boiling water for 10 minutes, then drain, reserving the cooking water. Melt the butter with the Gorgonzola in a small pan over very low heat, stirring constantly and adding a few tablespoons of milk if necessary. Do not let the mixture boil. Remove the pan from the heat. Heat the oil in a shallow pan. Add the garlic clove and cook over low heat, stirring frequently, for a few minutes until lightly browned. Remove the garlic with a slotted spoon and discard. Add the cauliflower to the pan and cook, stirring occasionally, for 5 minutes. Sprinkle with the thyme and season with salt and pepper. Cook the pappardelle in the reserved cooking water, topped up with more boiling water if necessary, for 2–3 minutes until al dente. Drain, tip into the pan with the cauliflower, and stir. Stir in the Gorgonzola mixture, remove from the heat, and serve sprinkled with the grated cheese.

Preparation time: 25 minutes

Cooking time: 25 minutes

Serves 4

7 ounces cauliflower, cut into florets

1½ tablespoons butter

5 ounces Gorgonzola cheese, diced

3–4 tablespoons milk (optional)

2–3 tablespoons olive oil

1 garlic clove

1 tablespoon chopped fresh thyme

10 ounces Pappardelle (see opposite)

⅓ cup grated Parmesan cheese

salt and pepper

PAPPARDELLE WITH CHICKEN LIVERS

Melt the butter with the oil in a pan. Add the carrot, onion, and celery and cook over low heat, stirring occasionally, for 10 minutes. Add the chicken livers, drizzle with the Marsala, and cook until the alcohol has evaporated. Mix the tomato paste with 2 tablespoons water and stir into the pan. Season with salt and simmer for 10 minutes. Cook the pappardelle in plenty of salted boiling water for 2–3 minutes until al dente. Drain, tip into a warmed serving, dish and pour the sauce over. Sprinkle with the Parmesan and serve immediately.

Preparation time: 15 minutes

Cooking time: 30 minutes

Serves 4

2 tablespoons butter

2 tablespoons olive oil

1 carrot, chopped

1 onion, chopped

1 celery stalk, chopped

7 ounces chicken livers, trimmed and chopped

scant ½ cup dry Marsala wine

1 tablespoon tomato paste

2 tablespoons water

10 ounces Pappardelle (see opposite)

⅔ cup grated Parmesan cheese

salt

PAPPARDELLE ARETINA

Preparation time: 1 hour
Cooking time: 1 hour 50 minutes
Serves 4
2 tablespoons olive oil
generous ½ cup chopped prosciutto
1 onion, chopped
1 celery stalk, chopped
1 carrot, chopped
2¼-pound duckling, liver reserved, cut into
serving pieces
scant 1 cup dry white wine
7 ounces canned chopped tomatoes
1 sprig fresh sage
1 sprig fresh basil
10 ounces Pappardelle (see page 188)
2 tablespoons butter, chilled
½ cup grated Parmesan cheese
salt and pepper

Heat the oil in a shallow pan. Add the prosciutto, onion, celery, and carrot and cook over low heat, stirring occasionally, for 5 minutes. Add the pieces of duckling and cook, stirring frequently, until lightly browned all over. Pour in the wine and cook until the alcohol has evaporated. Stir in the tomatoes, add the sage and basil, and season with salt and pepper. Cover and simmer, stirring occasionally, for about 1½ hours until the meat is tender. Ten minutes before the end of cooking, add the liver. Remove the pieces of duckling from the pan and keep warm. Pass the sauce through a strainer into a bowl, pressing with the back of a wooden spoon. Cook the pappardelle in plenty of salted boiling water for 2–3 minutes until al dente. Drain and return to the pan, then pour the sauce over, add the butter, and toss. Sprinkle with Parmesan, transfer to a warmed serving dish, and serve immediately. Serve the duckling separately.

Tuscan cuisine is simple but full of flavor, with an emphasis on all types of meat—roasted on a spit, grilled or coated with tasty sauces. Pappardelle is a worthy match, mainly with duck, hare and wild boar sauces.

PAPPARDELLE WITH MIXED MEAT SAUCE

Preparation time: 30 minutes
Cooking time: 45 minutes
Serves 4
4 tablespoons butter • 2 tablespoons olive oil
½ onion, chopped • ½ carrot, chopped
1 celery stalk, chopped
2½ tablespoons pancetta or bacon, diced
7 ounces ground beef or pork
pinch of freshly grated nutmeg
scant 1 cup red wine
9 ounces canned chopped tomatoes
3½ ounces chicken livers, trimmed and chopped
10 ounces Pappardelle (see page 188)
½ cup grated Parmesan cheese
salt and pepper

Melt half the butter with the oil in a shallow pan. Add the onion, carrot, celery, and pancetta or bacon and cook over low heat, stirring occasionally, for 10 minutes. Stir in the ground meat, season with salt and pepper, and add the nutmeg. Cook over low heat, stirring frequently, for 5–8 minutes until the meat is lightly browned. Pour in the wine and cook until the alcohol has evaporated, then add the tomatoes. Cover and simmer over low heat, stirring occasionally and adding a little hot water if the sauce is too thick, for 15 minutes. Melt the remaining butter in a small skillet. Add the chicken livers and cook over low heat, stirring frequently, for 10 minutes, then season with salt and pepper. Cook the pappardelle in plenty of salted boiling water for 2–3 minutes until al dente. Drain, tip into a warmed tureen, pour the sauce over, and add the chicken livers. Stir, sprinkle with the Parmesan, and serve immediately.

GARLIC-FLAVORED PAPPARDELLE

PAPPARDELLE AL PROFUMO D'AGLIO

Preparation time: 1 hour 10 minutes,
plus 1 hour resting
Cooking time: 40 minutes
Serves 4

3 garlic cloves
2¾ cups all-purpose flour, preferably Italian type 00, plus extra for dusting
½ cup durum wheat semolina flour
3 eggs • salt
For the sauce
3 tablespoons olive oil
1 large eggplant, diced
9 ounces canned chopped tomatoes
1 tablespoon chopped fresh flat-leaf parsley
1 cup grated Parmesan cheese
salt and pepper

Make the pasta dough. Cook the garlic cloves in boiling water for 15–20 minutes until softened. Drain, peel, and mash in a bowl until smooth. Sift together both types of flour into a mound on a counter and make a well in the center. Break the eggs into the well and add the mashed garlic and a pinch of salt. Knead thoroughly, shape into a ball, cover with a clean dish towel, and let rest for 1 hour. Meanwhile, make the sauce. Heat the oil in a pan. Add the eggplant and cook over low heat, stirring frequently, for 10 minutes until almost cooked through. Add the tomatoes, season with salt and pepper, and stir in the parsley. Simmer, stirring occasionally, for 10 minutes, then remove the pan from the heat. Roll out the dough on a lightly floured counter into a sheet. Cut into 1¼-inch wide strips. Cook the pappardelle in plenty of salted boiling water for 2–3 minutes until al dente. Drain, tip into the pan with the sauce, and toss well. Transfer to a warmed serving dish, sprinkle with the Parmesan, and serve immediately.

PAPPARDELLE WITH RABBIT SAUCE

PAPPARDELLE AL SUGO DI CONIGLIO

Preparation time: 20 minutes
Cooking time: 40 minutes
Serves 4

3 tablespoons olive oil
1 onion, finely chopped
1 celery stalk, finely chopped
1 sprig finely chopped fresh flat-leaf parsley
1 garlic clove, finely chopped
1 pound 2 ounces boneless rabbit, ground
scant ½ cup dry white wine
1½ cups bottled strained tomatoes
4–5 tablespoons vegetable stock
10 ounces Pappardelle (see page 188)
salt and pepper

Heat the oil in a shallow pan. Add the onion, celery, parsley, and garlic and cook over very low heat, stirring occasionally, for 5 minutes. Season with salt and pepper and cook, stirring occasionally, for another 10 minutes. Add the rabbit meat and cook, stirring frequently, for 5 minutes, then pour in the wine and cook until the alcohol has evaporated. Stir in the bottled strained tomatoes and simmer for 20 minutes, stirring in a little stock if the sauce is too thick. Cook the pappardelle in plenty of salted boiling water for 2–3 minutes until al dente. Drain, tip into a warmed serving dish, pour the sauce over, and serve.

→

PAPPARDELLE WITH SEA SCALLOPS

PAPPARDELLE ALLE CAPPESANTE

Preparation time: 18 minutes

Cooking time: 25 minutes

Serves 4

2 tablespoons olive oil

1 shallot, finely chopped

1 sprig finely chopped fresh tarragon

12 sea scallops, shelled

scant 1 cup dry white wine

7 ounces canned chopped tomatoes

10 ounces Pappardelle (see page 188)

1 tablespoon finely chopped fresh flat-leaf parsley

salt and pepper

Heat the oil in a pan. Add the shallot and tarragon and cook over low heat, stirring occasionally, for 5 minutes. Add the sea scallops, drizzle with the wine, and cook until the alcohol has evaporated. Simmer for 10 minutes, then add the tomatoes, season with salt and pepper, and simmer for another 5 minutes. Cook the pasta in plenty of salted boiling water for 2–3 minutes until al dente. Drain, tip into a warmed serving dish, and pour the sauce over. Sprinkle with the parsley and serve immediately.

PAPPARDELLE EN CROÛTE

PAPPARDELLE IN CROSTA

Preparation time: 50 minutes

Cooking time: 55 minutes

Serves 6

1¼ cups baby peas

1 quantity béchamel sauce (see Baked Rigatoni, page 144)

scant 1 cup grated Gruyère cheese

5 ounces ham in a single slice, diced

pinch of freshly grated nutmeg

1 tablespoon chopped fresh flat-leaf parsley

12 ounces Pappardelle (see page 188)

butter, for greasing

14 ounces ready-made pie dough, thawed if frozen

all-purpose flour, for dusting

1 egg yolk

1 tablespoon milk

salt and pepper

Cook the peas in lightly salted boiling water for about 10 minutes until tender. Meanwhile, gently heat the béchamel sauce in another pan, stirring occasionally. Drain the peas and stir into the sauce with the Gruyère, ham, nutmeg, and parsley. Season with pepper and remove from the heat. Cook the pappardelle in plenty of salted boiling water for 2–3 minutes until al dente. Drain, return to the pan, pour in the béchamel mixture, and stir. Preheat the oven to 400°F and grease a baking pan with butter. Roll out the dough on a lightly floured counter and cut out two rounds, one twice the size of the other. Use the larger round to line the base and sides of the prepared pan, then spoon in the pasta mixture. Cover with the smaller round, brushing the edge with water and pressing to seal. Beat the egg yolk with the milk in a small bowl and brush the surface of the pie with the mixture, then prick with a toothpick. Bake for about 20 minutes until golden. Remove from the oven and serve.

STRACCI

Typical of the Piedmont and Liguria regions in the northwest of Italy, stracci, meaning "rags," is a type of home-made pasta that is long and flat, similar to lasagna but narrower. The shapes are cut irregularly and the dough is often made softer with oil and milk. Spinach is sometimes added to give it a green color. Stracci is most often combined with seafood sauces.

STRACCI WITH LOBSTER

STRACCI AGLI ASTICI

Preparation time: 30 minutes
Cooking time: 30 minutes
Serves 6
2 tablespoons butter
1 onion, chopped
1 celery stalk, cut into 1¼-inch batons
½ fennel bulb, cut into 1¼-inch batons
5 tablespoons olive oil
1 garlic clove
2 sprigs chopped fresh flat-leaf parsley
1 zucchini, cut into 1¼-inch batons
½ eggplant, cut into 1¼-inch batons
2 live lobsters
3 plum tomatoes, peeled and diced
12 ounces fresh stracci
(see Stracci with Zucchini Sauce, page 198)
salt and pepper

Melt the butter in a pan, add the onion, and cook over low heat, stirring occasionally, for 5 minutes until softened. Parboil the celery and fennel for a few minutes, then drain. Heat 3 tablespoons of the oil in a pan, add the garlic and parsley, and cook for a few minutes. Add the onion, zucchini, eggplant, celery, and fennel, season, and cook, stirring frequently, for about 10 minutes until tender.

Meanwhile, prepare the lobsters. If you put them into the freezer for 2 hours before cooking, they will die painlessly from hypothermia. Plunge them into a pan of salted water, cover, and cook for 8 minutes, drain, and extract the meat (see Linguine with Lobster, page 38). Heat the remaining oil in a pan, add the lobster meat and tomatoes, and cook for 5 minutes. Cook the stracci in a pan of salted, boiling water for 2–3 minutes until al dente, drain, and add to the vegetables. Mix well, add the lobster mixture, and transfer to a warmed serving dish.

STRACCI WITH ZUCCHINI SAUCE

STRACCI ALLA SALSA DI ZUCCHINE

Preparation time: 50 minutes,
plus 1 hour resting
Cooking time: 20 minutes
Serves 4

2 tablespoons olive oil
1 pound 5 ounces zucchini, sliced
1 shallot, chopped
3 tablespoons vegetable stock
1½ quantity Fresh Pasta Dough (see page 163)
all-purpose flour, for dusting
½ cup grated Parmesan cheese
salt and pepper

Heat the oil in a pan. Add half the zucchini and the shallot and cook over medium-low heat, stirring occasionally, for 10 minutes. Put the remaining zucchini into a food processor, add the stock and a pinch each of salt and pepper, and process to a purée. Roll out the pasta on a lightly floured counter to a thin sheet and cut into uneven wide pieces. Cook in plenty of salted boiling water for 2–3 minutes until al dente. Drain, transfer to the pan with the zucchini, and stir. Add the zucchini purée and toss the stracci for 2 minutes. Transfer to a warmed serving dish, sprinkle with the Parmesan, and serve immediately.

STRACCI WITH CLAMS

STRACCI ALLE VONGOLE

Preparation time: 30 minutes
Cooking time: 30 minutes
Serves 4

2¼ pounds live clams
4 garlic cloves
2 tablespoons olive oil
7 ounces canned chopped tomatoes
14 ounces fresh stracci
(see Stracci with Zucchini Sauce, above)
1 sprig fresh flat-leaf parsley, chopped
salt and pepper

Scrub the clams under cold running water and discard any with damaged shells or that do not shut immediately when sharply tapped. Put them into a shallow pan, add the garlic cloves and pour in half the oil. Cover and cook over high heat, shaking the pan occasionally, for 3–5 minutes until opened. Lift out the clams with a slotted spoon. Strain the cooking liquid through a cheesecloth-lined strainer into a bowl and set aside.

Chop the remaining garlic clove. Heat the remaining oil in a pan. Add the tomatoes and chopped garlic, cover, and simmer, stirring occasionally, for 10 minutes. Add the clams, pour in 1 cup of the reserved cooking liquid, season with salt and pepper and cook over high heat for 5 minutes. Cook the stracci in plenty of salted boiling water for 2–3 minutes until al dente. Drain, tip into the pan with the clam sauce, and toss. Sprinkle with the parsley and serve.

TAGLIATELLE

These long, pale gold ribbons are made with a flour and egg dough, rolled out very thin and cut into strips ¼–⅜ inch wide. The name comes from tagliare, "to cut," and tagliatelle is usually home-made but can be found commercially, both fresh and dried. It originated in the city of Bologna in Emilia-Romagna, in northern Italy, where the chamber of commerce displays a gold reproduction of a perfect tagliatella. The classic sauce to accompany tagliatelle is the iconic Bolognese, but it goes equally well with other meat or creamy sauces. Tagliatelle comes in different sizes, such as the smaller version tagliatelline, and can also be colored. The green is usually achieved by adding spinach to the dough, the black by adding squid ink. A dish of green tagliatelle mixed with ordinary tagliatelle is called Paglia e Fieno (see page 214), meaning "straw and hay." Pizzocheri is another type of thick tagliatelle (¾ inch wide) originating from Valtellina, a valley in Lombardy in northern Italy, made with a mixture of buckwheat flour and all-purpose wheat flour (see Valtellina Pizzocheri page 216).

TAGLIATELLE WITH ARTICHOKES

TAGLIATELLE CON CARCIOFI

Roll out the pasta dough on a lightly floured counter into a sheet. Cut into strips about ¼–⅜ inch wide and let dry on floured dish towels. Break off the artichoke stalks and remove the tough outer leaves and the chokes. Rub all over with lemon juice to prevent discoloration. Cook in lightly salted boiling water for 7 minutes, then drain, and slice thinly. Heat the oil in a skillet, add the garlic, and cook for a few minutes until browned. Remove and discard the garlic and add the artichokes, basil, parsley, and tomatoes to the skillet. Season with salt and cook over low heat for 10 minutes. Cook the tagliatelle in a large pan of salted boiling water for 2–3 minutes until al dente, then drain, and add to the skillet. If necessary, add a few tablespoonfuls of the pasta cooking water to thin the sauce. Drizzle with olive oil and sprinkle with the Parmesan. Remove and discard the parsley, transfer the tagliatelle to a warmed serving dish, and serve.

Preparation time: 1 hour, plus 1 hour resting

Cooking time: 30 minutes

Serves 4

1 quantity Fresh Pasta Dough (see page 163)

4 globe artichokes

juice of 1 lemon, strained

4 tablespoons olive oil, plus extra for drizzling

1 garlic clove

6 fresh basil leaves

1 sprig fresh flat-leaf parsley

5 canned tomatoes, drained and chopped

4 tablespoons grated Parmesan cheese

salt

SPICY TAGLIATELLE WITH CAULIFLOWER

Preparation time: 30 minutes
Cooking time: 30 minutes
Serves 6
1 small cauliflower, cut into florets
2 tablespoons olive oil
2 garlic cloves, lightly crushed
1 tablespoon fresh bread crumbs
½ dried red chile, crumbled
1–2 tablespoons chopped fresh thyme
1 egg yolk
scant 1 cup heavy cream
14 ounces fresh tagliatelle
(see Tagliatelle with Artichokes, page 199)
salt

Cook the cauliflower florets in lightly salted boiling water for 10 minutes, then drain, reserving the cooking water. Heat the oil in a shallow pan. Add the garlic cloves and cook over low heat, stirring frequently, for a few minutes until golden brown. Remove with a slotted spoon and discard. Add the bread crumbs, chile, and cauliflower to the pan and stir. Sprinkle with the thyme, pour in 5 tablespoons of the reserved cooking water, and simmer for 10 minutes. Remove the pan from the heat, beat in the egg yolk, and then gently stir in the cream. Cook the tagliatelle in the remaining reserved cooking water, topped up with more boiling water if necessary, for 2–3 minutes until al dente. Drain, tip into a warmed serving dish, and pour the sauce over. Serve immediately.

TAGLIATELLE WITH ARTICHOKES AND SWEETBREADS

Preparation time: 25 minutes
Cooking time: 30 minutes
Serves 4
2 tablespoons olive oil
1 garlic clove
4 young globe artichokes, trimmed and sliced
7 ounces sweetbreads, soaked
in several changes of water for 5–8 hours and drained
2 tablespoons butter
10 ounces fresh tagliatelle (see Tagliatelle with Artichokes, page 199)
salt and pepper

Heat the oil in a shallow pan. Add the garlic clove and cook over low heat, stirring frequently, until lightly browned. Remove the garlic with a slotted spoon and discard. Add the artichokes and 2 tablespoons water to the pan, season with a pinch each of salt and pepper, cover, and simmer for 15 minutes. Put the sweetbreads into a pan, pour in water to cover, and bring to a boil. Remove from the heat and drain, then dice. Melt the butter in a skillet. Add the sweetbreads and cook over low heat, stirring occasionally, for 2 minutes. Cook the tagliatelle in plenty of salted boiling water for 2–3 minutes until al dente. Drain, tip into a warmed serving dish, and pour the artichokes and sweetbreads over. Stir well and serve immediately.

TAGLIATELLE BOLOGNESE

TAGLIATELLE ALLA BOLOGNESE

**Preparation time: 30 minutes,
plus 30 minutes soaking
Cooking time: 1 hour 20 minutes
Serves 6**

1 cup dried mushrooms
2 tablespoons olive oil
1 garlic clove
1 small carrot, finely chopped
1 celery stalk, finely chopped
½ onion, finely chopped
⅓ cup finely chopped prosciutto
7 ounces ground pork
¾ cup red wine
1¾ cup bottled strained tomatoes
pinch of freshly grated nutmeg
4–5 tablespoons hot vegetable stock (optional)
14 ounces fresh tagliatelle (see Tagliatelle
with Artichokes, page 199)
⅓ cup grated Parmesan cheese
salt and pepper

Put the mushrooms into a heatproof bowl, pour in lukewarm water to cover, and let soak for 30 minutes. Drain and squeeze out the excess liquid. Heat the oil in a flameproof earthenware dish. Add the garlic clove and cook over low heat, stirring frequently, for a few minutes until lightly browned. Remove the garlic with a slotted spoon and discard. Add the carrot, celery, onion, and prosciutto and cook over low heat, stirring occasionally, for 8 minutes until lightly browned. Increase the heat to medium, add the ground pork and mushrooms, and cook, stirring frequently, for 8–10 minutes, until lightly browned. Pour in the wine and cook until the alcohol has evaporated. Add the bottled strained tomatoes and nutmeg, season with salt and pepper, lower the heat, cover, and simmer for 1 hour. Add a little hot stock occasionally if the sauce begins to dry out. Cook the tagliatelle in plenty of salted boiling water for 2–3 minutes until al dente. Drain, tip into a warmed serving dish, pour the sauce over, and sprinkle with the Parmesan. Serve immediately

This fresh pasta dish, made at home using a board and rolling pin, has brought worldwide fame to the cuisine of Emilia-Romagna in northern Italy. Characteristically, simple ingredients contrast with incredibly rich and robust flavors. The meat sauce from Bologna differs from the recipes of other towns by the addition of prosciutto, instead of sausage.

TAGLIATELLE WITH OLIVES

TAGLIATELLE CON OLIVE

**Preparation time: 5 minutes
Cooking time: 5 minutes
Serves 4**

4 tablespoons butter
11 ounces fresh tagliatelle (see Tagliatelle
with Artichokes, page 199)
24 green olives, pitted
fresh basil leaves, to garnish
salt

Melt the butter in a heatproof bowl set over a pan of simmering water. Cook the tagliatelle in plenty of salted boiling water for 2–3 minutes, until al dente. Drain and tip onto a warmed serving dish. Toss with the melted butter and olives, sprinkle with a few small basil leaves, and serve immediately.

TAGLIATELLE WITH CREAM, PEAS, AND HAM

TAGLIATELLE PANNA, PISELLI E PROSCIUTTO

Preparation time: 10 minutes

Cooking time: 35 minutes

Serves 4

2 tablespoons butter

2 tablespoons olive oil

1 onion, very thinly sliced

1¾ shelled peas

scant ½ cup heavy cream

2 cooked ham slices, diced

10 ounces fresh tagliatelle (see Tagliatelle with Artichokes, page 199)

⅔ cup grated Parmesan cheese • salt

Heat the butter and oil in a pan, add the onion, and cook over low heat, stirring occasionally, for 5 minutes until softened. Add the peas and cook, stirring occasionally, for 20 minutes, then stir in the cream. Cook for 5 minutes, then add the ham. Cook the tagliatelle in a large pan of salted boiling water for 2–3 minutes until al dente, then drain, and toss with the Parmesan and hot sauce. Transfer to a warmed serving dish.

TAGLIATELLE WITH MUSHROOMS

TAGLIATELLE AI FUNGHI

Preparation time: 30 minutes

Cooking time: 45 minutes

Serves 4

½ cup dried mushrooms

1 small onion

2 tablespoons olive oil

½ cup water

5 tablespoons dry white wine

3 tablespoons concentrated tomato paste

10 ounces fresh tagliatelle (see Tagliatelle with Artichokes, page 199)

½ cup grated Parmesan cheese • salt

Place the mushrooms in a bowl, add warm water to cover, and let soak for 20 minutes. Drain, squeeze out the liquid, and chop finely with the onion. Heat the oil in a pan, add the mushrooms and onion, and cook over low heat, stirring occasionally, for 5 minutes. Stir in the water and season lightly with salt. Add the white wine and cook until the alcohol has evaporated, then stir in the tomato paste. Simmer over low heat for 30 minutes. Cook the tagliatelle in a large pan of salted boiling water for 2–3 minutes until al dente. Sprinkle with the Parmesan and toss with the mushroom sauce.

TAGLIATELLE WITH EGG AND RICOTTA SAUCE

TAGLIATELLE IN SALSA D'UOVO E RICOTTA

Beat the ricotta with a fork in a heatproof bowl, then beat in the egg yolks. Set the bowl over a pan of simmering water and heat through, whisking constantly. Season with salt and pepper and remove from the heat. Cook the tagliatelle in plenty of salted boiling water for 2–3 minutes until al dente. Drain, tip into the bowl with the ricotta mixture and toss well. Transfer to a serving dish and serve immediately.

Preparation time: 18 minutes

Cooking time: 10 minutes • Serves 4

7 ounces ricotta cheese • 3 egg yolks

10 ounces fresh tagliatelle

(see Tagliatelle with Artichokes, page 199)

salt and pepper

TAGLIATELLE WITH LANGOUSTINES AND ASPARAGUS

TAGLIATELLE CON SCAMPI AGLI ASPARAGI

Tie the asparagus together into a bunch and stand in a tall pan or asparagus pan. Add boiling water to reach just below the tips, cover, and simmer for 10 minutes. Drain, cut off the tips, and set aside. Put the remaining spears into a food processor or blender and process with half of the stock until smooth. Melt the butter in a shallow pan. Add the garlic and langoustines or lobsterettes and cook, stirring frequently, for 2 minutes. Pour in the brandy and cook until the alcohol has evaporated. Stir in the puréed asparagus cream, season with salt and pepper, and simmer for 5 minutes. Cook the tagliatelle in plenty of salted boiling water for 2–3 minutes until al dente. Drain, tip into the pan with the sauce, and toss for 30 seconds. Add the reserved asparagus tips, season with pepper, and serve immediately.

Preparation time: 25 minutes

Cooking time: 20 minutes

Serves 6

2¼ pounds asparagus, trimmed

1 cup vegetable stock

2 tablespoons butter

2 garlic cloves, finely chopped

2¼ pounds langoustines or lobsterettes, thawed if frozen, peeled, and deveined

½ cup brandy

14 ounces fresh tagliatelle (see Tagliatelle with Artichokes, page 199)

salt and pepper

TAGLIATELLE WITH LEEK BÉCHAMEL

TAGLIATELLE CON BESCIAMELLA AI PORRI

Melt the butter with the oil in a pan. Add the leeks and cook over low heat, stirring occasionally, for 5 minutes. Add the speck or bacon and cook, stirring occasionally, for 2 minutes, then stir the mixture into the béchamel sauce. Season with salt and pepper, stir in the parsley, and keep warm. Cook the tagliatelle in plenty of salted boiling water for 2–3 minutes until al dente. Drain, transfer to a warmed serving dish, pour the béchamel mixture over, and serve.

Preparation time: 20 minutes

Cooking time: 18 minutes • Serves 4

2 tablespoons butter • 2 tablespoons olive oil

2 leeks, white parts only, finely chopped

⅓ cup diced speck or smoked bacon

scant ½ cup béchamel sauce

(see Baked Rigatoni, page 144)

1 tablespoon chopped fresh flat-leaf parsley

10 ounces fresh tagliatelle (see Tagliatelle with Artichokes, page 199) • salt and pepper

TAGLIATELLE WITH EGGPLANT

TAGLIATELLE ALLE MELANZANE

Preparation time: 30 minutes

Cooking time: 30 minutes

Serves 4

6 tablespoons olive oil • 2 eggplants, thinly sliced

1 garlic clove

9 ounces tomatoes, peeled and chopped

10 fresh basil leaves • 10 ounces fresh tagliatelle

(see Tagliatelle with Artichokes, page 199)

scant 1 cup grated firm ricotta cheese

salt and pepper

Heat 4 tablespoons of the olive oil in a skillet, add the eggplant slices, and cook over low heat for 8–10 minutes until golden brown all over. Heat the remaining oil in a pan, add the garlic and the tomatoes, and cook over low heat for 10 minutes, then remove, and discard the garlic. Remove the pan from the heat and season with salt and pepper, then chop one of the basil leaves, and stir in. Cook the tagliatelle in a large pan of salted boiling water for 2–3 minutes until al dente, then drain, and place in a warmed serving dish. Cover with the ricotta, then spoon the tomato sauce over. Top with the eggplant slices and sprinkle with the remaining basil.

TAGLIATELLE WITH LEMON

TAGLIATELLE AL LIMONE

Preparation time: 25 minutes

Cooking time: 9 minutes

Serves 4

3 unwaxed lemons

4 tablespoons butter

¼ cup light cream

10 ounces fresh tagliatelle (see Tagliatelle

with Artichokes, page 199)

salt • grated Parmesan cheese, to serve

Grate the rind of 2 of the lemons. Peel the remaining lemon, removing all traces of pith from the rind and cut it into thin strips. Melt the butter in a skillet. When it foams, add the grated lemon rind and cook, stirring occasionally, for a few minutes, then stir in the cream and season with salt. Do not let the mixture boil. Cook the tagliatelle in plenty of salted boiling water for 2–3 minutes until al dente. Drain, tip into the skillet, and toss gently. Transfer the tagliatelle to a serving dish, sprinkle with plenty of Parmesan, and garnish with the strips of lemon rind.

TAGLIATELLE WITH ZUCCHINI SAUCE

TAGLIATELLE CON SALSA SAPORITA ALLE ZUCCHINE

Preparation time: 25 minutes

Cooking time: 26 minutes

Serves 4

3 tablespoons butter • 1 shallot, chopped

3 zucchini, thinly sliced

2 tablespoons heavy cream

12 ounces fresh tagliatelle (see Tagliatelle

with Artichokes, page 199)

¼ cup mascarpone cheese • salt and pepper

Melt the butter in a shallow pan. Add the shallot and cook over low heat, stirring occasionally, for 5 minutes. Add the zucchini and cook, stirring occasionally, for 10 minutes. Pour in the cream, season with salt and pepper, and simmer gently for another 10 minutes. Warm a serving dish and dot the base with the mascarpone. Cook the tagliatelle in plenty of salted boiling water until al dente. Drain, tip into the serving dish, and stir. Add the zucchini and serve.

TAGLIATELLE WITH LIGHTLY CURRIED VEGETABLES

TAGLIATELLE LIGHT AL CURRY

Preparation time: 25 minutes
Cooking time: 30 minutes
Serves 4
2 tablespoons olive oil
1 shallot, chopped • 3 leeks, chopped
3 zucchini, thinly sliced
⅔ cup strained plain yogurt
1 tablespoon curry powder
10 ounces fresh tagliatelle (see Tagliatelle with Artichokes, page 199)
salt and pepper

Heat the oil in a pan. Add shallot and leeks and cook over low heat, stirring occasionally, for 5–8 minutes until softened. Increase the heat to medium-high, add the zucchini, and cook, stirring occasionally, for 15 minutes. Stir in the yogurt, sprinkle with the curry powder, and heat through, stirring constantly. Do not let the mixture boil. Cook the tagliatelle in plenty of salted boiling water for 2–3 minutes until al dente. Drain, tip into the pan with the sauce, and toss over the heat for 30 seconds. Transfer to a warmed serving dish, season to taste with pepper, and serve immediately.

TAGLIATELLE WITH ASPARAGUS TIPS

TAGLIATELLE ALLE PUNTE DI ASPARAGI

Preparation time: 25 minutes
Cooking time: 30 minutes
Serves 4
1½ pounds asparagus spears, trimmed
4 tablespoons butter • 1 onion, chopped
10 ounces fresh tagliatelle (see Tagliatelle with Artichokes, page 199)
½ cup grated Parmesan cheese
salt

Cook the asparagus in salted boiling water for 10 minutes, then drain. Melt 3 tablespoons of the butter in a shallow pan. Add the onion and cook over low heat, stirring occasionally, for 5 minutes. Do not let it color. Add the asparagus and cook for another 5 minutes. Cook the tagliatelle in plenty of salted boiling water for 2–3 minutes until al dente. Drain, tip into a warmed serving dish, and pour the asparagus sauce over. Add the remaining butter and the Parmesan and toss lightly. Serve immediately.

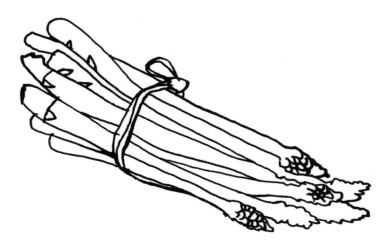

TAGLIATELLE WITH SAGE AND TARRAGON CHICKEN SAUCE

TAGLIATELLE CON RAGÙ DI GALLINA AL DRAGONCELLO E SALVIA

Melt the butter in a shallow pan. Add the shallots and carrots and cook over low heat, stirring occasionally, for 5 minutes. Add the chicken, increase the heat to medium, and cook, stirring occasionally, for about 8 minutes until lightly browned. Pour in the wine and cook until the alcohol has evaporated. Pour in the stock, stir in the tomato paste, lower the heat, cover, and simmer gently for 15 minutes. Stir in the tarragon and lemon rind. Cook the tagliatelle in plenty of salted boiling water for 2–3 minutes until al dente. Drain, tip into the pan with the sauce and toss for 1 minute. Add the remaining butter and the Parmesan, transfer to a warmed serving dish, and garnish with the fried sage leaves.

Preparation time: 30 minutes

Cooking time: 30 minutes

Serves 6

2 tablespoons butter

2 shallots, finely chopped

2 carrots, finely chopped

2 skinless boneless chicken breasts, diced

scant 1 cup dry white wine

1¾ cups chicken stock

1 teaspoon tomato paste

1 sprig chopped fresh tarragon

grated rind of 1 lemon

14 ounces fresh tagliatelle (see Tagliatelle with Artichokes, page 199)

½ cup grated Parmesan cheese

12 large fresh sage leaves, fried in butter

salt

TAGLIATELLINE WITH CHICKEN LIVERS

TAGLIATELLINE AI FEGATINI DI POLLO

Roll out the pasta dough on a lightly floured counter into a sheet. Cut into strips about ¼ inch wide and let dry on floured dish towels. Melt the butter in a small skillet. Add the onion and celery and cook over low heat, stirring occasionally, for 5 minutes. Add the ground veal and cook, stirring occasionally, for 10 minutes until lightly browned. Add the chicken livers, mix well, and pour in the bottled strained tomatoes. Simmer gently for another 10 minutes. Cook the pasta in plenty of salted boiling water for 2–3 minutes until al dente. Drain and toss with the sauce, then stir in a pat of butter if you like.

Preparation time: 1 hour, plus 1 hour resting

Cooking time: 30 minutes

Serves 4

1 quantity Fresh Pasta Dough (see page 163)

2 tablespoons butter, plus extra for serving

½ small onion, chopped

½ celery stalk, chopped

2 ounces ground veal

3½ ounces chicken livers, trimmed and coarsely chopped

1¼ cups bottled strained tomatoes

salt

TAGLIATELLE WITH SALMON

TAGLIATELLE AL SALMONE

Preparation time: 5 minutes
Cooking time: 15 minutes
Serves 4
4 tablespoons butter
3½ ounces smoked salmon, chopped
juice of ½ lemon, strained
scant ½ cup heavy cream
5 tablespoons whiskey
10 ounces fresh tagliatelle (see Tagliatelle
with Artichokes, page 199)
salt and pepper

Melt the butter in a pan, add the salmon, stir, and sprinkle with the lemon juice. Cook for a few minutes, then add the cream and whiskey and season with salt and pepper. Cook over low heat for 5 minutes. Cook the tagliatelle in a large pan of salted boiling water for 2–3 minutes until al dente, drain, add to the sauce, and cook for a few minutes. Toss gently and transfer to a warmed serving dish.

Tip: This recipe also works with dried short pasta like penne.

TAGLIATELLE WITH SPINACH

TAGLIATELLE CON SPINACI

Preparation time: 20 minutes
Cooking time: 20 minutes
Serves 4
5 tablespoons butter, plus extra for greasing
1½ pounds spinach
1 onion, finely chopped
1⅓ cups grated Parmesan cheese
10 ounces fresh tagliatelle (see Tagliatelle
with Artichokes, page 199)
scant 1 cup heavy cream
salt and pepper

Preheat the oven to 400°F and grease an ovenproof dish with butter. Cook the spinach, in just the water clinging to the leaves after washing, for 5 minutes, then drain, and chop. Heat half the butter in a pan, add the onion, and cook over low heat, stirring occasionally, for 5 minutes until softened. Add the spinach and cook for a few minutes more. Season with salt and pepper and sprinkle with half the Parmesan. Cook the tagliatelle in a large pan of salted boiling water for 2–3 minutes until al dente, then drain, return to the pan, and toss with the remaining butter. Make layers of tagliatelle, most of the remaining Parmesan, and the spinach in the prepared dish, ending with a layer of spinach. Pour the cream on top, sprinkle with the rest of the Parmesan, and bake for 10 minutes until golden and bubbling.

TAGLIATELLE WITH STURGEON

Heat the oil in a skillet. Add the leeks and cook over low heat, stirring occasionally, for 5 minutes. Add the fish, stir gently, and cook for 2 minutes, then add the tomatoes. Cook the tagliatelle in plenty of salted boiling water for 2–3 minutes until al dente, then drain, and tip into the skillet. Mix lightly and serve immediately.

Preparation time: 10 minutes

Cooking time: 15 minutes

Serves 4

4 tablespoons olive oil

2 small leeks, thinly sliced

5 ounces sturgeon fillet, skinned and diced

2 plum tomatoes, peeled and chopped

9 ounces fresh tagliatelle (see Tagliatelle with Artichokes, page 199)

salt

TAGLIATELLE WITH MOZZARELLA

Cook the tagliatelle in plenty of salted boiling water for 2–3 minutes until al dente. Drain and toss with the mozzarella and ham, then transfer to a serving dish. Sprinkle the curls of butter over the surface, season lightly with pepper, and garnish with the Parmesan. Serve immediately.

Preparation time: 15 minutes

Cooking time: 6 minutes

Serves 4

12 ounces fresh tagliatelle (see Tagliatelle with Artichokes, page 199)

4 ounces diced mozzarella cheese

½ cup diced ham

3 tablespoons butter, shaved into curls

½ cup grated Parmesan cheese

salt and pepper

TAGLIATELLE, FAVE E CALAMARETTI

TAGLIATELLE WITH FAVA BEANS AND BABY SQUID

Preparation time: 25 minutes

Cooking time: 35 minutes

Serves 4

¾ cup shelled fava beans

4 tablespoons butter

1 shallot, chopped

11 ounces baby squid, cleaned and cut into strips

scant 1 cup dry white wine

14 ounces fresh tagliatelle

(see Tagliatelle with Artichokes, page 199)

salt

Pop the fava beans out of their skins by pressing gently between your finger and thumb. Melt half the butter in a shallow pan. Add the shallot and cook over very low heat, stirring occasionally, for 5 minutes. Add the squid and cook, stirring occasionally, for 10 minutes. Season lightly with salt, drizzle with the wine, and cook until the alcohol has evaporated. Add the beans and a pinch of salt and simmer for 20 minutes. Cook the tagliatelle in plenty of salted boiling water for 2–3 minutes until al dente. Drain, tip into the pan of sauce, and toss over the heat for 1 minute. Serve immediately.

TAGLIATELLE AL NERO DI SEPPIA

CUTTLEFISH INK TAGLIATELLE

Preparation time: 30 minutes

Cooking time: 5 minutes

Serves 4

1¾ cups all-purpose flour, preferably Italian type 00, plus extra for dusting

2 eggs, lightly beaten

1 or 2 cuttlefish ink sacs

5 ounces canned tuna in oil, drained and flaked

1 tablespoon capers, rinsed

3 tablespoons olive oil

salt

Sift the flour with a pinch of salt into a mound on the counter and make a well in the center. Add the eggs and cuttlefish ink and gradually incorporate the flour with your fingers. Knead the dough until soft and smooth, then roll out into a sheet on a lightly floured counter, fold over several times, and cut into ¼–⅜-inch wide tagliatelle. Combine the tuna, capers, and olive oil in a bowl. Cook the tagliatelle in a large pan of salted boiling water for 2–3 minutes until al dente, then drain, and toss with the tuna sauce. Transfer to a warmed serving dish and serve immediately.

PAGLIA E FIENO WITH SPECK

Preparation time: 50 minutes, plus 1 hour resting

Cooking time: 15 minutes

Serves 4

scant ½ cup heavy cream

⅔ cup grated Parmesan cheese

3 tablespoons butter

1 sprig fresh rosemary

½ cup diced speck or smoked bacon

1 quantity Green Pasta Dough (see page 163)

5 ounces fresh tagliatelle (see Tagliatelle

with Artichokes, page 199)

salt and pepper

Roll out the green pasta dough on a lightly floured counter into a sheet. Cut into strips about ¼–⅜ inch wide and let dry on floured dish towels. Combine the cream and Parmesan in a tureen. Melt the butter in a pan. Add the rosemary and speck or bacon, season with salt and pepper, and cook over low heat, stirring frequently, for 5 minutes. Remove and discard the rosemary and transfer the speck or bacon into the tureen. Cook both types of tagliatelle in plenty of salted boiling water for 2–3 minutes until al dente. Drain, tip into the tureen, stir and serve.

Tip: Green tagliatelle is slightly moist because of the spinach used to color it. To prevent the ribbons from sticking together when they are left to rest, sprinkle the cloth they are laid on with semolina flour rather than all-purpose flour.

PAGLIA E FIENO WITH GIBLETS

Preparation time: 30 minutes

Cooking time: 40 minutes

Serves 6

7 ounces chicken giblets (hearts, gizzards, and livers)

2 tablespoons butter

1 shallot, chopped

2 tablespoons olive oil

11 ounces canned chopped tomatoes

1 tablespoon chopped fresh flat-leaf parsley

5 ounces fresh spinach tagliatelle (see above)

5 ounces fresh tagliatelle

(see Tagliatelle with Artichokes, page 199)

½ cup grated Parmesan cheese

salt and pepper

Slice the chicken hearts, slit open the gizzards on the fleshy side, and discard the gravel sacs. Trim the livers and chop. Melt the butter in a shallow pan. Add the shallot and chicken hearts and gizzards, season lightly with salt and pepper, and cook over medium-low heat, stirring frequently, for 15 minutes. Add the chicken liver and cook, stirring frequently, for 2 minutes.

Heat the oil in another shallow pan. Add the tomatoes, and cook for 10–15 minutes until thickened, then season lightly with salt, and stir into the chicken mixture. Sprinkle with the chopped parsley. Cook the pasta in plenty of salted boiling water for 2–3 minutes until al dente. Drain, tip into the pan with the sauce, and toss over the heat for 1 minute. Transfer to a warmed serving dish, sprinkle with the Parmesan, and serve immediately.

TAGLIATELLINE WITH ONIONS

TAGLIATELLINE ALLE CIPOLLE

Preparation time: 10 minutes
Cooking time: 15 minutes
Serves 4
3 tablespoons butter • 4 tablespoons olive oil
14 ounces white onions, thinly sliced
10 ounces fresh tagliatelline
(see Tagliatelline with Chicken Livers, page 209)
⅔ cup grated Parmesan cheese
salt and pepper

Heat the butter and oil in a flameproof casserole. Add the onions and cook over low heat, stirring occasionally, for 5–10 minutes until translucent, then season with salt. Meanwhile, cook the tagliatelline in a large pan of salted boiling water for 2–3 minutes until al dente, then drain, and tip into the casserole. Season lightly with pepper and toss. Remove from the heat and sprinkle with the Parmesan.

VALTELLINA PIZZOCCHERI

PIZZOCCHERI DELLA VALTELLINA

Preparation time: 50 minutes
plus 30 minutes resting
Cooking time: 45 minutes
Serves 6
1¼ cups buckwheat flour
¾ cup all-purpose flour, preferably Italian type 00, plus extra for dusting
1 egg, lightly beaten
2 tablespoons milk
salt
For the sauce
14 ounces savoy cabbage, shredded
1 potato, chopped
scant ½ cup butter
1 onion, thinly sliced
1 garlic clove, thinly sliced
4 shredded fresh sage leaves
5 ounces sliced low-fat cheese
1 cup grated Parmesan cheese
salt and pepper

Sift together both flours and a pinch of salt into a mound on the counter and make a well in the center. Add the egg, 1 tablespoon warm water, and the milk and gradually incorporate the flour with your fingers, adding more warm water if necessary. Knead until smooth. Roll in a damp dish towel and let rest for 30 minutes. Meanwhile, put the cabbage and potato into a pan, add water to cover, and season with salt and pepper. Bring to a boil, then lower the heat, and simmer for 20 minutes until the cabbage is tender and the potato is almost disintegrating. Divide the butter between three small pans and cook the onion, garlic, and sage in the separate pans until soft and golden brown. Roll out the pasta dough into a fairly thick sheet on a lightly floured counter and cut into ½-inch wide ribbons about 8 inches long. Add the pizzoccheri to the pan of vegetables, cook for 5 minutes, then drain, and transfer to a large dish. Pour the hot butters over the mixture and toss lightly. Arrange a layer of vegetables and pizzoccheri on the base of a soup tureen, place a layer of cheese slices on top, and sprinkle with the Parmesan. Continue making alternating layers until all the ingredients are used. Serve hot.

Buckwheat flour, originally from Asia, is often replaced by cornstarch in Italian cooking. However, buckwheat is still produced near Carnia in Friuli-Venezia Giulia, northeast Italy, and in Valtellina in Lombardy, in the north, where Pizzoccheri is a traditional dish.

BAKED TAGLIATELLE AND SPINACH

PASTICCIO DI TAGLIATELLE E SPINACI

Preparation time: 1 hour,
plus 2–2½ hours rising
Cooking time: 55 minutes
Serves 6
For the bread dough
oil, for brushing
4 cups strong white bread flour,
plus extra for dusting
1 tablespoon salt
1 envelope rapid-rise yeast
1 tablespoon olive oil
1¾ cups lukewarm water
6 tablespoons butter, plus extra for greasing
7 ounces spinach, coarse stalks removed
scant ½ cup milk • ¼ cup heavy cream
11 ounces fresh tagliatelle
(see Tagliatelle with Artichokes, page 199)
scant 1 cup diced ham
3 eggs
⅔ cup grated Parmesan cheese
salt and pepper

Make the bread dough. Brush a bowl with oil. Sift together the flour and salt onto a counter, mix in the yeast, and shape into a mound. Make a well in the center and pour the oil and half the lukewarm water into it. Knead thoroughly, gradually incorporating the dry ingredients and adding more water to make a firm dough (you may not need all the water.) Shape into a ball, put it into the prepared bowl, cover with a damp dish towel, and let rise in a warm place for 2–2½ hours. Preheat the oven to 350°F and grease an ovenproof dish with butter. Punch down the dough and roll out on a lightly floured counter into a sheet ⅛–¼ inch thick. Put it into the base of the prepared dish, trimming off any excess. Put the spinach into a pan with just the water clinging to the leaves after washing and cook over low heat, turning occasionally, for 5–10 minutes until tender. Add the butter, pour in the milk and cream, stir well, and season with salt and pepper. Cook the tagliatelle in plenty of salted boiling water for 2–3 minutes until al dente. Drain, return to the pan, and add the spinach mixture and ham. Spoon the mixture into the dish. Beat the eggs with the Parmesan and a pinch of salt in a bowl, then pour the mixture over the tagliatelle. Bake for about 30 minutes, remove from the oven, and serve.

SPICY TAGLIATELLE MOLD

SFORMATO DI TAGLIATELLE PICCANTI

Preparation time: 30 minutes
Cooking time: 25 minutes
Serves 4
½ cup diced smoked pancetta or bacon
8¾ cups milk
10 ounces fresh tagliatelle (see Tagliatelle with Artichokes, page 199)
3 eggs, separated
¾ cup grated Gruyère cheese
1 teaspoon paprika
butter, for greasing
salt and pepper

Preheat the oven to 350°F and grease an ovenproof dish with butter. Dry-fry the pancetta or bacon in a small pan over low heat, stirring occasionally, for 4–5 minutes until lightly browned. Remove the pan from the heat. Pour the milk into a large pan and bring just to a boil. Add the tagliatelle and cook for 2–3 minutes until al dente. Drain, reserving scant 1 cup of the cooking liquid. Beat the egg yolks with the cheese and paprika in a large bowl and season with salt and pepper. Stir in the reserved cooking liquid, then stir in the tagliatelle and pancetta or bacon. Stiffly whisk the egg whites in a grease-free bowl and fold into the mixture. Pour the mixture into the prepared dish and bake for 10–15 minutes until the mold is golden brown and has risen slightly. Serve immediately.

SUNDAY TAGLIATELLE

TAGLIATELLE DOMENICALI

Melt half the butter with the oil in a shallow pan. Add the onions, celery, and carrots and cook over low heat, stirring occasionally, for 5 minutes. Add the ground meat, increase the heat to medium, and cook, stirring frequently and breaking it up with a wooden spoon, for 8–10 minutes until lightly browned. Pour in the wine and cook until the alcohol has evaporated. Add the peas and tomatoes, season with salt and pepper, lower the heat, cover, and simmer, stirring occasionally, for 30 minutes.

Remove the pan from the heat and transfer the mixture to a food processor. Process in pulses until thoroughly combined, then scrape into a bowl. Shape scoops of the mixture into small balls with your hands and dust with flour. Heat the oil in a deep-fryer 350–375°F or until a cube of day-old bread browns in 30 seconds. Add the meatballs, in batches if necessary, and cook until browned all over. Remove with a slotted spoon and drain on paper towels. Preheat the oven to 325°F. Cook the tagliatelle in plenty of salted boiling water for 2–3 minutes until al dente. Drain and arrange in an ovenproof dish in alternating layers with the mozzarella, tomato sauce, meatballs, and pecorino until all the ingredients are used up. Dot with the remaining butter and bake for about 10 minutes until golden. Remove fr m the oven, sprinkle with pecorino, and season with pepper. Serve immediately.

Preparation time: 1 hour

Cooking time: 1 hour 15 minutes

Serves 4–6

4 tablespoons butter

2 tablespoons olive oil

2 onions, finely chopped

1 celery stalk, finely chopped

4 carrots, finely chopped

14 ounces ground meat

scant 1 cup dry white wine

1 cup cooked or frozen baby peas

11 ounces canned chopped tomatoes

all-purpose flour, for dusting

oil, for deep-frying

14 ounces fresh tagliatelle (see Tagliatelle with Artichokes, page 199)

10 ounces diced mozzarella cheese

scant ½ cup tomato sauce (see Angel Hair Mold, page 30)

⅔ cup grated pecorino cheese, plus extra to serve

salt and pepper

TAGLIATELLE AND CHEESE PIE

Preparation time: 1 hour, plus
2–2½ hours rising
Cooking time: 25 minutes
Serves 6
butter, for greasing
½ quantity bread dough (see Baked
Tagliatelle and Spinach, page 218)
all-purpose flour, for dusting
⅔ cup ricotta cheese
3½ ounces diced robiola cheese
3 ounces diced mild Gorgonzola cheese
9 ounces fresh tagliatelle (see Tagliatelle
with Artichokes, page 199)
2 eggs
½ cup grated Parmesan cheese
salt and pepper

Preheat the oven to 350°F and lightly grease an ovenproof dish with butter. Roll out the bread dough on a lightly floured counter into a thin sheet and use to line the base of the prepared dish. Crumble the ricotta into a bowl, add the robiola and Gorgonzola, season lightly with pepper, and mix together. Cook the tagliatelle in plenty of salted boiling water for 2–3 minutes until al dente. Drain, tip into the cheese, and toss. Spoon the mixture into the dish on top of the bread base. Beat the eggs with the Parmesan in another bowl and season with salt and pepper. Pour the mixture over the tagliatelle and bake for about 20 minutes until golden brown. Remove from the oven and let stand for 5 minutes, then serve.

TAGLIATELLE WITH WHITE TRUFFLE

Preparation time: 10 minutes
Cooking time: 20 minutes
Serves 4
5 tablespoons butter, plus extra for greasing
1 garlic clove
1 sprig fresh rosemary
14 ounces fresh tagliatelle (see Tagliatelle
with Artichokes, page 199)
1 egg yolk
pinch of freshly grated nutmeg
1 quantity hot béchamel sauce (see Baked
Rigatoni, page 144)
1 white truffle, thinly shaved
⅔ cup grated Parmesan cheese
salt and pepper

Preheat the oven to 350°F and grease an ovenproof dish with butter. Melt 4 tablespoons of the butter in a skillet. Add the garlic clove and rosemary sprig and cook over low heat for a few minutes, but do not let the garlic burn, then remove, and discard. Cook the tagliatelle in plenty of salted boiling water for 2–3 minutes until al dente. Drain, tip into the skillet, and toss in the flavored butter. Beat the egg yolk and nutmeg into the béchamel sauce and season with salt and pepper. Gently stir the sauce and truffle shavings into the tagliatelle and sprinkle with the grated cheese. Transfer the mixture to the prepared dish, dot with the remaining butter, and bake for 10 minutes. Serve immediately.

TAGLIERINI

A type of fresh pasta also known as tagliolini, taglierini is a very thin version of tagliatelle that originated in northern Italy and is about ⅛ inch wide. Rolled out into a sheet and cut with a knife in the old-fashioned way, home-made taglierini is made from rich egg dough, whereas industrial taglierini is made from durum wheat semolina flour and water. Taglierini is suitable for serving with a sauce, but can also be cooked in stock. It is ideal with delicate and creamy sauces based on butter, eggs, and cheese, as well as with fish and shellfish.

FALL TAGLIERINI

TAGLIERINI D'AUTUNNO

Preparation time: 1 hour 10 minutes, plus 1 hour resting
Cooking time: 22 minutes
Serves 6

1½ quantity Fresh Pasta Dough (see page 163)
4 tablespoons butter
5 ounces smoked pancetta or bacon, cut into strips
2¾ cups sliced porcini mushrooms
2 tablespoons heavy cream
1 tablespoon chopped fresh flat-leaf parsley
salt and pepper

Roll out the pasta dough on a lightly floured counter into a sheet. Cut into strips about ⅛ inch wide and let dry on floured dish towels. Melt the butter in a small pan. Add the pancetta or bacon and cook over low heat, stirring occasionally, for 4–5 minutes until lightly browned. Increase the heat to high, add the mushrooms, season with salt, and cook, stirring occasionally, for 10 minutes. Cook the taglierini in plenty of salted boiling water for 2–3 minutes until al dente. Drain and tip into the pan with the mushrooms. Lower the heat, add the cream, and heat through, stirring constantly. Transfer to a warmed serving dish, sprinkle with the parsley, and season with pepper. Serve immediately.

GREEN TAGLIERINI WITH SHRIMP AND BRANDY

TAGLIERINI VERDI AI GAMBERI SFUMATI AL COGNAC

Preparation time: 40 minutes

Cooking time: 30 minutes

Serves 4

3 young globe artichokes, trimmed and thinly sliced

juice of ½ lemon, strained

20 cooked shrimp

3 tablespoons butter

4 tablespoons heavy cream

½ cup brandy

10 ounces fresh taglierini (see Fall Taglierini, opposite)

8–12 fresh basil leaves

salt

Put the artichokes into a pan, add the lemon juice and a pinch of salt, and pour in water just to cover. Bring to a boil, lower the heat, cover, and simmer for 10 minutes. Meanwhile, reserve 8 shrimp for the garnish and peel, devein, and chop the remainder. Drain the artichokes, transfer to a food processor, and process to a purée. Melt 1 tablespoon of the butter in a small pan. Add the artichoke purée and cook over low heat, stirring frequently, for 5 minutes. Stir in the cream and heat through over low heat, stirring constantly, for a few minutes.

Melt the remaining butter in a skillet. Add the chopped shrimp and cook over low heat, stirring frequently, for 5 minutes. Drizzle with the brandy and cook until the alcohol has evaporated. Cook the taglierini in plenty of salted boiling water for 2–3 minutes until al dente. Drain, tip into the pan with the shrimp and toss for 2 minutes. Pour a small ladleful of artichoke purée onto each of 4 individual plates and top with the taglierini rolled into a turban shape. Garnish with the reserved whole shrimp and a few basil leaves.

TAGLIERINI FANTASIA

TAGLIERINI FANTASIA

Preparation time: 15 minutes

Cooking time: 8 minutes

Serves 4

1¾ cups low-fat cream cheese

2 egg yolks

generous ½ cup diced prosciutto

2 tablespoons heavy cream

10 ounces fresh taglierini (see Fall Taglierini, opposite)

2 tablespoons butter

½ cup grated Parmesan cheese

salt and pepper

Beat the cream cheese in a bowl, then stir in the egg yolks, prosciutto, and cream, and season with salt and pepper. Cook the taglierini in plenty of salted boiling water for 2–3 minutes until al dente. Drain, tip onto a warmed serving dish, pour the sauce over, and add the butter. Serve immediately, handing the Parmesan separately.

COCOA TAGLIERINI

Make the pasta dough. Sift together the flour and unsweetened cocoa powder into a mound on a counter and make a well in the center. Break the eggs into the well and add a pinch of salt. Knead thoroughly, shape into a ball, cover with a clean dish towel and let rest for 30 minutes. Roll out the dough on a lightly floured counter to a thin sheet. Roll it up and cut into ⅛-inch wide strips. Make the sauce. Melt the butter in a pan. Add the garlic and bay leaves and cook over low heat, stirring occasionally, for a few minutes until the garlic is lightly browned. Remove the garlic and bay leaves with a slotted spoon and discard. Stir the mascarpone and chile into the pan. Cook the taglierini in plenty of salted boiling water for 2–3 minutes until al dente. Drain, tip into the pan with the sauce, and toss for 30 seconds. Transfer to a warmed serving dish, sprinkle with the Parmesan, and serve immediately.

Preparation time: 50 minutes,

plus 1 hour resting

Cooking time: 15 minutes

Serves 4

1¼ cups all-purpose flour, plus extra for dusting

3 tablespoons unsweetened cocoa powder

2 eggs

salt

For the sauce

3 tablespoons butter

1 garlic clove

3 bay leaves

⅓ cup mascarpone cheese

½ dried red chile, crumbled

½ cup grated Parmesan cheese

CHESTNUT FLOUR TAGLIERINI WITH ONION BUTTER

Make the pasta dough. Sift both types of flour into a mound on a counter and make a well in the center. Break the eggs into the well and add a pinch of salt. Knead thoroughly, shape into a ball, cover with a clean dish towel and let rest for 1 hour. Meanwhile, make the sauce. Melt half the butter in a small shallow pan. Add the onion, season lightly with salt, and cook over low heat, stirring occasionally, for 10 minutes. Remove the pan from the heat and set aside. Roll out the dough into a fairly thick sheet, then roll it up, and slice into ⅛-inch rounds. Dice the remaining butter and put it into a serving dish with the onion butter and both types of cheese. Cook the taglierini in plenty of salted boiling water for 2–3 minutes until al dente. Drain, leaving it slightly wet, tip into the serving dish, and toss well. Serve immediately.

Preparation time: 1 hour, plus 1 hour resting

Cooking time: 20 minutes

Serves 4

1¼ cups chestnut flour

2¼ cups all-purpose flour, preferably Italian type 00, plus extra for dusting

1 egg

salt

For the sauce

2 tablespoons butter

1 small onion, finely chopped

2 ounces diced mild fontina cheese

1½ ounces finely diced fontina valdostana cheese

salt

PINK TAGLIERINI

Melt the butter with the oil in a pan. Add the onion and garlic and cook over low heat, stirring occasionally, for 5 minutes. Add the tomatoes and salmon and cook, stirring occasionally, for 10 minutes. Drizzle with the wine and cook until the alcohol has evaporated. Stir in the cream and thyme, season with salt and pepper, and heat through gently. Cook the taglierini in plenty of salted boiling water for 2–3 minutes until al dente. Drain, tip into the pan with the sauce, and toss for a few minutes. Sprinkle with the chives and serve immediately.

Preparation time: 10 minutes

Cooking time: 25 minutes

Serves 4

2 tablespoons butter

2 tablespoons olive oil

1 onion, chopped

1 garlic clove, chopped

3½ ounces canned chopped tomatoes

3 ounces smoked salmon, cut into strips

scant 1 cup dry white wine

2 tablespoons heavy cream

1 teaspoon chopped fresh thyme

10 ounces fresh taglierini (see Fall Taglierini, page 222)

1 tablespoon snipped fresh chives

salt and pepper

TAGLIERINI WITH BUTTER AND WHITE WINE

Melt half the butter in a shallow pan. Add the lemon rind, stir, drizzle with the wine, and cook until the alcohol has evaporated. Stir in the chile and cream and simmer gently for 10 minutes. Remove the pan from the heat and keep warm. Cook the taglierini in plenty of salted boiling water for 2–3 minutes until al dente. Drain, tip into the pan with the sauce, set over medium-high heat and toss for a few minutes. Remove from the heat, transfer to a warmed serving dish, drizzle with the lemon juice, and stir. Add the remaining butter, Parmesan and parsley, and serve immediately.

Preparation time: 15 minutes

Cooking time: 15 minutes

Serves 4

3 tablespoons butter

grated rind and strained juice of ½ lemon

scant 1 cup dry white wine

1 dried red chile, crumbled

3 tablespoons heavy cream

14 ounces fresh taglierini (see Fall Taglierini, page 222)

½ cup grated Parmesan cheese

1 tablespoon chopped fresh flat-leaf parsley

salt

TAGLIERINI WITH HAZELNUTS

TAGLIERINI ALLE NOCCIOLE

Preparation time: 10 minutes
Cooking time: 15 minutes
Serves 4
2 tablespoons olive oil
1 onion, chopped
⅓ cup diced pancetta or bacon
scant ½ cup dry white wine
3 tablespoons butter
scant 1 cup chopped hazelnuts
9 ounces fresh taglierini
(see Fall Taglierini, page 222)
salt and pepper

Heat the oil in a pan. Add the onion and cook over low heat, stirring occasionally, for 5 minutes. Increase the heat to medium, add the pancetta or bacon, and cook, stirring frequently, for 2 minutes. Pour in the wine and cook until the alcohol has evaporated. Beat the butter in a bowl until creamy, then beat in the chopped hazelnuts. Stir the mixture into the pan, season with salt and pepper, remove from the heat, and keep warm. Cook the taglierini in plenty of salted boiling water for 2–3 minutes until al dente. Drain, tip into a warmed serving dish, and pour the sauce over. Serve immediately.

TAGLIERINI WITH MASCARPONE

TAGLIERINI AL MASCARPONE

Preparation time: 15 minutes
Cooking time: 20 minutes
Serves 4
2 tablespoons milk
⅓ cup mascarpone cheese
grated rind and strained juice of ½ lemon
10 ounces fresh taglierini
(see Fall Taglierini, page 222)
salt and freshly ground white pepper

Heat the milk in a small pan. Add the mascarpone and cook over very low heat, stirring constantly, until melted. Remove from the heat, stir in the lemon rind, and season with salt and white pepper. Stir well and keep warm. Pour the strained lemon juice onto a warmed serving dish. Cook the taglierini in plenty of salted boiling water for 2–3 minutes until al dente. Drain, tip onto the serving dish, and pour the mascarpone sauce over. Toss well and serve immediately.

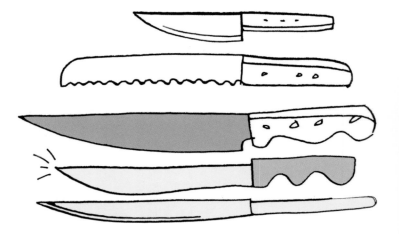

TAGLIERINI WITH LUMPFISH ROE

TAGLIERINI ALLE UOVA DI LOMPO

Combine the cream and tomato paste in a bowl. Heat the oil in a pan. Add the onion and cook over low heat, stirring occasionally, for 5 minutes. Drizzle with the wine and cook until the alcohol has evaporated. Stir in the cream mixture and lumpfish roe. Cook the taglierini in plenty of salted boiling water for 2–3 minutes until al dente. Drain, tip into the pan with the sauce, stir, and season lightly with pepper. Remove from the heat and sprinkle with the chives. Serve immediately.

Preparation time: 18 minutes

Cooking time: 12 minutes

Serves 4

3 tablespoons heavy cream

½ teaspoon tomato paste

3 tablespoons olive oil

1 small onion, chopped

scant ½ cup dry white sparkling wine

¼ cup red lumpfish roe

10 ounces fresh taglierini

(see Fall Taglierini, page 222)

1 tablespoon snipped fresh chives

salt and pepper

TAGLIERINI WITH MASCARPONE AND BELL PEPPERS

TAGLIERINI CON MASCARPONE E PEPERONI

Peel the bell peppers with a paring knife, halve, and seed, then cut the flesh into thin strips. Heat the oil in a pan with the chopped onion until it becomes translucent. Add the bell pepper strips and cook over low heat, stirring occasionally, for 15 minutes. Season with salt and pepper, add the mascarpone, and stir until melted. Cook the taglierini in plenty of salted boiling water until al dente. Drain, tip into the pan with the sauce, and toss gently for a few seconds. Transfer to a warmed serving dish and serve immediately.

Preparation time: 15 minutes

Cooking time: 30 minutes

Serves 4

2 red bell peppers

2 tablespoons olive oil

1 tablespoon chopped onion

⅓ cup mascarpone cheese

10 ounces fresh taglierini

(see Fall Taglierini, page 222)

salt and pepper

TAGLIERINI WITH SHALLOTS

Preparation time: 10 minutes
Cooking time: 20 minutes
Serves 4
4 tablespoons butter
2 shallots, thinly sliced
10 ounces fresh taglierini (see Fall
Taglierini, page 222)
½ cup grated Gruyère cheese
generous ⅓ cup grated Parmesan cheese
salt

Melt the butter in a skillet. Add the shallots and cook over very low heat, stirring occasionally, for 25–30 minutes until golden brown and caramelized. Cook the taglierini in plenty of salted boiling water for 2–3 minutes until al dente. Drain and immediately tip the pasta into the hot skillet. Toss well, transfer to a warmed serving dish, sprinkle with the Gruyère and Parmesan, and serve immediately.

TAGLIERINI WITH TRUFFLES

Preparation time: 14 minutes
Cooking time: 8 minutes
Serves 4
4 tablespoons butter
1 tablespoon heavy cream
1-ounce tube truffle paste
10 ounces fresh taglierini (see Fall
Taglierini, page 222)
½ cup grated Parmesan cheese, to serve
salt and freshly ground white pepper

Melt the butter in a heatproof bowl set over a pan of simmering water. Add the cream and mix well. Add about 4 inches of the truffle paste and mix well again. Taste and, if necessary, add more truffle paste. Cook the taglierini in plenty of salted boiling water for 2–3 minutes until al dente. Drain, transfer to a warmed serving dish, and toss with the truffle butter. Season with white pepper, sprinkle with Parmesan, and serve immediately.

TAGLIERINI WITH RICOTTA

TAGLIERINI ALLA RICOTTA

Preparation time: 30 minutes
Cooking time: 25 minutes
Serves 4
2 small eggplants, diced
6 tablespoons olive oil
scant 1 cup ricotta cheese
10 ounces fresh taglierini (see Fall
Taglierini, page 222)
1 sprig fresh flat-leaf parsley, chopped
salt and pepper

Spread out the eggplants on a plate, sprinkle with salt, and let drain for 30 minutes. Rinse under cold running water and pat dry with paper towels. Heat 5 tablespoons of the oil in a large skillet. Add the eggplants and cook over low heat, stirring frequently, for 8–10 minutes until golden brown. Remove with a slotted spoon and drain on paper towels. Keep warm. Combine the ricotta and remaining oil in a bowl and season with salt and pepper. Cook the taglierini in plenty of salted boiling water for 2–3 minutes until al dente. Drain, return to the pan, and add the ricotta mixture and eggplants. Sprinkle with the parsley, stir, and serve immediately.

TAGLIERINI WITH ROSEMARY

TAGLIERINI AL ROSMARINO

Preparation time: 10 minutes
Cooking time: 25 minutes
Serves 4
3 tablespoons butter
1 tablespoon olive oil
1 garlic clove, finely chopped
1 onion, finely chopped
1 sprig finely chopped fresh rosemary
⅓ cup finely chopped pine nuts
scant 1 cup dry white wine
10 ounces fresh taglierini (see Fall
Taglierini, page 222)
½ cup grated pecorino cheese
1 dried red chile, crumbled
salt and pepper

Melt half the butter with the oil in a shallow pan. Add the garlic and onion and cook over low heat, stirring occasionally, for 5 minutes. Add the rosemary and pine nuts and cook, stirring constantly, for a few minutes. Drizzle with the wine and cook until the alcohol has evaporated, then stir, season with salt and pepper, lower the heat, and simmer for 10 minutes. Cook the taglierini in plenty of salted boiling water for 2–3 minutes until al dente. Drain, tip into a warmed serving dish, and pour the sauce over. Sprinkle with pecorino and chile, and serve immediately.

TAGLIERINI WITH TUNA

TAGLIERINI AL TONNO

Preparation time: 15 minutes

Cooking time: 28 minutes

Serves 4

Heat the oil in a shallow pan. Add the onion and garlic clove and cook over low heat, stirring occasionally, for 5 minutes. Remove the garlic with a slotted spoon when it becomes golden brown and discard. Add the tuna and anchovy, stir, and cook for 3 minutes, then stir in the chopped tomatoes, and season with salt and pepper. Cover and simmer, stirring occasionally, for 15 minutes. Cook the taglierini in plenty of salted boiling water for 2–3 minutes until al dente. Drain, tip into a warmed serving dish, pour the tuna sauce over, and serve.

2 tablespoons olive oil

1 small onion, chopped

1 garlic clove

3 ounces canned tuna in oil, drained and flaked

1 canned anchovy fillet, drained and chopped

7 ounces canned chopped tomatoes

10 ounces fresh taglierini (see Fall

Taglierini, page 222)

salt and pepper

TAGLIERINI AND PEA TIMBALE

TIMBALLO DI TAGLIERINI AI PISELLI

Preparation time: 50 minutes

Cooking time: 1 hour

Serves 6

Melt half the butter with the oil in a shallow pan. Add the onion and cook over low heat, stirring occasionally, for 5 minutes. Add the peas and lukewarm water, cover, and simmer for 30 minutes. Preheat the oven to 350°F. Grease an ovenproof dish with butter and sprinkle with bread crumbs. Line the dish with the slices of ham. Cook the taglierini in plenty of salted boiling water for 2–3 minutes until al dente. Drain, tip into the pan with the peas, and stir, then remove the pan from the heat. Beat the eggs with the grated cheese and a pinch of pepper in a bowl, then stir into the pasta mixture. Spoon the mixture over the ham, dot with the remaining butter, and bake for about 20 minutes. Remove from the oven and let stand for 5 minutes, then serve.

4 tablespoons butter, plus extra for greasing

2 tablespoons olive oil

½ onion, chopped

1¾ cups shelled peas

scant ½ cup lukewarm water

5–6 tablespoons fresh bread crumbs

3½ ounces ham, sliced

15 ounces fresh taglierini (see Fall

Taglierini, page 222)

2 eggs

½ cup grated Parmesan cheesed

salt and pepper

TAGLIERINI PIE

**Preparation time: 1 hour 10 minutes,
plus 30 minutes resting
Cooking time: 45 minutes
Serves 6**

2 egg yolks

2 tablespoons superfine sugar

scant ½ cup butter, melted and cooled, plus
extra for greasing

1¾ cups all-purpose flour, plus extra for dusting

1 quantity béchamel sauce (see
Baked Rigatoni, page 144)

salt

For the filling

14 ounces fresh taglierini
(see Fall Taglierini, page 222)

2 tablespoons butter

1 quantity hot meat sauce
(see Tagliatelle Bolognese, page 202)

½ cup grated Parmesan cheese

salt

Make the dough. Beat the egg yolks with the sugar, a pinch of salt, and the cooled melted butter in a bowl. Gradually add the flour and knead until smooth. Shape the dough into a ball and let rest for 30 minutes.

Preheat the oven to 400°F and grease a springform cake pan with butter. Cut the dough into 2 pieces, one larger than the other. Roll out on a lightly floured counter into 2 thin sheets. Use the large sheet to line the base and sides of the prepared cake pan, overlapping the sides. Cook the taglierini in plenty of salted boiling water for 2–3 minutes until al dente. Drain, return to the pan, and toss with the butter, then make a layer in the prepared pan. Spread a layer of the hot meat sauce on top using a teaspoon, cover with a layer of béchamel sauce, and sprinkle with grated cheese. Continue making layers in this way until all the ingredients have been used. Cover with the smaller sheet of dough, pressing down firmly on the edges. Trim off any excess. Bake for about 30 minutes until golden. Remove from the oven and let stand for 5 minutes, then serve.

TAGLIOLINI WITH BUTTER AND TRUFFLE

**Preparation time: 14 minutes
Cooking time: 8 minutes
Serves 4**

6 tablespoons butter

pinch of freshly grated nutmeg

1 quantity Fresh Pasta Dough (see page 163)

1 cup grated Parmesan cheese

1 small white truffle

salt and pepper

Roll out the pasta dough on a lightly floured counter into a sheet. Cut into strips about ⅛ inch wide and let dry on floured dish towels. Melt the butter in a small pan and season with the nutmeg and a pinch each of salt and pepper. Cook the tagliolini in a large pan of salted boiling water for 2–3 minutes until al dente, then drain, and tip into a warmed serving dish. Pour the melted butter over the pasta, sprinkle with the Parmesan and then shave the truffle over the top.

BAKED TAGLIOLINI WITH CREAM AND HAM

Preparation time: 20 minutes

Cooking time: 20 minutes

Serves 4

3 tablespoons butter, plus extra for greasing

2 egg yolks

3 tablespoons heavy cream

3½ ounces ham in a single slice, cut into strips

12 ounces fresh tagliolini (see Fall Taglierini, page 222)

½ cup grated Parmesan cheese

salt and pepper

Preheat the oven to 350°F and grease an ovenproof dish with butter. Beat the egg yolks with the cream in a bowl, season with salt and pepper, and stir in the ham. Cook the tagliolini in plenty of salted boiling water for 2–3 minutes until al dente. Drain, return to the pan, and add the butter and grated cheese. Transfer to the prepared dish, pour the ham and cream mixture over it, and stir. Bake for 10 minutes, then remove from the oven, and let stand for 5 minutes before serving.

It is said that Catherine de' Medici was the first ambassador for pasta in France. As wife of Henry II of France she brought cooks from Florence who introduced pasta to the French court. Later the powerful Cardinal Mazarin followed in her footsteps when he recommended pasta to the clergymen of France as a wholesome, vegetarian food.

TAGLIOLINI WITH SEA SCALLOPS AND LETTUCE

Preparation time: 18 minutes

Cooking time: 20 minutes

Serves 4

3 tablespoons olive oil

2 garlic cloves

7 ounces shelled sea scallops with coral

scant ½ cup white wine

2½ cups shredded lettuce

2 tablespoons butter

pinch of chile powder

1 tablespoon chopped fresh flat-leaf parsley

10 ounces fresh tagliolini (see Fall Taglierini, page 222)

salt

Heat the oil in a pan, add the garlic, and cook for 30 seconds. Remove and discard the garlic and add the sea scallops to the pan. Sprinkle in the wine, cook until it has evaporated, then season with salt. Add the lettuce and butter and stir well. Stir in the chile powder and parsley. Cook the tagliolini in a large pan of salted boiling water for 2–3 minutes until al dente, then drain, and add to the sauce. Toss gently and transfer to a warmed serving dish.

GRANA

TAGLIOLINI WITH LANGOUSTINES

TAGLIOLINI AGLI SCAMPI

Peel the langoustines or lobsterettes, reserving the shells. Put the shells in a pan with the onion, carrot, and celery, add water to cover and a pinch of salt. Bring to a boil, lower the heat, and simmer for 15 minutes, then strain into a bowl. Reserve some of the stock. Heat the oil in a skillet, add the langoustines or lobsterettes and cook for 3 minutes, then sprinkle with the parsley. Stir the tomato paste with a little of the shellfish stock in a bowl and add to the pan. Cook the tagliolini in a large pan of salted boiling water for 2–3 minutes until al dente, then drain, toss with the sauce, and transfer to a warmed serving dish.

Preparation time: 35 minutes

Cooking time: 25 minutes

Serves 4

14 ounces langoustines or lobsterettes

1 onion • 1 carrot

1 celery stalk

3 tablespoons olive oil

1 tablespoon chopped fresh flat-leaf parsley

1 teaspoon concentrated tomato paste

10 ounces fresh tagliolini

(see Fall Taglierini, page 222)

salt

TAGLIOLINI WITH MASCARPONE AND LEMON

TAGLIOLINI AL MASCARPONE E LIMONE

Heat the milk in a small pan. Add the mascarpone and stir over very low heat until melted. Remove the pan from the heat, add the lemon rind and peppercorns, and season to taste with salt and a little white pepper. Stir well, set aside, and keep warm. Pour the lemon juice into a warmed serving dish. Cook the tagliolini in plenty of salted boiling water for 2–3 minutes until al dente. Drain and tip into the prepared serving dish. Add the mascarpone sauce and toss to coat. Serve immediately.

Preparation time: 10 minutes

Cooking time: 10 minutes

Serves 4

2 tablespoons milk

⅓ cup mascarpone cheese

grated rind and strained juice of ½ lemon

1 tablespoon green peppercorns

12 ounces fresh tagliolini (see Fall Taglierini, page 222)

salt and freshly ground white pepper

237

TRENETTE

Ribbons of fresh, narrow, and flat pasta, trenette is very similar to linguine, but slightly thinner, with a width of ½ inch. It originates from Liguria in the northwest of Italy, and is commonly served with pesto, as in the most traditional recipe Trenette con il Pesto (Trenette with Pesto, see below). Trenette also goes well with other delicate fish and shellfish sauces.

TRENETTE WITH PESTO

TRENETTE CON IL PESTO

Preparation time: 1 hour 10 minutes, plus 1 hour resting
Cooking time: 25 minutes
Serves 4

1 quantity Fresh Pasta Dough (see page 163)
2 potatoes
scant 1 cup green beans, trimmed

For the pesto
10 fresh basil leaves
½ cup pine nuts
½ cup grated Parmesan cheese
½ cup grated pecorino cheese
½ cup olive oil
salt

Roll out the pasta dough on a lightly floured counter into a sheet. Cut into strips about ½ inch wide and let dry on floured dish towels. Peel and cut the potatoes into thin batons and put them into a bowl of cold water. To make the pesto, put the basil, pine nuts, both cheeses, a pinch of salt, and the oil in a food processor and process at medium speed until blended. Alternatively, pound the ingredients in a mortar with a pestle until a smooth paste is obtained. Cook the potatoes and green beans in plenty of salted boiling water for 10–15 minutes until tender. Remove them from the pan and in the same water, cook the pasta for 2–3 minutes until al dente. Drain, leaving it quite moist, and tip into a warmed serving dish. Add the green beans and potatoes, spoon the sauce over the top, and serve immediately.

TRENETTE WITH ANCHOVIES

TRENETTE CON LE ALICI

Preparation time: 25 minutes
Cooking time: 20 minutes
Serves 4
3 tablespoons olive oil
1 garlic clove
1 fresh red chile, seeded and chopped
2 ounces canned anchovy fillets,
drained and chopped
1 sprig chopped fresh flat-leaf parsley
14 oz canned tomatoes, drained and chopped
12 ounces fresh trenette
(see Trenette with Pesto, page 238)
salt

Heat the oil in a shallow pan. Add the garlic clove and chile and cook over low heat, stirring frequently, for a few minutes until the garlic is lightly browned. Remove the garlic with a slotted spoon and discard. Add the anchovy fillets and parsley to the pan and cook, stirring constantly, for 4 minutes. Add the tomatoes, season with salt, cover, and simmer gently, stirring occasionally, for about 10 minutes until thickened. Cook the trenette in plenty of salted boiling water until al dente. Drain, tip into a warmed serving dish, pour the hot sauce over, and serve.

TRENETTE WITH LANGOUSTINES

TRENETTE AGLI SCAMPI

Preparation time: 10 minutes
Cooking time: 10 minutes
Serves 4
3 tablespoons olive oil
1 garlic clove
1 chile
12 ounces langoustines or lobsterettes,
thawed if frozen, peeled
12 ounces fresh trenette (see Trenette
with Pesto, page 238)
chopped fresh flat-leaf parsley, to garnish
salt

Heat the oil in a skillet. Add the garlic clove and chile and cook, stirring frequently, for a few minutes until lightly browned. Remove the garlic and chile with a slotted spoon and discard. Add the langoustines or lobsterettes to the skillet, season with salt, and cook for 3–5 minutes. Meanwhile, cook the trenette in plenty of salted boiling water for 2–3 minutes until al dente. Drain, tip into the skillet, and toss to mix. Serve immediately, garnished with chopped parsley.

TROFIE

These tiny dumplings are a specialty of the coastal area in Liguria (northwest Italy) from Camogli to Bogliasco and, along with trenette, trofie is the most typical pasta from Liguria. The name derives from the dialect word "strufuggià," meaning "to rub," referring to the way in which it is made—by rolling pieces of pasta into thin twists. Trofie is typically served with pesto sauce (see overleaf). The classic version is to boil potatoes and green beans in the same pan and add the trofie at the end of cooking. In some areas, trofie is often mixed with boiled fresh white beans. A small amount of chestnut flour can sometimes be added to the white flour: This sweetens the trofie and complements the pesto.

TROFIE WITH ARUGULA

TROFIE ALLA RUCOLA

Preparation time: 20 minutes
Cooking time: 10 minutes
Serves 4

1 green bell pepper
¾ cup arugula
¼ cups pine nuts
1 garlic clove
3 tablespoons olive oil
½ cup grated sharp pecorino cheese
11 ounces fresh trofie
(see Trofie with Pesto, page 242)
salt and pepper

Preheat the oven to 400°F. Put the bell pepper onto a cookie sheet and roast, turning occasionally, for 30 minutes until charred. Remove from the oven and when cool enough to handle, peel, seed, and coarsely chop the flesh. Put the bell pepper, arugula, pine nuts, garlic, oil, and a pinch of salt into a food processor and process until smooth. Pour the mixture into a large bowl and mix with the grated pecorino. Cook the trofie in plenty of salted boiling water until al dente. Drain, tip into the bowl with the sauce, season with pepper, and serve.

TROFIE WITH PESTO

**Preparation time: 30 minutes,
plus 1 hour resting
Cooking time: 4–5 minutes
Serves 4**

3 cups all-purpose flour, plus extra for dusting

salt

pesto, to serve (see Trenette
with Pesto, page 238)

Sift the flour into a mound on a counter and make a well in the center. Add a pinch of salt and enough water to make a fairly firm dough. Knead well, then break off very small pieces of dough, and roll them on the worktop to make 1¼–1½-inch long rolls that are thicker at the center and thinner at the ends. Let dry on floured dish towels for up to 1 hour. Cook the trofie in plenty of salted boiling water for 2–3 minutes until al dente. Drain, toss with pesto, and serve immediately.

TROFIE WITH POTATOES AND TURNIP GREENS

*TROFIE CON PATATE E
BROCCOLETTI*

**Preparation time: 50 minutes
Cooking time: 50 minutes
Serves 4**

9 ounces turnip greens

2 potatoes

2 tablespoons olive oil

1 onion, chopped

1 garlic clove

12 ounces fresh trofie (see Trofie
with Pesto, above)

3 ounces diced crescenza cheese

½ cup grated pecorino cheese

salt and pepper

Blanch the turnip greens in salted boiling water for 5 minutes, then drain, squeeze out the excess liquid, and chop. Cook the potatoes in boiling salted water for 20–30 minutes until tender but not falling apart. Drain, peel, and dice. Heat the oil in a shallow pan. Add the onion and garlic clove and cook over low heat, stirring occasionally, for 5 minutes and removing the garlic clove when it becomes golden brown. Stir the potatoes into the pan, then add the turnip greens. Season with salt and pepper and cook, stirring occasionally, for 10–15 minutes. Cook the trofie in plenty of salted boiling water for 2–3 minutes until al dente. Drain, tip into a warmed serving dish, sprinkle with the crescenza, and stir. Add the turnip greens and potatoes, sprinkle with grated pecorino, season with pepper, and serve.

The Italian word "broccoletti" refers both to broccoli and turnip greens ("cime di rapa"). They are very similar, but broccoli requires a longer cooking time (8 minutes).

FILLED PASTA

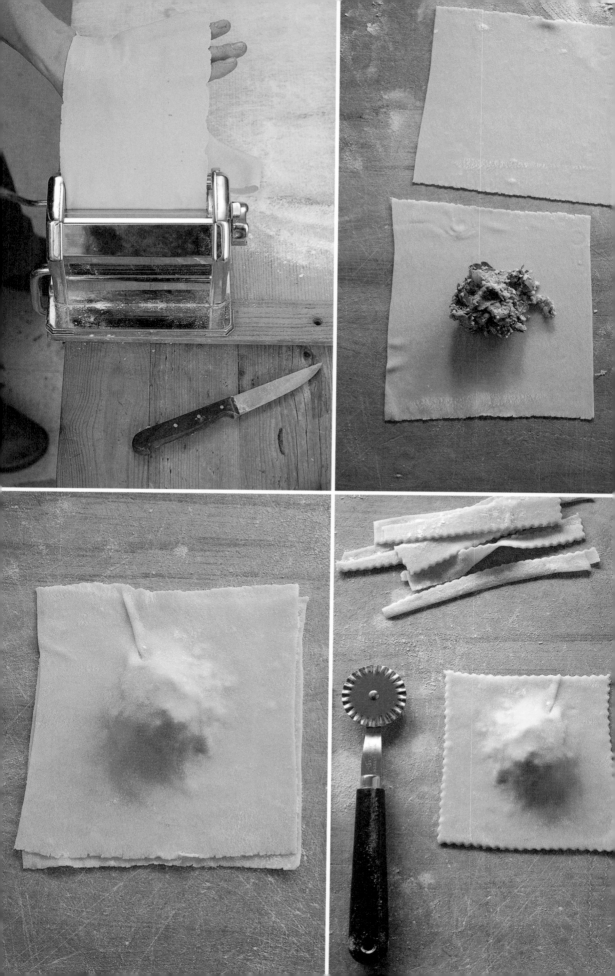

AGNOLOTTI

Agnolotti, a specialty of the Piedmont region in northwest Italy, is a square or round type of filled pasta. The alleged story behind its name is that the Marquis of Monferrato asked his chef, Angelot, to prepare a feast to celebrate a long-awaited victory. Using the few ingredients that were available to him, Angelot created the diminutive pieces for his piat d'Angelot (Angelot's dish), which eventually became agnolotti. The filling generally consists of cooked meat, and agnolotti is typically served with a simple dressing of either the meat juices saved from the filing or melted butter. For Agnolotti alla Piemontese (Agnolotti Piedmontese, see below), the most traditional recipe, the filling calls for a mixture of veal and pork, or braised beef.

AGNOLOTTI PIEDMONTESE

AGNOLOTTI ALLA PIEMONTESE

Make the pasta dough with the quantities specified (see Fresh Pasta Dough, page 163) and let rest for 1 hour. Blanch the spinach in boiling water, drain, chop, and combine with the beef in a bowl. Stir in the egg yolks, whole egg, Parmesan, and ham and season with salt and pepper. If the mixture is a little dry, soften with a few tablespoons of gravy from the braised beef. Roll out the pasta dough into strips on a lightly floured counter. Put mounds of filling at regular intervals along one strip, place another strip on top, and press down well around the filling. Cut square agnolotti with a pasta or pastry wheel. Cook in salted boiling water for about 10 minutes. Drain and dress with gravy from the braised beef or melted butter and Parmesan.

Preparation time: 1 hour 15 minutes,
plus 1 hour resting
Cooking time: 25 minutes
Serves 6

2⅔ cups all-purpose flour, preferably Italian type 00, plus extra for dusting

3 eggs, lightly beaten • salt

For the filling

9 ounces spinach

14 ounces braised beef, ground

2 egg yolks, lightly beaten

1 egg, lightly beaten

⅔ cup grated Parmesan cheese,
plus more to serve

scant 1 cup chopped cooked ham

salt and pepper

PUMPKIN AGNOLOTTI

AGNOLOTTI DI ZUCCA

**Preparation time: 45 minutes,
plus 1 hour resting**
**Cooking time: 45 minutes,
Serves 4**

3½ cups all-purpose flour,
preferably Italian type 00

4 eggs

salt

For the filling

olive oil, for brushing

1 pound 2 ounces pumpkin, seeded,
and cut into chunks

½ onion, chopped

⅓ cup chopped walnuts

1 tablespoon chopped fresh sage

salt and pepper

For the sauce

generous ⅓ cup golden raisins

2 tablespoons butter

1 shallot, chopped

4 tablespoons medium sherry

salt and pepper

Preheat the oven to 400°F and brush an ovenproof dish with oil. Meanwhile, make the pasta dough with the quantities specified (see Fresh Pasta Dough, page 163) and let rest for 1 hour. Cover with a damp dish towel and let rest for 30 minutes. Put the pieces of pumpkin in the prepared dish and bake in the oven for 30 minutes until softened. Remove the pumpkin from the oven and when it is cool enough to handle, scoop the pulp from the skin and mash well. Discard the skin. Add the onion, walnuts, and sage and season with salt and pepper.

Roll out the pasta dough on a lightly floured counter or with a pasta machine into thin strips. Put small mounds—about 1 teaspoon—of the filling at regular intervals along one strip, place another strip on top and press down well around the filling. Cut square agnolotti with a pasta or pastry wheel. To make the sauce, put the golden raisins into a heatproof bowl, pour in warm water to cover, and let soak and plump up. Melt the butter in a skillet. Add the shallot and cook over low heat, stirring occasionally, for 5 minutes. Add the sherry and cook for a few minutes until the alcohol has evaporated. Drain the golden raisins and add to the pan, then season with salt and pepper. Cook the agnolotti in plenty of salted boiling water until it floats to the counter and is al dente. Drain, toss with the sauce, and serve immediately.

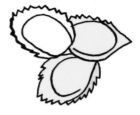

ANOLINI

Anolini is a type of fresh, filled pasta of ancient origin, from the city of Parma in the northern Italian region of Emilia-Romagna. It is made by placing small portions of the filling on a sheet of pasta, about 1¾ inches apart. A second sheet is placed over this, and the pieces are cut out using a stamp about 1¼ inches in diameter. Anolini is also common in Piacenza, in the same region, where the pieces are smaller and the meat for the filling is stewed in wine. Anolini can also be served in brodo, or beef stock.

ANOLINI WITH PARMESAN

ANOLINI AL PARMIGIANO

Make the pasta dough. Sift the flour into a mound on a counter and make a well in the center. Break the eggs into the well and add a pinch of salt. Knead thoroughly, shape into a ball, cover with a clean dish towel, and let rest in a cool place for 1 hour. Meanwhile, make the filling. Put the bread crumbs into a heatproof bowl, add a pinch each of salt and pepper, pour in 2 tablespoons of the boiling stock, and stir well. Add the eggs and then stir in the Parmesan. The mixture must be fairly firm but if it is too dry, add the remaining tablespoon of stock. Roll out the dough on a lightly floured counter into a thin sheet. Cut out 1¼-inch rounds with a pasta wheel or stamp out with a cookie cutter. Put a small mound of filling in the center of each, fold the dough over, and shape into a half moon. Alternatively, put a mound of filling in the center of half the rounds and cover with the remaining rounds, pressing the edges to seal. Bring the beef stock to a boil in a large pan. Add the anolini, bring back to a boil, and cook until al dente. Serve immediately in the hot stock.

Preparation time: 1 hour 30 minutes,
plus 1 hour resting
Cooking time: 25 minutes
Serves 6
generous 2¾ cups all-purpose flour,
plus extra for dusting
3 eggs
4 cups beef stock
salt
For the filling
1¾ cups fresh bread crumbs
2–3 tablespoons boiling vegetable stock
2 eggs
3 cups grated Parmesan cheese
salt and pepper

CANNELLONI

Cannelloni, meaning "large tubes," is a type of fresh pasta related to lasagna. These 4-inch squares of pasta dough are covered with a thin layer of filling and then rolled up to enclose it. For this reason, cannelloni is sometimes confused with manicotti, meaning "sleeves," which is a pre-fabricated tube. The composer Gioachino Rossini from Pesaro, in the central Italian region of Marche, allegedly invented the shape in the nineteenth century, and cannelloni is therefore common in both the Marche and in Abruzzo, further south. Cannelloni lends itself to a wide variety of fillings, including meat, vegetables and cheese, and is frequently served with thick sauces.

CANNELLONI (basic recipe)

CANNELLONI (ricetta base)

Preparation time: 35 minutes, plus 1 hour resting
Cooking time: 5 minutes
Makes about 12 cannelloni
3½ cups all-purpose flour, preferably Italian type 00
4 eggs
salt

Sift the flour into a mound on a counter and make a well in the center. Break the eggs into the well and add a pinch of salt. Knead thoroughly, then roll out on a lightly floured counter into a thin sheet. Cut into 4-inch squares. Cook the pasta squares, a few at a time in plenty of salted boiling water for a few minutes. Remove with a slotted spoon, refresh under cold running water, and spread out on clean dish towels to dry. They are then ready for your chosen filling.

CANNELLONI WITH RADICCHIO CREAM

CANNELLONI ALLA CREMA DI RADICCHIO

Blanch the radicchio leaves in lightly salted water for 2 minutes, then drain, squeeze out the excess liquid, and chop. Melt the butter with the oil in a shallow pan. Add the shallot and cook over low heat, stirring occasionally, for 5 minutes. Stir in the chicken, season with salt and pepper, drizzle with the hot water, cover, and simmer, stirring occasionally, for 20 minutes. Add the chopped radicchio and cook for another 5 minutes. Preheat the oven to 400°F and grease an ovenproof dish with butter. Spread 1 tablespoon of the béchamel sauce on each cannelloni square, put a slice of fontina on top, add a little of the radicchio mixture, and roll them up. Put the rolls into the prepared dish, pour the remaining béchamel sauce over, and sprinkle with the Parmesan. Bake for about 20 minutes until golden brown. Remove from the oven and let stand for 5 minutes, then serve.

Preparation time: 40 minutes

Cooking time: 1 hour

Serves 4

1 quantity Cannelloni (see opposite)

For the filling

14 ounces radicchio, trimmed and coarse leaves removed

3 tablespoons butter, plus extra for greasing

2 tablespoons olive oil

1 shallot, finely chopped

5 ounces ground chicken breast

2 tablespoons hot water

½ quantity béchamel sauce (see Baked Rigatoni, page 144)

5 ounces thinly sliced fontina cheese

2 tablespoons grated Parmesan cheese

salt and pepper

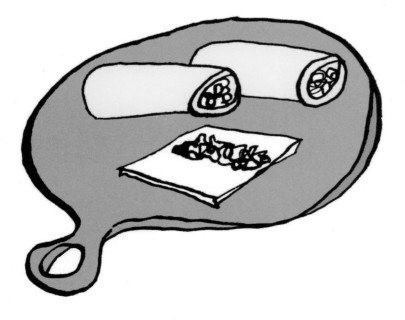

ARTICHOKE CANNELLONI

Preheat the oven to 400°F and grease an ovenproof dish with butter. Half-fill a large bowl with water and stir in the lemon juice. Break off the artichoke stalks and remove and discard the coarse outer leaves. Thinly slice, discarding the chokes, then add to the acidulated water to avoid discoloration.

Melt the butter in a pan. Add the onion, garlic, and parsley and cook over low heat, stirring occasionally, for 5 minutes. Drain the artichokes, add to the pan, and cook over medium-low heat, stirring occasionally. Sprinkle in the flour and nutmeg and stir well to mix. Gradually pour in the stock, stirring until smooth and thoroughly combined, and bring to a boil, stirring constantly. Remove the pan from the heat, let cool slightly, then transfer the mixture to a food processor, and process until smooth. Alternatively, push the mixture through a meat grinder. Transfer the mixture to a bowl, if necessary. Stir in the egg, and a little Parmesan, and béchamel sauce.

Spread a little artichoke mixture on each cannelloni square and roll up. Put them into the prepared dish in a single layer, pour the remaining béchamel sauce over and sprinkle with the remaining Parmesan. Bake for 20–25 minutes, remove from the oven and let stand for 5 minutes, then serve.

Preparation time: 30 minutes

Cooking time: 55 minutes

Serves 4

1 quantity Cannelloni (see page 250)

For the filling

4 tablespoons butter, plus extra for greasing

juice of ½ lemon, strained

6 globe artichokes

1 small onion, finely chopped

1 garlic clove, finely chopped

1 tablespoon finely chopped fresh flat-leaf parsley

2 tablespoons all-purpose flour

pinch of freshly grated nutmeg

scant 1 cup beef stock

1 egg, lightly beaten

1 cup grated Parmesan cheese

1 quantity béchamel sauce

(see Baked Rigatoni, page 144)

salt and pepper

CANNELLONI FROM PIACENZA

Preparation time: 50 minutes

Cooking time: 1 hour

Serves 4

3 tablespoons butter

1¾ cups all-purpose flour

2 eggs

2 egg yolks

2¼ cups milk

salt

For the filling

1¾ pounds spinach, coarse stalks removed

2⅔ cups ricotta cheese

1 small garlic clove, coarsely chopped

scant ½ cup mascarpone cheese

1 egg

1 egg yolk

pinch of freshly grated nutmeg

salt

For the sauce

⅓ cup grated Parmesan cheese

5 tablespoons butter, melted

Melt 1 tablespoon of the butter in a heatproof bowl set over a pan of simmering water, then remove from the heat. Sift the flour with a pinch of salt into a bowl and make a well in the center. Break the eggs into the well, add the egg yolks and melted butter, and mix well. Gradually stir in the milk, a little at a time, and continue stirring for 10 minutes to make a fairly thick batter. Melt the remaining butter in a small skillet. Pour in a ladleful of the batter and cook until the underside is set. Flip over and cook the second side, then remove from the skillet. Continue making fritters in this way until all the batter has been used.

Preheat the oven to 350°F. To make the filling, put the spinach into a pan with just the water clinging to its leaves after rinsing and cook over low heat, turning occasionally, for 5–10 minutes until tender. Drain and squeeze out the excess liquid. Put the spinach into a food processor or blender, add the ricotta, and garlic and process until thoroughly combined. Transfer to a bowl and stir in the mascarpone, egg, egg yolk, and nutmeg, and season with salt. Divide the filling among the fritters, roll them up, and put them into an ovenproof dish. Sprinkle with Parmesan and drizzle with the melted butter. Bake for about 30 minutes until golden brown. Serve immediately.

CANNELLONI WITH BÉCHAMEL SAUCE

CANNELLONI ALLA BESCIAMELLA

Preheat the oven to 400°F. Grease an ovenproof dish with butter. Cook the spinach in just the water clinging to the leaves after washing, for 5 minutes. Drain well and pass through a food processor, then combine with the veal, ham, Parmesan, and egg, and season to taste. Put some of the spinach mixture and a little béchamel sauce on each cannelloni square and roll up from one long side. Arrange the cannelloni in a single layer in the prepared dish, pour the remaining béchamel sauce over, and dot with the butter. Bake for 20 minutes, then let rest for 5 minutes before serving.

Preparation time: 1 hour

Cooking time: 35 minutes

Serves 4

1 quantity Cannelloni (see page 250)

For the filling

2 tablespoons butter, plus extra for greasing

11 ounces spinach

7 ounces roast veal, chopped

1 slice cooked ham, chopped

2 tablespoons grated Parmesan cheese

1 egg, lightly beaten

1 quantity béchamel sauce (see Baked Pumpkin Pasta, page 272)

salt and pepper

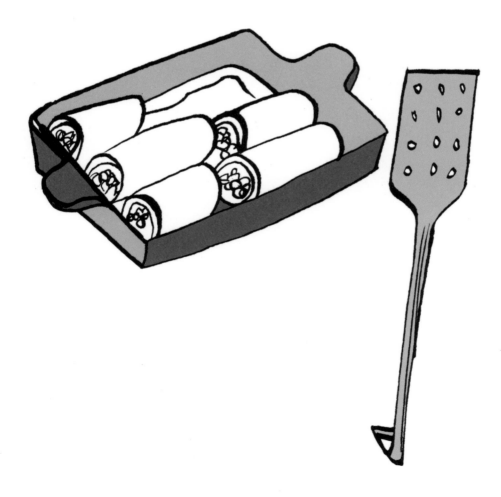

CANNELLONI NAPOLETANA

CANNELLONI ALLA NAPOLETANA

To make the filling, finely chop the meat with the salami. Heat the oil in a flameproof shallow earthenware dish. Add the meat mixture and pieces of sausage, season lightly with salt and pepper, and cook over low heat, stirring occasionally, for 30 minutes until thickened. Remove the dish from the heat and let cool. Preheat the oven to 350°F and grease an ovenproof dish with butter. Stir the hard-cooked eggs into the cooled meat mixture. Reserve a quarter of this mixture and divide the rest among the cannelloni squares, then roll them up. Put the cannelloni into the prepared dish, spoon the reserved filling over them, sprinkle with the pecorino, and drizzle with a little olive oil. Bake for about 20 minutes until golden brown. Remove from the oven and let stand for 5 minutes, then serve.

The aroma of freshly cooked "ragù" (or meat sauce) is a permanent feature in Naples and the whole region of Campania in southern Italy. Neapolitans dedicate a great deal of time and patience to its preparation, using an earthenware pan to perfectly blend the flavors of the various ingredients. Ragù can accompany a variety of pasta types and it also makes a rich and tasty timbale with macaroni, lasagna or cannelloni.

Preparation time: 40 minutes

Cooking time: 1 hour 5 minutes

Serves 4

1 quantity Cannelloni (see page 250)

butter, for greasing

⅓ cup grated pecorino cheese

olive oil, for drizzling

salt

For the filling

12 ounces lean beef or pork or a mixture

3 ounces Neapolitan salami

2 tablespoons olive oil

3½ ounces Italian sausage, skinned and cut into pieces

2 hard-cooked eggs, chopped

salt and pepper

CANNELLONI WITH STRACCHINO AND VEGETABLES

Preparation time: 1 hour

Cooking time: 1 hour 25 minutes

Serves 6

butter, for greasing

1½ quantity Cannelloni (see page 250)

½ cup grated Parmesan cheese

salt

For the filling

3 young globe artichokes, trimmed

2 carrots, sliced

scant 1 cup green beans, trimmed

2 zucchini, sliced

4 tablespoons butter

1 leek, chopped

1 firm tomato, cut into strips

7 ounces stracchino cheese

1 cup grated Parmesan cheese

salt and pepper

For the béchamel sauce

scant 1 cup shelled peas

4 tablespoons butter

¼ cup all-purpose flour

2½ cups lukewarm milk

salt and pepper

To make the filling, blanch the artichokes, carrots, beans, and zucchini in boiling water for a few minutes, then drain. Melt the butter in a pan. Add the leek and cook over low heat, stirring occasionally, for 5 minutes. Season with salt and pepper, add the blanched vegetables, and cook over low heat, stirring occasionally, for 30 minutes. Stir in the tomato, remove the pan from the heat, and let cool. Meanwhile, briefly blanch the peas in boiling water, then drain and stir in half the butter.

Make the béchamel sauce. Melt the remaining butter in a pan. Stir in the flour and cook over medium heat, stirring constantly, for 2–3 minutes until golden brown. Gradually stir in the milk, a little at a time. Bring to a boil, stirring constantly, lower the heat, and simmer gently, stirring constantly, for 20 minutes until thickened and smooth. Remove the pan from the heat, season with salt, and stir in the peas. Stir the stracchino and Parmesan into the cooled vegetable filling.

Preheat the oven to 350°F and grease an ovenproof dish with butter. Divide the filling among the cannelloni squares and roll up. Spoon a little of the béchamel sauce over the base of the prepared dish, put the cannelloni on top, and cover with the remaining béchamel sauce. Sprinkle with the grated cheese and bake for about 20 minutes until golden brown. Remove from the oven and let stand for 5 minutes, then serve.

CAPPELLACCI

Cappellacci is a type of fresh egg pasta from the Ferrara area in the northern Italian region of Emilia-Romagna, known locally as "caplaz." The name refers to a type of informal cap. Cappellacci is bigger than cappelletti and looks like round ravioli. It is made by placing a small amount of filling in the center of a square of pasta dough; the pasta dough is then folded in half, and the two opposing corners are joined and twisted closed. The most traditional filling for cappellacci consists of a mixture of pumpkin and Parmesan cheese, served with melted butter and Parmesan. Cappellacci is also often combined with tomato, meat or sausage sauces.

PUMPKIN CAPPELLACCI

CAPPELLACCI DI ZUCCA

Make the pasta dough. Sift the flour into a mound on a counter and make a well in the center. Break the eggs into the well and add a pinch of salt. Knead thoroughly, shape into a ball, cover with a clean dish towel, and let rest for 1 hour. Meanwhile, make the filling. Preheat the oven to 350°F. Put the pumpkin or squash on a cookie sheet and bake for 20 minutes until softened. Remove from the oven, halve, and scoop out and discard the seeds. Scoop out the flesh and pass it through a strainer into a bowl. Beat in the egg, Parmesan, and nutmeg and season with salt and pepper. Stir well and add bread crumbs if the mixture is too runny. Roll out the dough on a lightly floured counter into a thin sheet and cut out 2½-inch squares. Put a mound of filling in the center of each and fold the dough in half diagonally to make a triangle, pressing the edges firmly together. Bring the tips of the longest side together, one on top of the other, pressing firmly to seal but without flattening the cappellacci. Cook in plenty of salted boiling water until they rise to the counter and are all dente. Drain, transfer to a warmed serving dish, pour the melted butter over, and sprinkle with Parmesan. Serve immediately.

Preparation time: 1 hour 10 minutes, plus 1 hour resting

Cooking time: 30 minutes

Serves 6

4½ cups all-purpose flour, plus extra for dusting

5 eggs

salt

For the filling

1¾ pounds pumpkin or butternut squash

1 egg

½ cup grated Parmesan cheese

pinch of freshly grated nutmeg

1–2 tablespoons fresh bread crumbs

salt and pepper

For the sauce

6 tablespoons butter, melted

⅔ cup grated Parmesan cheese

CAPPELLETTI

Cappelletti is a type of filled pasta originating from the northern Italian region of Emilia-Romagna. It resembles small miter hats, hence its name, which means "small caps." In the Middle Ages, cappelletti was known as "galoza" and was mentioned as early as the thirteenth century. Cappelletti is made by cutting sheets of dough into 1¼-inch squares and placing a small amount of filling in the center. The squares are folded into triangles and the two corners are joined at the base and pressed together.

CAPPELLETTI WITH TOMATO SAUCE

CAPPELLETTI CON SUGO DI POMODORO

**Preparation time: 45 minutes,
plus 1 hour resting
Cooking time: 5 minutes
Serves 4**

1¾ cups all-purpose flour, plus extra for dusting

2 eggs

1 tablespoon grated Parmesan cheese

salt and pepper

For the sauce

1 quantity tomato sauce
(see Angel Hair Mold, page 30)

butter, for tossing

grated Parmesan cheese, for sprinkling

Put the flour in a mound on a counter. Make a well in the center and break the eggs into it. Add the Parmesan and a pinch of salt and knead quickly to make a smooth, pliable dough. Shape the dough into a ball, cover, and let rest for 1 hour. Roll out on a lightly floured counter into a thin sheet or use a pasta machine. Cut the dough into 1¼-inch squares. Fold the squares in half diagonally and pinch the opposite corners together to form triangles. Join the corners of the longest side, without flattening the triangles, to form small miter-like hats—cappelletti. Cook in plenty of boiling salted water until al dente. Drain and toss with the tomato sauce and butter and serve immediately sprinkled with the Parmesan.

CARAMELLE

Caramelle, so called because of its resemblance to wrapped candies, is a type of filled egg-based pasta. It is made by cutting out 2-inch squares from a sheet of pasta dough, placing a small amount of filling in the center, and then twisting the two sides of the square in opposite directions. Caramelle is typically filled with cheese.

CARAMELLE WITH CREAMY CHEESE FILLING

CARAMELLE ALLA CREMA DI FORMAGGIO

Preparation time: 1 hour 25 minutes, plus 1 hour resting
Cooking time: 10 minutes
Serves 4

2¼ cups all-purpose flour, plus extra for dusting
2 eggs
melted butter, for brushing
For the filling
scant 1 cup ricotta cheese
3½ ounces diced stracchino cheese
scant ½ cup low-fat cream cheese
1 cup grated Parmesan cheese
pinch of freshly grated nutmeg
salt and pepper
For the sauce
4 tablespoons butter, melted
black truffle, thinly sliced

First make the pasta dough. Sift the flour into a mound on a counter and make a well in the center. Break the eggs into the well and add a pinch of salt. Knead thoroughly, shape into a ball, cover with a clean dish towel, and let rest for 1 hour. Meanwhile, make the filling. Pass the ricotta through a strainer into a bowl, beat in the stracchino, cream cheese, Parmesan, and nutmeg, and season with salt and pepper. Cover and chill in the refrigerator. Roll out the dough on a lightly floured counter into a thin sheet and cut out 2-inch squares with a pasta wheel. Lightly brush the surface of each square with melted butter and put a teaspoon of the cheese mixture on top. Roll up into a tube and twist the ends in opposite directions to resemble a paper-wrapped taffy. Cook the caramelle in plenty of salted boiling water until they rise to the counter and are al dente. Drain and transfer to a warmed serving dish. Pour the melted butter over, garnish with slices of truffle, and serve immediately.

CASÔNSÈI

Casônsèi dates back to the fourteenth century and is a specialty of Brescia in the Lombardy region of northern Italy. It is also known as casunzièi in Belluno, in the northeastern region of Veneto. The word casônsèi comes from the ancient term "cassoncelle," which probably meant "small caskets." Similar to ravioli, these half-moon-shaped parcels are made of an egg-based dough and can have a variety of fillings. The Renaissance version was bittersweet in taste, combining cinnamon and almonds. In the traditional cuisine of Brescia, casônsèi is typically filled with a mixture of sausage, bread dipped in milk, and grated Parmesan.

CASÔNSÈI FROM VAL CAMONICA

CASÔNSÈI DELLA VAL CAMONICA

Preparation time: 1 hour,
plus 30 minutes resting
Cooking time: 20 minutes
Serves 4

2¾ cups all-purpose flour,
plus extra for dusting

3 eggs

1 tablespoon olive oil

salt

For the filling

1 pound 2 ounces potatoes, diced

14 ounces Swiss chard, stalks removed

3 tablespoons butter

1 garlic clove, finely chopped

1 sprig chopped fresh parsley

1 leek, chopped

7 ounces Italian sausage, skinned and chopped

¾ cups bread crumbs

generous 1 cup grated Parmesan cheese

1 egg, lightly beaten

salt and pepper

For the sauce

4 tablespoons butter, melted

⅔ cup grated Parmesan cheese

Make the pasta dough. Sift the flour into a mound on a counter and make a well in the center. Break the eggs into the well and add the oil and a pinch of salt. Knead to a soft dough, shape into a ball, cover with a clean dish towel, and let rest for 30 minutes.

Meanwhile, make the filling. Cook the potatoes in lightly salted boiling water for 15–20 minutes until tender. Drain and mash. Cook the chard leaves in just enough boiling water to cover for 5–10 minutes until tender. Drain, squeeze out the excess liquid, and chop. Melt the butter in a pan. Add the garlic and parsley and cook over low heat, stirring frequently for a few minutes. Add the leek and sausage and cook, stirring occasionally, for 10 minutes. Remove the pan from the heat and let cool. Combine the sausage mixture, mashed potatoes, chard, bread crumbs, Parmesan, and egg in a bowl and season to taste with salt and pepper.

Roll out the dough on a lightly floured counter into a thin sheet. Cut out rectangles about 3¼ × 6¼ inches. Put a mound of filling on each one, roll the dough up, and press the edges well to seal, then gently bend into a horseshoe shape. Cook the casônsèi in plenty of salted boiling water for 5 minutes until al dente. Drain, transfer to a warmed serving dish, pour the melted butter over them, and sprinkle with Parmesan. Serve immediately.

FAGOTTINI

Fagottini, meaning "small bundles" in Italian, is a type of filled pasta similar to ravioli. It is made by cutting 4½-inch squares out of a sheet of pasta and drawing all four corners up together to create small parcels. This shape is ideally suited to vegetable fillings.

ASPARAGUS AND CHEESE FAGOTTINI

FAGOTTINI DI PUNTE D'ASPARAGI E FORMAGGI

Preheat the oven to 350°F and grease an ovenproof dish with butter. To make the filling, melt the butter in a pan. Add the onion and asparagus and cook over low heat, stirring occasionally, for 15 minutes. Season with salt, remove the pan from the heat, and stir in the Gorgonzola and fontina until thoroughly combined. Cut the pasta dough into long thin strips and then into squares. Briefly blanch in boiling salted water and drain. Put a small mound of the filling on each one and roll up to make parcels or bundles. Put them into the prepared dish, pour the béchamel over, and dot with the butter. Bake for 20 minutes until golden brown. Serve immediately.

Preparation time: 25 minutes

Cooking time: 25 minutes

Serves 4

1½ quantity Fresh Pasta Dough (see page 163)

For the filling

2 tablespoons butter, plus extra for greasing

1 onion, chopped

1 pound 5 ounces asparagus spears,

trimmed and chopped

6 ounces crumbled Gorgonzola cheese

3 ounces diced fontina cheese

salt

For the sauce

½ quantity béchamel sauce (see Baked Rigatoni, page 144)

butter

FAGOTTINI WITH PUMPKIN, ONION, AND RAISIN FILLING

FAGOTTINI RIPIENI DI ZUCCA, CIPOLLA E UVETTA

Preparation time: 1 hours 30 minutes, plus 1 hour resting

Cooking time: 1 hour

Serves 4

2¼ cups all-purpose flour, plus extra for dusting

2 eggs

16 blanched fresh chives

butter, for greasing • salt

For the filling

1 tablespoon olive oil

1½ cups pumpkin or butternut squash, peeled, seeded and diced

2 small white onions, finely chopped

generous 1 cup ricotta cheese

2 tablespoons raisins

salt

For the sauce

4 tablespoons butter

½ cup all-purpose flour

2¼ cups hot milk

salt and pepper

Make the pasta dough. Sift the flour into a mound on a counter and make a well in the center. Break the eggs into the well and add a pinch of salt. Knead thoroughly, shape into a ball, cover with a clean dish towel, and let rest for 1 hour. Meanwhile, make the filling. Put the raisins into a heatproof bowl, pour in hot water to cover, and let soak. Heat the oil in a pan. Add the pumpkin, season with salt and pepper, and cook over low heat, stirring occasionally, for 15 minutes. Add the onions and cook, stirring occasionally, for another 5 minutes. Taste and adjust the seasoning if necessary. Beat the ricotta in a bowl, then stir in the pumpkin and onion mixture. Drain the raisins, squeeze out the excess liquid, and stir into the bowl.

Roll out the dough on a lightly floured counter and cut into 8 fairly large squares. Cook in plenty of salted boiling water until al dente. Drain and spread out on clean dish towels. Put a generous tablespoon of the filling in the center of each square, bring the 4 corners together holding them fairly high, and tie at the base with 2 blanched chives.

Preheat the oven to 350°F and grease an ovenproof dish with butter. To make the sauce melt the butter in a pan. Stir in the flour and cook over medium heat, stirring constantly, for 2–3 minutes until golden brown. Gradually stir in the milk, a little at a time. Bring to a boil, stirring constantly, lower the heat, and simmer gently, stirring constantly, for 20 minutes until thickened and smooth. Put the fagottini in the prepared dish, pour the sauce over, and bake for 10–15 minutes. Remove from the oven and let stand for 5 minutes, then serve.

LASAGNA

The starting point for a huge family of fresh pasta, this large flat sheet of egg dough cut into strips is considered the basis for all fresh pasta. It was already popular with the Greeks as early as the first millennium BC. The name itself is of Greek origin, from the word "laganon," referring to a flat sheet of pasta cut into strips The dough is cut into rectangular sheets, measuring 4×8 inches, arranged in layers alternating with sauce, and then baked in the oven. Lasagnette, popular in the northern region of Emilia-Romagna and in central and southern Italy, is a narrower version and is also known as pappardelle in Tuscany. Lasagna itself is popular throughout Italy, but the classic lasagna recipe remains Lasagne alla Bolognese (Lasagna Bolognese, see page 274), which layers pasta, meat sauce, béchamel sauce and grated Parmesan.

LASAGNA (basic recipe)

LASAGNE (ricetta base)

**Preparation time: 40 minutes,
plus 15 minutes resting
Cooking time: 5 minutes
Serves 6
Makes about 12 lasagna sheets**

2¾ cups all-purpose flour,
plus extra for dusting
3 eggs
1 tablespoon olive oil
salt

Sift the flour into a mound on a counter and make a well in the center. Break the eggs into the well and add a pinch of salt. Knead for about 10 minutes, adding a little flour if it is too soft or a little water if it is too firm. Shape into a ball, cover with a clean dish towel, and let rest for 15 minutes. Roll out into a fairly thick sheet on a lightly floured counter, then cut into 4×8-inch wide rectangles. Cook, a few at a time, in plenty of salted boiling water to which the oil has been added, until al dente, then remove, and spread out to dry on clean dish towels.

LASAGNA VERDI
(basic recipe)

LASAGNE VERDI (ricetta base)

Sift the flour into a mound on a counter and make a well in the center. Break the eggs into the well and add the chopped spinach and a pinch of salt. Knead for a few minutes, adding more flour, a little at a time, if the spinach has made the dough too wet. Shape into a ball, cover with a clean dish towel, and let rest for 15 minutes. Roll out into a fairly thick sheet on a lightly floured counter, then cut into 4 × 8-inch wide rectangles. Cook, a few at a time, in plenty of salted boiling water to which the oil has been added, until al dente, then remove, and spread out to dry on clean dish towels.

Preparation time: 40 minutes,

plus 15 minutes resting

Cooking time: 5 minutes

Serves 6

2¾ cups all-purpose flour, plus extra for dusting

3 eggs

1⅔ cups cooked spinach, chopped

1 tablespoon olive oil

salt

EGGPLANT AND
RICOTTA LASAGNA

LASAGNE CON MELANZANE E RICOTTA

Put the eggplant slices in a colander, sprinkle with salt, and let drain for 1 hour. Rinse, pat dry, and cook under a preheated broiler until tender. Preheat the oven to 350°F. Grease an ovenproof dish with butter. Arrange a layer of lasagna sheets on the base of the prepared dish, place half the eggplant slices on top, and sprinkle with half the pine nuts, half the ricotta, 4 tablespoons of the tomato paste and 6 of the basil leaves. Drizzle with olive oil and repeat the layers. Sprinkle with the Parmesan, bake for about 40 minutes and serve.

Preparation time: 1 hour 15 minutes

Cooking time: 50 minutes

Serves 4

1 quantity Lasagna (see page 270)

1 large eggplant, sliced

butter, for greasing

½ cup pine nuts, chopped

⅔ cup crumbled ricotta cheese

½ cup concentrated tomato paste

12 fresh basil leaves

olive oil, for drizzling

4 tablespoons grated Parmesan cheese

salt

ROTELLINA

BAKED PUMPKIN PASTA

PASTICCIO DI PASTA DI ZUCCA

**Preparation time: 1 hour,
plus 15 minutes resting
Cooking time: 1 hour
Serves 4**

butter, for greasing
7 ounces cooked pumpkin or canned
unsweetened pumpkin purée
2¾ cups all-purpose flour,
plus extra for dusting
1 egg
salt

For the filling
1 cup dried mushrooms
2 tablespoons butter
½ shallot, chopped
½ carrot, chopped
salt and pepper

For the béchamel sauce
4 tablespoons butter
½ cup all-purpose flour
2¼ cups lukewarm milk
salt and pepper

Make the filling. Put the mushrooms into a heatproof bowl and pour in hot water to cover. Let soak for 30 minutes, then drain, squeeze out the excess liquid, and chop. Melt the butter in a shallow pan. Add the shallot and carrot and cook over low heat, stirring occasionally, for 5 minutes. Add the mushrooms and cook, stirring occasionally, for 30 minutes. Meanwhile, make the béchamel sauce. Melt the butter in a pan. Stir in the flour and cook over medium heat, stirring constantly, for 2–3 minutes until golden brown. Gradually stir in the milk, a little at a time. Bring to a boil, stirring constantly, lower the heat, and simmer gently, stirring constantly, for 20 minutes until thickened and smooth. Remove the pan from the heat, season with salt and pepper, and stir in the mushroom mixture. Preheat the oven to 400°F and grease an ovenproof dish with butter.

Make the pasta dough. Put the cooked pumpkin into a food processor or blender, add a pinch of salt, and process to a purée. Combine the pumpkin purée with the flour and egg and knead well. Roll out on a lightly floured counter into a sheet and cut out 10 rectangles. Cook in plenty of salted boiling water until al dente. Drain and arrange them alternately with the béchamel mixture in the prepared dish. Bake for 10 minutes, then serve.

BUCKWHEAT LASAGNA WITH
BROCCOLI AND SAVOY CABBAGE

Combine the buckwheat flour, all-purpose flour, and semolina flour, shape into a mound on a counter, and make a well in the center. Break the eggs into the well, add a pinch of salt, and knead to a smooth and elastic dough. Shape into a ball, cover with a clean dish towel, and let rest for 1 hour. Meanwhile, make the filling. Briefly blanch the broccoli and savoy cabbage in separate pans of salted boiling water, then drain. Melt the butter in a wide shallow pan. Add the pancetta or bacon and shallots and cook over low heat, stirring occasionally, for 5 minutes. Add the broccoli and cabbage and cook, stirring occasionally, for about 10 minutes until tender. Remove the pan from the heat and let cool.

Roll out the dough on a lightly floured counter into a thin sheet and cut into rectangles. Cook in plenty of salted boiling water to which the oil has been added, until al dente. Drain and spread out on clean dish towels to dry. Meanwhile, make the cheese sauce. Melt the butter in a shallow pan. Stir in the flour and cook over medium heat, stirring constantly, for 2–3 minutes until golden brown. Gradually stir in the milk and stock, a little at a time. Bring to a boil, stirring constantly, lower the heat and simmer, stirring constantly, for 20 minutes. Remove the pan from the heat, stir in the fontina and Emmenthal, and season with salt and pepper.

Preheat the oven to 400°F and grease an ovenproof dish with butter. Stir the ricotta, Parmesan, and nutmeg into the cooled filling mixture and season with salt and pepper. Make a layer of lasagna in the base of the prepared dish, spread a layer of the filling on top, and cover with cheese sauce. Continue making layers in this way until all the ingredients have been used, ending with a layer of cheese sauce. Bake for 20 minutes until golden brown. Remove from the oven and let stand for 10 minutes, then serve.

Preparation time: 1 hour 30 minutes,
plus 15 minutes resting
Cooking time: 1 hour
Serves 6

⅔ cup buckwheat flour

1¾ cups all-purpose flour, preferably Italian type 00, plus extra for dusting

½ cup durum wheat semolina flour

4 eggs

1 tablespoon olive oil

butter, for greasing

salt

For the filling

4½ pounds broccoli, cut into florets

6½ cups savoy cabbage, shredded

2 tablespoons butter

2 ounces smoked pancetta or bacon, cut into thin strips

2 shallots, sliced

scant ½ cup ricotta cheese

⅔ cup grated Parmesan cheese

pinch of freshly grated nutmeg

salt and pepper

For the cheese sauce

6 tablespoons butter

¾ cup all-purpose flour

1¾ cups lukewarm milk

1¾ cups lukewarm vegetable stock

9 ounces diced fontina cheese

3½ ounces diced Emmenthal cheese

salt and pepper

GOLDEN LASAGNA

LASAGNE DORATE

Preparation time: 45 minutes

Cooking time: 45 minutes

Serves 6

1 quantity Lasagna (see page 270)

For the filling

4 tablespoons butter, thinly sliced, plus extra for greasing

2 egg yolks, lightly beaten

1 quantity hot béchamel sauce (see Baked Rigatoni, page 144)

½ cup grated Gruyère cheese

4 hard-cooked eggs, sliced

⅔ cup chopped ham

9 ounces fontina cheese, sliced

salt

Preheat the oven to 350°F and grease an ovenproof dish with butter. Beat the egg yolks into the béchamel sauce and stir in the Gruyère. Make a layer of lasagna sheets on the base of the prepared dish and cover with a layer of hard-cooked egg, and then a layer of chopped ham. Sprinkle with some of the butter, cover with slices of fontina, and top with béchamel sauce. Continue making layers in this way until all the ingredients have been used, ending with a topping of béchamel sauce dotted with butter. Bake for 30 minutes, until golden brown, then serve.

LASAGNA BOLOGNESE

LASAGNE ALLA BOLOGNESE

Preparation time: 30 minutes, plus 15 minutes resting

Cooking time: 1 hour and 20 minutes

Serves 4

1 quantity Fresh Pasta Dough (see page 163)

For the filling

3 tablespoons olive oil

1 carrot, chopped

1 onion, chopped

11 ounces ground beef

scant ½ cup dry white wine

1 cup bottled strained tomatoes

2 tablespoons butter, plus extra for greasing

1 quantity béchamel sauce (see Baked Pumpkin Pasta, page 272)

scant 1 cup grated Parmesan cheese

salt and pepper

Heat the olive oil in a pan, add the carrot and onion, and cook over low heat, stirring occasionally, for 5 minutes. Add the meat and cook until browned, then pour in the wine, and cook until it has evaporated. Season with salt, add the tomatoes, and simmer for 30 minutes, then season with pepper. Preheat the oven to 400°F. Grease an ovenproof dish with butter. Roll out the pasta dough into a sheet on a lightly floured counter. Cut into 4 × 8-inch rectangles and cook, a few at a time, in plenty of lightly salted, boiling water for a few minutes. Drain and place on a damp dish towel. Arrange a layer of lasagna on the base of the prepared dish, spoon some of the meat sauce, then some of the béchamel sauce on top, sprinkle with some of the Parmesan, and dot with some of the butter. Repeat the layers until all the ingredients have been used, ending with a layer of béchamel sauce. Bake for 30 minutes.

LASAGNA NAPOLETANA

LASAGNE ALLA NAPOLETANA

For the filling, heat 3 tablespoons of the oil in a pan, add the onion, carrot, celery, and garlic, and cook over low heat, stirring occasionally, for 5 minutes, then add the tomatoes. Season with salt and pepper and simmer for about 1 hour. Meanwhile, boil 4 of the eggs for 12 minutes, then refresh in cold water, shell, and slice. Combine the ground beef, Parmesan, and remaining egg in a bowl and season with salt. Shape the mixture into small balls. Heat 2 tablespoons of the butter and the remaining oil in a skillet, add the meatballs, and cook until browned all over, then add them to the tomato sauce.

Make the pasta (see Fresh Pasta Dough, page 163) with the quantities specified and roll out into 2 thin sheets. Cut into 4-inch squares and cook, a few at a time, in plenty of salted boiling water for a few minutes. Drain and place on a damp dish towel. Preheat the oven to 325°F. Grease a large ovenproof dish with butter, arrange a layer of lasagna on the base, and cover with the tomato sauce with meatballs, then the mozzarella and a few slices of hard-cooked eggs. Repeat the layers until all the ingredients have been used, ending with a layer of tomato sauce. Dot the top with the remaining butter, cover the dish with aluminium foil or baking paper and bake for about 1 hour. Let stand for 10 minutes before serving.

Preparation time: 1 hour,
plus 15 minutes resting
Cooking time: 2 hours 30 minutes
Serves 6

2¾ cups all-purpose flour, preferably Italian type 00, plus extra for dusting

3 eggs, lightly beaten

salt

For the filling

5 tablespoons olive oil

1 onion, chopped

1 carrot, chopped

1 celery stalk, chopped

½ garlic clove, chopped

4 cups bottled strained tomatoes

5 eggs

11 ounces ground beef

⅔ grated Parmesan cheese

3 tablespoons butter, plus extra for greasing

5 ounces mozzarella cheese, sliced

salt and pepper

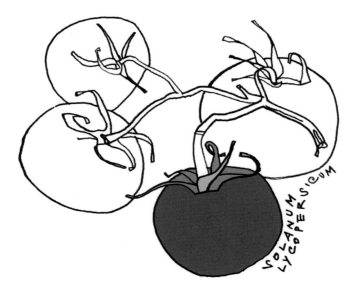

SOLANUM LYCOPERSICUM

LASAGNA VERDI WITH PORCINI MUSHROOMS

LASAGNE VERDI AI FUNGHI PORCINI

Preparation time: 25 minutes

Cooking time: 50 minutes

Serves 6

1 quantity Lasagna Verdi (see page 271)

2 tablespoons butter, plus extra for greasing

salt

For the filling

2 tablespoons olive oil

2 garlic cloves, lightly crushed

2¾ cups sliced porcini mushrooms

1 tablespoon chopped fresh thyme

scant 1 cup dry white wine

pinch of freshly grated nutmeg

1 quantity béchamel sauce (see Baked Rigatoni, page 144)

⅔ cup grated Parmesan cheese

salt and pepper

To make the filling, heat the oil in a shallow pan. Add the garlic cloves and cook over low heat, stirring frequently, for a few minutes until lightly browned. Remove the garlic with a slotted spoon and discard. Add the mushrooms, sprinkle with the thyme, drizzle with the wine, and cook until the alcohol has evaporated. Season with salt and pepper and simmer, stirring occasionally, for 10 minutes, then remove from the heat. Stir the nutmeg into the béchamel sauce. Preheat the oven to 350°F and grease an ovenproof dish with butter. Place a layer of lasagna in the base of the prepared dish, cover with a layer of mushrooms, top with béchamel sauce, and sprinkle with Parmesan. Continue making layers in this way until all the ingredients have been used, ending with a layer of béchamel sauce. Dot with the butter and bake for about 20 minutes until golden brown. Sprinkle Parmesan over and serve immediately.

LASAGNA WITH MUSHROOMS AND PARMESAN CREAM

LASAGNE CON CREMA DI PARMIGIANO E FUNGHI

Preparation time: 40 minutes

Cooking time: 1 hour

Serves 6

1 quantity Lasagna (see page 270)

1 tablespoon butter, plus extra for greasing

salt

For the filling

6 tablespoons butter

4–5 fresh sage leaves

¼ cup heavy cream

generous 1 cup grated Parmesan cheese

2 tablespoons olive oil

1 garlic clove

7¼ cups chanterelle mushrooms, chopped

salt and pepper

To make the filling, melt the butter in a pan. Add the sage leaves and cook over low heat until lightly browned, then remove and discard. Pour in the cream and bring just to a boil. Stir in the Parmesan, remove from the heat, and set aside. Heat the oil in another shallow pan. Add the garlic clove and cook over low heat, stirring frequently, until lightly browned. Remove the garlic with a slotted spoon and discard. Add the mushrooms to the pan, season with salt and cook over low heat, stirring occasionally, for 30 minutes. Meanwhile, preheat the oven to 350°F and grease an ovenproof dish with butter. Make a layer of lasagna in the base of the prepared dish, cover with the Parmesan and cream mixture and top with mushrooms. Continue making layers until all the ingredients have been used, ending with a layer of pasta. Dot with the butter and bake for 20 minutes until golden brown. Remove from the oven and let stand for 5 minutes, then serve.

PUMPKIN LASAGNA

LASAGNE ALLA ZUCCA GIALLA

Preparation time: 30 minutes

Cooking time: 55 minutes

Serves 6

1 quantity Lasagna (see page 270)

2 tablespoons butter, plus extra for greasing

salt

For the filling

2 tablespoons butter

2 tablespoons olive oil

2 garlic cloves

3–4 fresh sage leaves

1 pound 2 ounces pumpkin, peeled, seeded, and sliced

4–5 tablespoons hot water

½ quantity béchamel sauce (see Baked Rigatoni, page 144)

pinch of freshly grated nutmeg

1 cup grated Gruyère cheese

salt and pepper

To make the filling, melt the butter with the olive oil in a shallow pan. Add the garlic cloves and sage leaves and cook over low heat, stirring occasionally, for a few minutes until the garlic is lightly browned. Add the pumpkin, cover, and cook, stirring occasionally and adding a little hot water as required, for 30 minutes. Remove and discard the garlic and sage. Remove the pan from the heat and mash the pumpkin with a fork, then mix with the béchamel sauce. Stir in the nutmeg and season to taste with salt and pepper. Preheat the oven to 350°F and grease an ovenproof dish with butter. Make a layer of lasagna in the base of the prepared dish, spoon a layer of the pumpkin mixture on top, and sprinkle with Gruyère. Continue making layers in this way until all the ingredients have been used, ending with a layer of lasagna. Dot with butter and bake for 20 minutes until light golden brown. Remove from the oven and let stand for 5 minutes, then serve.

RADICCHIO LASAGNA

LASAGNE DI RADICCHIO

Preparation time: 40 minutes, plus 15 minutes resting

Cooking time: 1 hour 10 minutes

Serves 6

2¾ cups all-purpose flour, preferably Italian type 00, plus extra for dusting

3 eggs, lightly beaten

salt

For the sauce

3 tablespoons heavy cream

11 ounces radicchio, cut into strips

2 tablespoons butter, plus extra for greasing

1 quantity béchamel sauce (see Baked Pumpkin Pasta, page 272)

salt and pepper

Make the pasta (see Fresh Pasta Dough, page 163) with the quantities specified. Heat the cream in a pan over low heat, stir in the radicchio, add the butter, and cook until the radicchio is soft. Stir in the béchamel sauce and season with salt and pepper to taste. Preheat the oven to 300°F. Grease an ovenproof dish with butter. Cook the lasagna sheets, a few at a time, in a large pan of salted boiling water until al dente, drain, and place on a damp dish towel to cool. Place a layer of lasagna on the base of the prepared dish and top with a layer of radicchio sauce. Continue making alternate layers until all the ingredients have been used, ending with a layer of radicchio sauce. Bake for 30 minutes, then serve.

PASTA WITH BREAD CRUMBS AND CLAMS

PASTA DI PANGRATTATO CON VONGOLE VERACI

Make the pasta dough. Sift the flour onto a counter, add the bread crumbs, and shape into a mound. Make a well in the center, break the egg into the well, and add the oil and a pinch of salt. Knead thoroughly, adding a little lukewarm water if necessary to make a pliable dough. Shape into a ball, cover with a clean dish towel, and let rest for 1 hour.

Meanwhile, make the sauce. Scrub the clams under cold running water and discard any with damaged shells or that do not shut immediately when sharply tapped. Heat the oil with the garlic clove and bay leaves in a pan. Add the clams, pour in the wine, cover, and cook over high heat, shaking the pan occasionally, for 3–5 minutes until all the clams have opened. Remove the clams with a slotted spoon and take them out of their shells. Discard any that remain closed. Strain the cooking liquid into a pitcher. Melt the butter in another pan. Add the celery and shallot and cook over low heat, stirring occasionally, for 8–10 minutes until softened. Pour in the reserved cooking liquid, add the clams, and simmer for 5 minutes.

Roll out the dough on a lightly floured counter into a sheet ⅕-inch thick. Cut into 1½ × ¾-inch rectangles. Cook the pasta in plenty of salted boiling water until al dente. Drain, tip into the pan with the sauce, add the parsley, and season with pepper. Stir well and serve immediately.

Preparation time: 50 minutes,

plus 1 hour resting

Cooking time: 22 minutes

Serves 6

1¾ cups all-purpose flour, plus extra for dusting

3½ cups bread crumbs

1 egg

1 tablespoon olive oil

salt

For the sauce

4½ pounds live clams

1 tablespoon olive oil

1 garlic clove

2 bay leaves

scant 1 cup dry white wine

6 tablespoons butter

1¼ cups celery, diced

1 shallot, chopped

½ cup chopped fresh flat-leaf parsley

salt and pepper

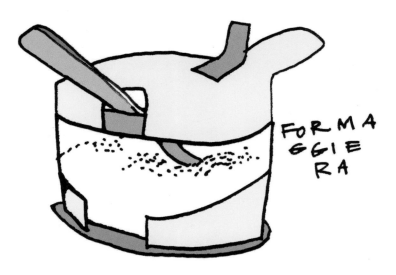

FORMA
GGIE
RA

SEAFOOD LASAGNA

For the filling, combine the tomatoes and pesto in a bowl. Heat the oil in a shallow pan over low heat. Add the sea scallops and cook for 2 minutes on each side. Remove from the pan and keep warm. Pour the wine into the pan, increase the heat to medium-high, and cook until reduced by half. Stir in the chives and cream and cook until reduced by half again. Meanwhile, preheat the oven to 350°F. Remove the pan from the heat, stir in the pecorino and crab meat, and season with salt and pepper. Make a layer of lasagna sheets in the base of an ovenproof dish, spoon some of the crab filling on top, and cover with a layer of seared sea scallops. Continue making layers in this way until all the ingredients have been used, ending with a layer of pasta. Cover with the pesto and tomato mixture. Turn off the oven and let the lasagna in the oven heat through for 10 minutes, then serve.

Preparation time: 40 minutes

Cooking time: 30 minutes

Serves 6

1 quantity Lasagna (see page 270)

salt

For the filling

2 canned tomatoes, drained and chopped

3 ounces pesto (see Trenette with Pesto, page 238)

2 tablespoons olive oil

7 ounces sea scallops, shelled

2½ cups dry white wine

½ bunch snipped fresh chives

1 cup heavy cream

½ cup grated mild pecorino cheese

7 ounces crab meat, drained if canned

salt and pepper

THREE-COLOR RICOTTA LASAGNA

To make the filling, rub the ricotta through a strainer into a bowl and beat well with a pinch of salt and pepper. Put one-third of the ricotta into another bowl and beat in the spinach purée. Put half the remaining ricotta into another bowl and beat in the tomatoes. Leave the remaining ricotta plain. Preheat the oven to 350°F and grease an ovenproof dish with butter. Make a layer of lasagna in the base of the prepared dish, spread the spinach and ricotta mixture on top, and sprinkle with grated pecorino. Make another layer of lasagna, spread the white ricotta on top and sprinkle with grated pecorino. Make a final layer of lasagna, spread the ricotta and tomato mixture on top, and sprinkle with the remaining pecorino. Dot with butter and bake for 20 minutes. Serve immediately.

Preparation time: 30 minutes

Cooking time: 25 minutes

Serves 6

1 quantity Lasagna (see page 270)

5 tablespoons butter, plus extra for greasing

salt

For the filling

2 cups ricotta cheese

3 ounces cooked spinach, drained and puréed

1 cup bottled strained tomatoes

1 cup grated pecorino cheese

salt and pepper

VINCISGRASSI

Preheat the oven to 350°F. Grease an ovenproof dish with butter. For the filling, put the mushrooms in a bowl, add hot water to cover, and let soak for 20 minutes, then drain, squeeze dry, and chop. Blanch the sweetbreads in boiling water for a few minutes, drain, and let cool, then dice.

Melt half the butter in a skillet, add the sweetbreads, and cook, stirring occasionally, for a few minutes. Heat the remaining butter with the oil in a pan, add the onion, and cook over low heat, stirring occasionally, for 5 minutes, then stir in the mushrooms, truffle, and stock. Add the chicken strips and cook over high heat until browned, then add the giblets, and cook for a few minutes more. Pour in the Marsala, lower the heat, and cook until half the wine has evaporated. Pour in just enough hot water to cover, season with salt and pepper, cover, and cook over low heat for about 30 minutes, then add the sweetbreads.

Make the pasta dough (see Fresh Pasta Dough, page 163) with the ingredients specified, then roll out into a sheet, and cut into strips about 4 inches wide and 20 inches long. Bring a large pan of salted water to a boil, add the pasta strips, and boil for a few minutes until half-cooked, then remove, and refresh in a bowl of cold water. Drain the pasta and spread out on a damp dish towel. Overlap pasta strips in the base of the prepared dish to cover the base, allowing the excess to overhang the sides. Cut the remaining strips into rectangles.

Fill the dish with alternate layers of filling and pasta, sprinkled with Parmesan and tablespoonfuls of béchamel sauce, ending with a layer of béchamel sauce. Fold over the overhanging ends of the pasta strips to make a pie. Place the dish in a roasting pan, add hot water to the tin to come about halfway up the sides of the dish, and bake for 30 minutes.

VINCISGRASSI

Preparation time: 1 hour,
plus 15 minutes resting
Cooking time: 1 hour and 30 minutes
Serves 6–8
butter, for greasing
3 cups all-purpose flour, preferably Italian type 00, plus extra for dusting
generous 1 cup semolina flour
3 tablespoons Vin Santo or Marsala
3 eggs, lightly beaten
salt
For the filling
½ cup dried mushrooms
3½ ounces sweetbreads
4 tablespoons butter
2 tablespoons olive oil
½ onion, chopped
1 black truffle, diced
2 tablespoons chicken stock
1 skinless chicken breast fillet, cut into strips
7 ounces chicken giblets, trimmed and chopped
5 tablespoons dry Marsala
1 cup grated Parmesan cheese
1 quantity béchamel sauce (see Baked Pumpkin Pasta, page 272)
salt and pepper

ARTICHOKE LASAGNETTE

Preparation time: 1 hour 20 minutes,
plus 15 minutes resting
Cooking time: 30 minutes
Serves 4
1 quantity Fresh Pasta Dough (see page 163)
juice of ½ lemon, strained
4 globe artichokes
4 tablespoons olive oil
½ onion, chopped
5 ounces ham, cut into strips
⅔ cup grated Parmesan cheese
salt and pepper

Roll out the dough into a fairly thick sheet on a lightly floured counter, then cut into strips about 2½ inches long and ½ inch wide. Partly fill a bowl with water and stir in the lemon juice. Break off the stems and remove and discard the coarse outer leaves from the artichokes, then slice. As you prepare each artichoke, put them into the acidulated water to prevent discoloration. Heat the oil in a pan. Add the onion and cook over low heat, stirring occasionally, for 5 minutes, until softened. Drain the artichokes, add them to the pan, cover, and cook, stirring occasionally, for 10–15 minutes until tender. Add the strips of cooked ham to the artichoke mixture and sauté, stirring occasionally, for 2 minutes, then remove the pan from the heat. Cook the lasagnette in plenty of salted boiling water until al dente, then drain and toss with the artichoke mixture. Sprinkle with the Parmesan and serve immediately.

POTATO LASAGNETTE

Preparation time: 40 minutes,
plus 15 minutes resting
Cooking time: 30 minutes
Serves 4
2¼ pounds starchy potatoes
3 eggs, lightly beaten
generous 1 cup grated Parmesan cheese
1¾–2¾ cups all-purpose flour, plus extra for dusting
4 tablespoons butter, softened
salt

Steam the potatoes for about 20 minutes, until tender, then mash well with a potato masher. Turn them out and make a mound on the counter. Make a well in the center and stir in the eggs, 3 tablespoonfuls of the Parmesan, and as much flour as required to make a soft, pliable dough. Shape the dough into a ball, flatten slightly, and roll out on a lightly floured counter into a fairly thick sheet. Cut into strips about 2½ inches long and ½ inch wide. Bring a large pan of salted water to a boil, then lower heat to a gentle simmer. Meanwhile, dot a warmed serving dish with the butter. Carefully add the dough strips to the simmering water and cook for a few minutes until they rise to the counter. Remove with a slotted spoon and transfer to the prepared dish. Sprinkle with the remaining Parmesan and serve immediately.

LASAGNETTE WITH EEL

LASAGNETTE ALL'ANGUILLA

Heat the oil in a shallow pan. Add the garlic clove, tomatoes, and basil leaves and cook over low heat, stirring occasionally, for 5 minutes. Season with salt and pepper and stir. Remove the garlic with a slotted spoon and discard. Add the eel to the pan, increase the heat to medium, and cook for 30 minutes. Meanwhile, preheat the oven to 400°F. Cook the lasagnette in plenty of salted boiling water until al dente, then drain. Make alternating layers of pasta, sauce, and parsley in an ovenproof dish. Bake for 20 minutes, then remove from the oven and let stand for 10 minutes. Serve immediately.

Preparation time: 15 minutes

Cooking time: 55 minutes

Serves 6

3 tablespoons olive oil

1 garlic clove

11 ounces canned chopped tomatoes

4 fresh basil leaves

14 ounces fresh lasagnette (see Artichoke

Lasagnette, opposite)

11 ounces eel slices

2 tablespoons chopped fresh flat-leaf parsley

salt and pepper

PASTA
PASTICCIATA

PANSOTTI

Pansotti, a specialty of the city of Genoa in Liguria in northwest Italy, is a type of filled pasta that looks like large triangular ravioli. The name pansotti means "pot-bellied" in Italian. Pansotti is made from 2-inch squares of pasta, which are folded over to make a triangle. The edges may be either straight or serrated, and pansotti is typically served with a walnut sauce.

GENOESE PANSOTTI

PANSOTTI ALLA GENOVESE

**Preparation time: 1 hour 15 minutes,
plus 30 minutes resting
Cooking time: 20 minutes
Serves 6**

3½ cups all-purpose flour, preferably Italian type 00,
plus extra for dusting
1 tablespoon dry white wine
2 tablespoons butter, diced
⅔ cup grated Parmesan cheese
salt

For the filling

2¼ pounds borage, escarole, Swiss chard
or turnip tops
½ garlic clove
scant 1 cup ricotta cheese
2 eggs, lightly beaten
4–6 tablespoons grated Parmesan cheese

For the sauce

1 slice bread, crusts removed
2 tablespoons milk • 1¾ cups shelled walnuts
½ garlic clove
⅔ cup olive oil

Make the pasta dough (see Fresh Pasta Dough, page 163) with the flour, 5 tablespoons water, the wine, and a pinch of salt. To make the filling, cook the greens in salted, boiling water for 5 minutes or until tender. Drain, reserve some of the water, and chop the greens with the garlic, then mix with the ricotta, eggs, and enough Parmesan to thicken the mixture. Roll out the pasta dough into a thin sheet and place mounds of the filling at regular intervals on top. Cut the dough into squares around each mound, then fold them in half. To make the sauce, tear the bread into pieces, place in a bowl, add the milk, and let soak. Blanch the walnuts in boiling water and peel off the skins. Squeeze out the bread. Pound the walnuts, garlic, and bread in a mortar and gradually whisk in the oil to make a runny sauce. If necessary, add 1–2 tablespoons of the cooking water from the greens. Cook the pansotti in a large pan of salted boiling water until al dente, then drain, and transfer to a warmed serving dish. Add the walnut sauce, the butter, and Parmesan, mix well, and serve.

In Liguria, northwest Italy, there are numerous variations on this traditional dish. Pansotti can vary in shape and is found as squares, triangles, half-moons or tortelloni (see page 314), but it is always served with a walnut sauce.

RAVIOLI

Square, rectangular, or half-moon-shaped, ravioli is a popular type of filled pasta. Ravioli is also the generic name for all bite-size pasta shapes with fillings. Ravioli ranges in size from the small raviolini to the large raviolone, but commonly consists of $1\frac{1}{4} \times 1\frac{1}{4}$-inch squares. It is made by placing portions of filling on a sheet of dough, laying another sheet over it, and then cutting the pieces out using a serrated pasta wheel. The filling has changed over the centuries—wild herbs have been replaced by escarole, borage, chard or spinach, and pecorino cheese has often been replaced by Parmesan. Ravioli is usually served with melted butter or simple sauces flavored with aromatic herbs, with grated cheese on top. It can also be served in stock.

RAVIOLI WITH WHITE TRUFFLE

RAVIOLI AL TARTUFO BIANCO

**Preparation time: 1 hour,
plus 30 minutes resting
Cooking time: 8 minutes
Serves 4**

2¾ cups all-purpose flour, plus extra for dusting
3 eggs
salt

For the filling
1½ cups ricotta cheese
⅔ cup grated Parmesan cheese
1 egg • 2 pinches of freshly grated nutmeg
salt and pepper

For the sauce
6 tablespoons butter, melted
1 white truffle, shaved

Sift the flour into a mound on a counter and make a well in the center. Break the eggs into the well and add a pinch of salt. Knead thoroughly and form the dough into a ball. Cover with a clean dish towel and let rest for 30 minutes. Meanwhile, make the filling. Push the ricotta through a strainer into a large bowl, beat in the Parmesan, egg, and nutmeg, and season with salt and pepper.

Roll out the dough on a lightly floured counter into a thin sheet. Put small mounds of the filling in even rows over one half of the pasta sheet. Fold the other half of the dough sheet over and press around the filling with your fingers to seal. Cut out the ravioli and press the edges firmly together. Cook in plenty of salted boiling water until the ravioli rises to the counter and is al dente. Using a slotted spoon, transfer to a warmed serving dish, pour the melted butter over, and sprinkle with the truffle shavings. Serve immediately.

FISH RAVIOLI

*RAVIOLI CON RIPIENO
DI PESCE AZZURRO*

Make a fairly firm pasta dough (see Fresh Pasta Dough page 163) with the quantities specified. Cover with a damp dish towel and let rest for 30 minutes. Meanwhile, make the filling. Rub off the scales of the fish with your fingers or the back of a knife and rinse under cold running water. Cut the head off each fish. Gently squeeze the belly until the guts protrude, trap them with a knife, and pull them out. Rinse well, then slit open the belly of each fish, and place, skin side uppermost, on a cutting board. Press firmly along the backbone with your fingers until the fish is flat. Turn it over and gently pull out the bones, snipping the backbone at the tail end with kitchen scissors. Chop the flesh.

Tear the bread into pieces, put into a bowl and pour in water to cover. Let soak. Heat the oil in a skillet. Add the onion and cook over low heat, stirring occasionally, for 8–10 minutes until lightly browed. Add the fish and cook, stirring occasionally, for 2–3 minutes. Pour in the wine and cook for a few minutes until the alcohol has evaporated. Squeeze out the bread and stir into the skillet. Season with salt and pepper, remove the skillet from the heat, and let cool.

Roll out the pasta dough into a thin sheet on a lightly floured counter or use a pasta machine. Put small mounds—about 1 teaspoon—of the filling in even rows spaced about 1½ inches apart on half the sheet. Brush the spaces between the filling with beaten egg and fold over the other half of the sheet. Press down around the filling, pushing out any air. Using a ravioli cutter or sharp knife, cut into squares. Cook the ravioli in plenty of salted boiling water until it rises to the counter and is al dente, then remove from the pan, and drain. Melt the butter in a pan, add the ravioli, and toss gently over low heat for a few minutes. Tip into a warmed serving dish, sprinkle with the parsley, and serve immediately.

Preparation time: 1 hour 15 minutes,
plus 30 minutes resting
Cooking time: 25 minutes
Serves 4

3½ cups all-purpose flour, preferably Italian type 00, plus extra for dusting

4 eggs

2 tablespoons olive oil

beaten egg, for brushing

salt

For the filling

1¾ pounds mixed small oily fish such as anchovies and sardines

7 ounces bread, crusts removed

2 tablespoons olive oil

½ onion, chopped

scant ½ cup white wine

salt and pepper

To serve

6 tablespoons butter

chopped fresh flat-leaf parsley, to garnish

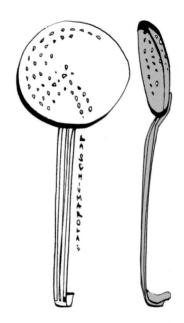

BUTTERED EGGPLANT RAVIOLI

Preparation time: 1 hour, plus 30 minutes resting

Cooking time: 1 hour 15 minutes

Serves 4

2¾ cups all-purpose flour, plus extra for dusting

3 eggs

salt

For the filling

1 pound 2 ounces eggplant, sliced

2 tablespoons butter

2 tablespoons olive oil

1 onion, chopped

2 garlic cloves, chopped

7 ounces tomatoes, peeled and diced

6 torn fresh basil leaves

½ cup grated Parmesan cheese

salt

For the sauce

3 tablespoons butter

½ cup grated Parmesan cheese

Preheat the oven to 200°F. Put the eggplant into an ovenproof dish, sprinkling salt between each layer, and dry out in the oven for 30 minutes. Meanwhile, make the pasta dough. Sift the flour into a mound on a counter and make a well in the center. Break the eggs into the well and add a pinch of salt. Knead thoroughly, shape into a ball, cover with a clean dish towel, and let rest for 30 minutes.

Remove the eggplant from the oven and leave until cool enough to handle, then peel, and finely chop the pulp. Melt the butter with the oil in a shallow pan. Add the onion and garlic and cook over low heat, stirring occasionally, for 5 minutes. Add the tomatoes and simmer, stirring occasionally, for 15 minutes. Add the eggplant flesh and cook for about 10 minutes until thickened. Remove the pan from the heat and stir in the basil and Parmesan.

Roll out the pasta dough on a lightly floured counter into a thin sheet. Put small mounds of the filling in even rows over one half of the pasta sheet. Fold over the other half of the sheet and press around the filling with your fingers to seal. Cut out the ravioli and press the edges together firmly. Cook in plenty of salted boiling water until the ravioli rises to the counter and is al dente. Drain and transfer to a pan with the butter and Parmesan, heat gently, and serve.

ZUCCHINI AND ALMOND RAVIOLI

Make the pasta dough. Sift the flour into a mound on a counter and make a well in the center. Break the eggs into the well and add the marjoram and a pinch of salt. Knead thoroughly, shape into a ball, cover with a clean dish towel, and let rest for 1 hour.

Meanwhile, make the filling. Heat the oil with 4 tablespoons water in a shallow pan. Add the shallots and cook over low heat, stirring occasionally, for 5 minutes. Add the grated zucchini and cook, stirring occasionally, for 15 minutes until tender and dry. Season with salt and pepper and stir in the marjoram. Transfer to a bowl and stir in the Parmesan, ground almonds, eggs, bread crumbs, and nutmeg.

Make the sauce. Using a citrus zester, cut long, thin strips of peel from 3 of the zucchini. Melt 2 tablespoons of the butter in a pan. Add the zucchini peel strips, season with salt and pepper, and cook over low heat, shaking the pan occasionally and taking care not to break them, for few minutes until softened. Remove the pan from the heat. Dice all the zucchini. Heat the oil in a shallow pan. Add the shallot and cook over low heat, stirring occasionally, for 5 minutes. Add the diced zucchini, pour in water to cover, season with salt and pepper and bring to a boil over medium heat. Lower the heat and simmer for 15 minutes. Stir in the cream and simmer for another 5 minutes. Remove the pan from the heat and add the marjoram. Transfer the mixture to a food processor and process to a purée. Return the sauce to the rinsed-out pan and reheat gently.

Roll out the pasta dough on a lightly floured counter into a thin sheet or use a pasta machine. Put small mounds of the filling in even rows over one half of the pasta sheet. Fold over the other half of the sheet and press around the filling with your fingers to seal. Cut out the ravioli and press the edges together firmly. Cook the ravioli in plenty of salted boiling water until it rises to the counter and is al dente. Drain, add to the pan with the sauce, and mix gently over the heat. Transfer the mixture to a warmed serving dish and garnish with the strips of zucchini peel, toasted almonds, pieces of cold butter, basil leaves, and Parmesan. Serve immediately.

Preparation time: 1 hour 20 minutes, plus 1 hour resting

Cooking time: 1 hour 10 minutes

Serves 6

2¾ cups all-purpose flour, plus extra for dusting

3 eggs

a pinch of dried marjoram

salt

For the filling

2 tablespoons olive oil

3 shallots, chopped

4⅔ cups grated zucchini

2 sprigs chopped fresh marjoram

1 cup grated Parmesan cheese

½ cup ground almonds

2 eggs, lightly beaten

3 tablespoons fresh bread crumbs

pinch of freshly grated nutmeg

salt and pepper

For the sauce

5 zucchini

6 tablespoons chilled butter

2 tablespoons olive oil

1 shallot, chopped

2 tablespoons heavy cream

¼ cup lightly toasted slivered almonds

4 torn fresh basil leaves

⅔ cup grated Parmesan cheese

salt and pepper

CHANTERELLE AND THYME RAVIOLI

RAVIOLI DI GALLINACCI AL TIMO

Make the pasta dough. Sift the flour into a mound on a counter and make a well in the center. Break 1 egg into the well and add the egg yolks, oil and a pinch of salt. Knead thoroughly, shape into a ball, cover with a clean dish towel, and let rest for 1 hour.

Meanwhile, make the filling. Heat the oil in a shallow pan. Add the onion and garlic and cook over low heat, stirring occasionally, for 5 minutes. Add the thyme and mushrooms, season with salt, and cook, stirring occasionally, for 20 minutes. Remove from the heat and let cool. Break up the cooled mixture, stir in the cheese, and season with salt and pepper. Lightly beat the remaining egg in a bowl.

Roll out the dough on a lightly floured counter into a thin sheet and cut out 3¼-inch rounds. Brush the counter of each with beaten egg, place a little filling on top, and fold the dough in half, pressing the edges to seal. Cook the ravioli in plenty of salted boiling water until it rises to the counter and is al dente. Meanwhile, make the sauce. Melt the butter in a shallow pan and stir in the thyme. Drain the ravioli, tip into the sauce, and toss lightly. Transfer to a warmed serving dish and serve immediately, handing the Parmesan separately.

Preparation time: 1 hour 15 minutes, plus 1 hour resting
Cooking time: 35 minutes
Serves 4

2¾ cups all-purpose flour, plus extra for dusting
2 eggs
2 egg yolks
1 tablespoon olive oil
salt

For the filling
2 tablespoons olive oil
1 onion, chopped
1 garlic clove, finely chopped
pinch of fresh thyme
7¼ cups chanterelle mushrooms, chopped
⅔ cup grated Parmesan cheese
salt and pepper

For the sauce
4 tablespoons butter
1 tablespoon chopped fresh thyme
½ cup grated Parmesan cheese

ONION RAVIOLI

**Preparation time: 1 hour 10 minutes,
plus 30 minutes resting**
Cooking time: 20 minutes
Serves 4–6

3½ cups all-purpose flour,
plus extra for dusting
4 eggs
salt
For the filling
4 tablespoons butter
1 pound 2 ounces onions, chopped
1 tablespoon chopped fresh pennyroyal or mint
generous 1 cup grated pecorino cheese
pepper
To serve
1 cup bottled strained tomatoes
grated pecorino cheese
pepper

Sift the flour into a mound on a counter and make a well in the center. Break the eggs into the well and add a pinch of salt. Knead thoroughly, shape into a ball, cover with a clean dish towel, and let rest for 30 minutes. Meanwhile, make the filling. Melt the butter in a pan. Add the onions and cook over low heat, stirring occasionally, for 10 minutes until softened. Remove from the heat, sprinkle with the pennyroyal or mint and the pecorino, and mix well. Divide the pasta dough in half and roll out each piece on a lightly floured counter into a thin sheet. Put small mounds of the filling in even rows on one sheet. Lift the second sheet on top and press around the filling with your fingers to seal. Using a ravioli cutter, stamp out square ravioli. Dust them lightly with flour and let rest for 15 minutes. Put the tomatoes into a heatproof bowl set over a pan of simmering water to heat through. Cook the ravioli in plenty of salted boiling water until it rises to the counter and is al dente. Remove with a slotted spoon and transfer to a warmed serving dish. Pour the tomatoes over, sprinkle with the pecorino, season with pepper, and serve.

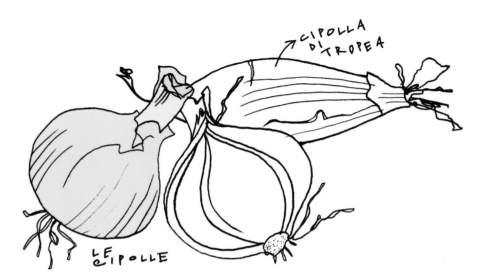

POTATO AND PORCINI MUSHROOM RAVIOLI

Make the pasta dough. Sift the flour into a mound on a counter and make a well in the center. Break the eggs into the well and add a pinch of salt. Knead thoroughly, shape into a ball, cover with a clean dish towel, and let rest for 1 hour.

Meanwhile, make the filling. Cook the potatoes in lightly salted boiling water for about 15 minutes until just tender, then drain. Meanwhile, melt 1 tablespoon of the butter with 1 tablespoon of the oil in a skillet. Add the mushrooms and cook over medium-high heat, stirring frequently, for 10 minutes. Remove from the skillet with a slotted spoon and set aside. Melt the remaining butter with the remaining oil in a pan. Add the drained potatoes, the garlic, and rosemary and cook over low heat, stirring occasionally, for 5 minutes. Remove from the heat and remove and discard the garlic and rosemary. Put the potatoes and porcini into a food processor and process until thoroughly combined. Transfer to a bowl and stir in the egg, Parmesan, pancetta or bacon, and season with salt and pepper.

Roll out the dough on a lightly floured counter to a thin sheet. Put small mounds of the filling in even rows over one half of the pasta sheet. Fold over the other half of the sheet and press around the filling with your fingers to seal. Cut out the ravioli and press the edges together firmly. Make the sauce. Put the spinach into a pan with just the water clinging to the leaves after washing and cook, turning occasionally, for 5–10 minutes until wilted. Drain and squeeze out the excess liquid, then put into the food proces,sor with the stock and mascarpone, season with salt and pepper and process. Cook the ravioli in plenty of salted boiling water until it rises to the counter and is al dente, then drain. Pour scant ½ cup water into a pan, add the thyme and ravioli, season with salt, and cook for 30 seconds. Pour in the spinach purée, stir, and serve garnished with pieces of chilled butter and sprinkled with Parmesan.

Preparation time: 1 hour 10 minutes,

plus 1 hour resting

Cooking time: 30 minutes

Serves 6

3½ cups all-purpose flour, plus extra for dusting

4 eggs

salt

For the filling

12 ounces potatoes, diced

3 tablespoons butter

3 tablespoons olive oil

2¾ cups porcini mushrooms, chopped

1 garlic clove

1 sprig fresh rosemary

1 egg, lightly beaten

½ cup grated Parmesan cheese

⅓ cup smoked pancetta or bacon, finely diced

For the sauce

3½ ounces spinach, coarse stalks removed

1 cup vegetable stock

1 tablespoon mascarpone cheese

1 sprig chopped fresh thyme

salt and pepper

To serve

½ cup chilled butter, diced

⅔ cup grated Parmesan cheese

RAVIOLI WITH CASTELMAGNO

RAVIOLI AL CASTELMAGNO

Preparation time: 1 hour 10 minutes,
plus 1 hour resting
Cooking time: 25 minutes
Serves 6

2¾ cups all-purpose flour,
plus extra for dusting

3 eggs

salt

For the filling

7 ounces diced Castelmagno cheese

¼ cup milk

scant ½ cup ricotta cheese

½ cup grated Parmesan cheese

3 egg yolks

salt

For the sauce

4 tablespoons butter

scant ½ cup vegetable stock

½-ounce truffle paste

To serve

½ white truffle

grated Parmesan cheese

Make the pasta dough. Sift the flour into a mound on a counter and make a well in the center. Break the eggs into the well and add a pinch of salt. Knead thoroughly, shape into a ball, cover with a clean dish towel, and let rest for 1 hour. Meanwhile, make the filling. Put the Castelmagno into a heatproof bowl, pour in the milk, and set over a pan of simmering water until softened. Remove from the heat and stir in the ricotta, Parmesan, and egg yolks, then season with salt and let cool.

Roll out the dough on a lightly floured counter into a thin sheet. Put small mounds of the filling in even rows over one half of the pasta sheet. Fold over the other half of the sheet and press around the filling with your fingers to seal. Cut out the ravioli and press the edges together firmly. Make the sauce. Melt the butter in a pan. Add the stock and truffle paste and simmer, stirring occasionally, until thickened. Cook the ravioli in plenty of salted boiling water until it rises to the counter and is al dente. Drain, transfer to the pan with the sauce, and toss for 1 minute. Transfer to a warmed serving dish and serve sprinkled with truffle shavings. Hand the Parmesan separately.

This recipe is from the Piedmont region in northwest Italy and uses the very best of autumnal produce, particularly truffles. This precious ingredient can be used in a multitude of dishes, from salads and risotto to filled pasta and fondues.

RAVIOLI NAPOLETANA

RAVIOLI ALLA NAPOLETANA

**Preparation time: 45 minutes,
plus 30 minutes resting
Cooking time: 20 minutes • Serves 6**

2¾ cups all-purpose flour, preferably Italian
type 00, plus extra for dusting • 3 eggs, lightly beaten
salt

For the filling

scant ½ cup ricotta cheese • 1 egg, lightly beaten
1 tablespoon chopped fresh flat-leaf parsley
generous 1 cup grated Parmesan cheese
generous ½ cup cooked ham, finely chopped
3½ ounces diced mozzarella cheese
1 quantity tomato sauce (see Angel Hair
Mold, page 30)

To serve

½ cup grated Parmesan cheese

Make the pasta dough (see Fresh Pasta Dough, page 163) with the quantities specified, cover with a damp dish towel, and let rest for 30 minutes. Meanwhile, beat the ricotta in a bowl with a wooden spoon, then stir in the egg, parsley, Parmesan, ham and mozzarella. Roll out the pasta dough on a lightly floured counter into a fairly thick sheet and place mounds of the filling at regular intervals on half the sheet. Fold over the dough and cut out ravioli, pressing the edges firmly to seal. Cook the ravioli in a large pan of salted boiling water until it rises to the counter and is al dente. Drain, toss with the tomato sauce, transfer to a warmed serving dish, and serve with Parmesan.

RAVIOLI WITH MARJORAM

RAVIOLI ALLA MAGGIORANA

**Preparation time: 1 hour,
plus 1 hour resting
Cooking time: 10 minutes
Serves 6**

3 cups all-purpose flour, plus extra for dusting
3 egg yolks
scant ½ cup dry white wine
salt

For the filling

scant 1 cup ricotta cheese • 1 egg
⅔ cup grated Parmesan cheese
1 cup finely chopped fresh marjoram
pinch of ground cinnamon
salt and pepper

For the sauce

scant ½ cup butter • ¼ cup superfine sugar
small pinch of ground cinnamon
⅓ cup finely chopped fresh marjoram

Make the pasta dough. Sift the flour into a mound on a counter and make a well in the center. Add the egg yolks, wine, and a pinch of salt to the well. Knead thoroughly, shape into a ball, cover with a clean dish towel, and let rest for 1 hour. Meanwhile, combine the ingredients for the filling, cover with plastic wrap, and store in the refrigerator until required. Roll out the dough on a lightly floured counter into a thin sheet. Put small mounds of the filling in even rows over one half of the pasta sheet. Fold over the other half of the sheet and press around the filling with your fingers to seal. Cut out the ravioli and press the edges together firmly. Make the sauce. Melt the butter in a shallow pan. Stir in the sugar and cinnamon. Cook the ravioli in plenty of salted boiling water until it rises to the counter and is al dente. Drain, tip into the pan, and toss gently. Transfer to a warmed serving dish, sprinkle with the marjoram, and serve.

RAVIOLI WITH DUCK FILLING

RAVIOLI CON RIPIENO D'ANATRA

Preheat the oven to 400°F. To make the filling, season the duckling with salt and pepper and put into a casserole with the rosemary, sage leaves, bay leaves, butter, and oil. Roast, drizzling occasionally with the brandy, for about 2 hours. Meanwhile, make the pasta dough. Sift the flour into a mound on a counter and make a well in the center. Break the eggs into the well and add a pinch of salt. Knead thoroughly, shape into a ball, cover with a clean dish towel, and let rest for 1 hour. To finish the filling, tear the bread into pieces, put it into a bowl, pour in the milk, and let soak. When the duckling is cooked, remove it from the oven. Reserve the cooking juices. Remove and discard the skin. Cut off and chop the meat from the breast, wings, and legs, and put it into a bowl. Squeeze out the bread and add it to the bowl with the prosciutto, egg, Parmesan, and nutmeg. Mix together well.

Roll out the dough on a lightly floured counter into a thin sheet. Put small mounds of the filling in even rows over one half of the pasta sheet. Fold over the other half of the sheet and press around the filling with your fingers to seal. Cut out the ravioli with a ravioli cutter and press the edges together firmly. To make the sauce, strain the reserved cooking juices into a pan, stir in the stock and orange rind, and heat, stirring frequently. Cook the ravioli in plenty of salted boiling water until it rises to the counter and is al dente. Drain, return to the pan, pour the sauce over, add the butter and plenty of Parmesan and toss lightly. Transfer to a warmed serving dish and serve immediately.

Preparation time: 1 hour 50 minutes,

plus 1 hour resting

Cooking time: 2 hours 10 minutes

Serves 6

4½ cups all-purpose flour, plus extra for dusting

5 eggs

salt

For the filling

6-pound duckling, thawed if frozen

1 sprig fresh rosemary

2 fresh sage leaves

2 bay leaves

2 tablespoons butter

2 tablespoons olive oil

scant ½ cup brandy

2 ounces bread, crusts removed

scant ½ cup milk

generous ½ cup chopped prosciutto

1 egg, lightly beaten

⅔ cup grated Parmesan cheese

pinch of freshly grated nutmeg

salt and pepper

For the sauce

⅔ cup chicken stock

grated rind of 1 orange

2 tablespoons butter

⅔ cup grated Parmesan cheese

RAVIOLI DI BACCALA E UVETTA

Preparation time: 1 hour 20 minutes,

plus 1 hour resting and 24 hours soaking

Cooking time: 1 hour 15 minutes

Serves 6

4½ cups all-purpose flour, plus extra for dusting

5 eggs

salt

For the filling

1 pound 2 ounces salt cod, soaked in several

changes of water for 24 hours

2 tablespoons olive oil

2 onions, sliced

3 tablespoons fresh bread crumbs

3 tablespoons milk

1 egg, lightly beaten

scant ½ cup ricotta cheese

2 tablespoons raisins

salt and pepper

For the sauce

scant ½ cup butter

1 bunch snipped fresh chives

1 garlic clove, finely chopped

sprigs fresh flat-leaf parsley, to garnish

SALT COD AND RAISIN RAVIOLI

Make the pasta dough. Sift the flour into a mound on a counter and make a well in the center. Break the eggs into the well and add a pinch of salt. Knead thoroughly, shape into a ball, cover with a clean dish towel, and let rest in a cool place for 1 hour.

Make the filling. Drain the cod, remove and discard the skin and bones, and chop the flesh. Heat the oil in a pan. Add the onions and cook over low heat, stirring occasionally, for 5 minutes. Add the cod and simmer, stirring occasionally, for 1 hour. Meanwhile, soak the bread crumbs in the milk for 10 minutes, then drain, and squeeze out. Remove the pan of fish from the heat, transfer the mixture to a food processor, and process to a purée. Transfer to a bowl, stir in the egg, ricotta, soaked bread crumbs, and 1½ tablespoons of the raisins, and season with salt and pepper.

Roll out the dough on a lightly floured counter into a thin sheet. Put small mounds of the filling in even rows over one half of the pasta sheet. Fold over the other half of the sheet and press around the filling with your fingers to seal. Cut out the ravioli and press the edges together firmly. To make the sauce, melt the butter in a pan. Pour in 4 tablespoons water, add the remaining raisins, the chives and garlic, and simmer gently. Cook the ravioli in plenty of salted boiling water until it rises to the counter and is al dente. Drain, add to the sauce, toss over the heat for 2 minutes, and serve immediately, garnished with parsley sprigs.

RAVIOLI DI RICOTTA CON ZUCCHINE AL BURRO E TIMO

Preparation time: 15 minutes

Cooking time: 20 minutes

Serves 4

14 ounces ready-made ricotta ravioli

For the sauce

3 tablespoons butter • 2 zucchini, diced

3 tablespoons heavy cream

1 tablespoon chopped fresh thyme • salt

RICOTTA RAVIOLI WITH BUTTERE ZUCCHINI AND THYME

To make the sauce, melt the butter in a shallow pan. Add the zucchini and cook over low heat, stirring occasionally, for a few minutes. Sprinkle with the thyme and drizzle with the cream, season with salt, and simmer, stirring occasionally, for 15 minutes. Cook the ravioli in plenty of salted boiling water until it rises to the counter and is al dente. Remove with a slotted spoon, add to the pan with the zucchini, and stir. Transfer to a warmed serving dish and serve immediately.

RAVIOLI WITH SHEEP MILK CHEESE

RAVIOLI AI FORMAGGI DI PECORA

Sift the flour into a mound on a counter and make a well in the center. Break the eggs into the well and add a pinch of salt. Knead thoroughly, then shape into a ball, cover with a clean dish towel, and let rest for 30 minutes. Meanwhile, make the filling. Combine the ricotta or goat cheese, grated cheeses, egg, orange rind, and lemon rind in a bowl and season with salt and pepper

Roll out the dough on a lightly floured counter into a thin sheet. Put small mounds of the filling in even rows over one half of the pasta sheet. Fold over the other half of the sheet and press around the filling with your fingers to seal. Cut out the ravioli and press the edges together firmly. To make the sauce, heat the oil in a pan. Add the shallot and cook over low heat, stirring occasionally, for 5 minutes. Add the tomatoes and basil, season with salt and pepper, and cook for 10 minutes. Remove from the heat and process in a food processor or blender, then return to a clean pan, and reheat gently.

Cook the ravioli in plenty of salted boiling water until it rises to the counter and is al dente. Drain, add to the pan with the sauce, and add the pieces of butter. Remove the pan from the heat and sprinkle with the Gruyère, pecorino and basil. Serve immediately.

Preparation time: 1 hour 20 minutes,

plus 30 minutes resting

Cooking time: 23 minutes

Serves 6

2¾ cups all-purpose flour, plus extra for dusting

3 eggs

salt

For the filling

3½ ounces sheep milk ricotta

or soft goat cheese

1 cup grated fresh pecorino sardo

1 cup grated sharp pecorino sardo

1 egg

grated rind of 1 orange

grated rind of 1 lemon

salt and pepper

For the sauce

1 tablespoon olive oil

1 shallot, chopped

6 tomatoes, peeled and diced

4 torn fresh basil leaves

salt and pepper

To serve

6 tablespoons chilled butter, cut into pieces

½ cup grated Gruyère cheese

⅓ cup grated mature pecorino cheese

4 torn fresh basil leaves

SEAFOOD RAVIOLI WITH BOTTARGA

RAVIOLI MARINARI ALLA BOTTARGA

**Preparation time: 1 hour 10 minutes,
plus 1 hour resting**

Cooking time: 45 minutes

Serves 4

3½ cups all-purpose flour, plus extra for dusting

4 eggs

salt

For the filling

2 tablespoons olive oil

1 onion, chopped

1 celery stalk, chopped

1 carrot, chopped

2 bay leaves

1 garlic clove

5 ounces cod fillet, skinned and cut into pieces

3½ ounces shelled langoustines, chopped

3½ ounces shelled shellfish, such as clams
or mussels

⅔ cup brandy

7 ounces canned chopped tomatoes

1 tablespoon grated bottarga (salted pressed
gray mullet or tuna roe)

1 tablespoon fresh bread crumbs

salt and pepper

For the sauce

3 tablespoons butter, melted

6 torn fresh basil leaves

1½ ounces bottarga, grated

First, make the pasta dough. Sift the flour into a mound on a counter and make a well in the center. Break the eggs into the well and add a pinch of salt. Knead thoroughly, shape into a ball, cover with a clean dish towel, and let rest for 1 hour.

Meanwhile, make the filling. Heat the oil in a shallow pan. Add the onion, celery, carrot, bay leaves, and garlic clove and cook over low heat, stirring occasionally, for 5 minutes. Add the cod, langoustines, and shellfish, stir, and cook for about 10 minutes. Pour in the brandy and cook until the alcohol has evaporated, then add the tomatoes. Season with salt and pepper and simmer for 5 minutes. Remove the pan from the heat, transfer the mixture to a food processor, and process to a purée. Transfer to a bowl and stir in the bottarga and bread crumbs.

Roll out the dough on a lightly floured counter into a thin sheet. Put small mounds of the filling in even rows over one half of the pasta sheet. Fold over the other half of the sheet and press around the filling with your fingers to seal. Cut out the ravioli and press the edges together firmly. Cook the ravioli in plenty of salted boiling water until it rises to the counter and is al dente. Drain and tip into a warmed serving dish. Pour the melted butter over and sprinkle with the basil and bottarga. Serve immediately.

RUCOLA

ARUGULA, ROBIOLA, RICOTTA AND MASCARPONE RAVIOLI

RAVIOLI DI RUCOLA, ROBIOLA, RICOTTA, MASCARPONE

To make the pasta dough, combine the flour and semolina flour, shape into a mound on a counter and make a well in the center. Break the eggs into the well and add a pinch of salt. Knead thoroughly, then shape into a ball, cover, and let rest for 2 hours.

Meanwhile, make the filling. Put the arugula into a small pan with just the water clinging to its leaves after washing and cook over low heat, turning occasionally, for 5 minutes. Drain, squeeze out the excess liquid, and chop. Melt the butter in a shallow pan. Add the shallot and garlic and cook over low heat, stirring occasionally, for 5 minutes, removing and discarding the garlic when it has turned golden brown. Stir in the arugula and ricotta, remove the pan from the heat, and let cool. Stir in the robiola, mascarpone, and bread crumbs, and add the stock if the mixture is too stiff. Season with salt and pepper and mix well.

To make the cream, pour the milk into a pan, add the butter and nutmeg, season with salt and pepper, and bring just to a boil. Immediately tip in all the sifted flour and stir vigorously. Cook, stirring constantly, for a few minutes until thickened, then stir in the cooled filling and Parmesan. Remove the pan from the heat and let cool. Add another pinch of bread crumbs if the mixture is too runny.

Roll out the pasta dough on a lightly floured counter into a thin sheet. Put small mounds of the filling in even rows over one half of the pasta sheet. Fold over the other half of the sheet and press around the filling with your fingers to seal. Cut out the ravioli and press the edges together firmly. Cook the ravioli in plenty of salted boiling water until it rises to the counter and is al dente, then drain. Make the sauce. Heat the oil in a shallow pan. Add the arugula and garlic and cook, stirring constantly, for 1 minute. Add the butter and the ravioli and toss gently. Add the tomatoes and heat through for a few seconds. Transfer the ravioli to a warmed serving dish and serve immediately.

Preparation time: 1 hour 10 minutes, plus 2 hours resting

Cooking time: 50 minutes

Serves 6

1½ cups all-purpose flour, plus extra for dusting

½ cup semolina flour

2 eggs

salt

For the filling

3 ounces arugula

1½ tablespoons butter

2 tablespoons shallot, chopped

½ garlic clove

3 ounces ricotta cheese

3 ounces robiola cheese

2½ tablespoons mascarpone cheese

pinch of fresh bread crumbs

1–2 tablespoons vegetable stock (optional)

salt and pepper

For the cream

5 tablespoons milk

1½ tablespoons butter

pinch of nutmeg, freshly grated

5 tablespoons all-purpose flour, sifted

4 tablespoons grated Parmesan cheese

salt and pepper

For the sauce

2 tablespoons olive oil

¾ cup arugula, shredded

1 garlic clove, very finely chopped

2 tablespoons butter

5 ounces tomatoes, seeded and diced

salt and pepper

SEA BASS RAVIOLI

Sift both kinds of flour into a mound on a counter and make a well in the center. Break the eggs into the well and add the egg yolks and a pinch of salt. Knead well, shape into a ball, cover with a clean dish towel, and let rest for 1 hour. Meanwhile, make the filling. Heat the oil in a shallow pan. Add the fish, season with salt and pepper, and cook over low heat, stirring occasionally, for 10 minutes. Remove from the pan and let cool, then combine with the mascarpone, lemon rind, and chives in a bowl. Roll out the dough on a lightly floured counter into a thin sheet. Put small mounds of the filling in even rows over one half of the pasta sheet. Fold over the other half of the sheet and press around the filling with your fingers to seal. Cut out the ravioli and press the edges together firmly. Cook the ravioli in plenty of salted boiling water until it rises to the counter and is al dente. Drain and toss in a pan over low heat with the butter and chives, then serve.

Preparation time: 1 hour 25 minutes,

plus 1 hour resting

Cooking time: 20 minutes

Serves 6

3 cups all-purpose flour, preferably Italian type 00,

plus extra for dusting

1¼ cups durum wheat semolina flour

3 eggs • 4 egg yolks

salt

For the filling

3 tablespoons olive oil

1½ pounds sea bass fillets, skinned and chopped

3 tablespoons mascarpone cheese

grated rind of 1 lemon

1 teaspoon snipped fresh chives

salt and pepper

For the sauce

6 tablespoons butter

1 tablespoon snipped fresh chives

VEGETABLE AND CHEESE FILLED RAVIOLI

For the filling, cook the spinach in just the water clinging to the leaves after washing for 5 minutes, then drain well, and chop. Beat the ricotta in a bowl with a wooden spoon and stir in the spinach. Stir in the eggs and Parmesan and season with salt and pepper to taste, stirring until very smooth. Make the pasta dough (see Fresh Pasta Dough, page 163) with the flour, eggs, and a pinch of salt. Roll out into a sheet, place mounds of the filling at regular intervals on half the sheet, fold over, and cut out ravioli (a little larger than normal). Press the edges to seal. Cook in a large pan of salted boiling water for about 10 minutes, then drain, and place in a warmed serving dish. Meanwhile melt the butter in a small pan and cook the sage leaves until golden. Sprinkle the ravioli with the ricotta and Parmesan, pour the sage butter over them, and serve.

Preparation time: 50 minutes

Cooking time: 20 minutes

Serves 6

2¾ cups all-purpose flour, preferably Italian type 00,

plus extra for dusting

3 eggs

4 tablespoons butter

8 fresh sage leaves

½ cup crumbled ricotta cheese

⅔ cup grated Parmesan cheese

salt

For the filling

3¼ pounds spinach • 2¼ cups ricotta cheese

2 eggs, lightly beaten

2 tablespoons grated Parmesan cheese

salt and pepper

RAVIOLINI VOL-AU-VENT

Preparation time: 25 minutes
Cooking time: 30 minutes
Serves 6
4 tablespoons butter
scant 1 cup shelled peas
2 tablespoons warm water
1 pound 2 ounces small ravioli
½ cup grated Parmesan cheese
1 large, ready-made vol-au-vent case,
about 6–8 inches in diameter
1 quantity béchamel sauce (see Baked
Pumpkin Pasta, page 272)
salt

Preheat the oven to 300°F. Line a cookie sheet with baking paper. Melt 2 tablespoons of the butter in a pan, add the peas and 2 tablespoons warm water, and cook for about 10 minutes until tender. Season with salt, drain, and set aside. Cook the ravioli in a large pan of salted boiling water until al dente, then drain, tip into a bowl, and gently toss with the remaining butter, 5 tablespoons of the Parmesan, and the peas. Fill the vol-au-vent case with the ravioli and spoon in the béchamel sauce. Sprinkle with the remaining Parmesan, place on the cookie sheet, and heat through in the oven.

WHOLE WHEAT RAVIOLI WITH PEA FILLING

Preparation time: 1 hour 10 minutes,
plus 1 hour resting
Cooking time: 50 minutes
Serves 6
1¼ cups whole wheat flour
1¼ cups all-purpose flour, preferably Italian
type 00, plus extra for dusting
3 eggs
salt
For the filling
5¼ cups shelled peas
2 tablespoons olive oil
¼ cup onion, chopped
salt and pepper
For the sauce
scant ½ cup chilled butter
1 cup grated Parmesan cheese
½ cup hazelnuts, chopped
juice of ½ lemon, strained
1 tablespoon chopped fresh flat-leaf parsley

Combine the two types of flour, shape into a mound on a counter and make a well in the center. Break the eggs into the well and add a pinch of salt. Knead thoroughly, shape into a ball, cover with a clean dish towel, and let rest for 1 hour. Meanwhile, make the filling. Cook the peas in salted boiling water for 10–15 minutes until tender. Drain well, transfer to a food processor or blender, and process to a purée. Heat the oil in a pan. Add the onion and cook over low heat, stirring occasionally, for 5 minutes. Add the pea purée, season lightly with salt and pepper, and cook, stirring frequently, for 10–15 minutes until the mixture is fairly dry. Remove the pan from the heat. Roll out the dough on a lightly floured counter into a thin sheet. Put small mounds of the pea filling in even rows over one half of the pasta sheet. Fold over the other half of the sheet and press around the filling with your fingers to seal. Cut out the ravioli and press the edges together firmly. Cook the ravioli in plenty of salted boiling water until it rises to the counter and is al dente. Transfer to a pan and toss with the butter, Parmesan, hazelnuts, lemon juice, and parsley over low heat. Serve immediately.

TORDELLI

Tordelli is a type of filled pasta typical of the city of Lucca in Tuscany. Tordelli is circular, similar to tortelli, and made with 3¼-inch dough rounds. Small mounds of filling are then put on each round, the dough is folded over, and the edges pressed together firmly to seal. Tordelli is traditionally accompanied by a sauce made from melted butter and sage.

TORDELLI FROM LUCCA

TORDELLI ALLA LUCCHESE

Preparation time: 1 hour 20 minutes, plus 30 minutes resting
Cooking time: 30 minutes
Serves 4–6

3½ cups all-purpose flour, plus extra for dusting
4 eggs
salt
For the filling
1 thick slice of bread, crusts removed
2 tablespoons olive oil
sprig of fresh thyme
5 ounces ground steak
5 ounces ground pork
2 ounces mortadella
2 eggs
½ cup grated Parmesan cheese
½ cup grated pecorino cheese
1 tablespoon chopped fresh flat-leaf parsley
pinch of nutmeg, freshly grated
salt and pepper
For the sauce
4 tablespoons butter, melted
4–6 chopped fresh sage leaves

Make the pasta dough. Sift the flour into a mound on a counter and make a well in the center. Break the eggs into the well and add a pinch of salt. Knead thoroughly, shape into a ball, cover with a clean dish towel, and let rest for 30 minutes.

Meanwhile, make the filling. Put the bread into a bowl, pour in water to cover, and let soak for 10 minutes, then drain, and squeeze out the excess liquid. Meanwhile, heat the oil in a shallow pan with the thyme sprig. Add the ground meat and cook over medium-low heat, stirring frequently, for about 10 minutes until lightly browned. Remove from the heat and let cool. Using a slotted spoon, transfer the ground meat to a cutting board, add the mortadella, and chop together. Transfer to a bowl and mix in the eggs, 2 tablespoons of the Parmesan, 1 tablespoon of the pecorino, the soaked bread, parsley, and nutmeg. Mix well and season with salt and pepper.

Roll out the pasta dough on a lightly floured counter into a thin sheet. Cut out 3¼-inch rounds with a pasta wheel. Put small mounds of filling on each round, fold over the dough, and press the edges firmly together to seal. Cook the tordelli in plenty of salted boiling water until it rises to the counter and is al dente. Drain, transfer to a warmed serving dish, pour the melted butter over, and sprinkle with the sage. Sprinkle with the remaining Parmesan and pecorino and serve immediately.

TORTELLI

A type of filled pasta similar to ravioli, tortelli takes its name from torta, meaning "tart," and can be square or half-moon-shaped. Originating in the Po Valley in northern Italy, tortelli is mentioned in recipes dating back to the twelfth century and was celebrated by poets in the Middle Ages. The most traditional filling comes from the Emilia-Romagna region and is made from ricotta and spinach. Fillings with potatoes or cured meats are also common.

BRANDY—FLAVORED POTATO TORTELLI

TORTELLI DI PATATE AL BRANDY

**Preparation time: 1 hour 15 minutes,
plus 30 minutes resting**
Cooking time: 40 minutes
Serves 6

3½ cups all-purpose flour, plus extra for dusting
4 eggs • salt
For the filling
1½ pounds potatoes
⅔ cup ricotta cheese
2 eggs
⅓ cup grated Parmesan cheese
pinch of nutmeg, freshly grated
5 tablespoons brandy
salt and pepper
For the sauce
6 tablespoons butter, melted
½ cup grated Parmesan cheese

Make the pasta dough. Sift the flour into a mound on a counter and make a well in the center. Break the eggs into the well and add a pinch of salt. Knead thoroughly, shape into a ball, cover with a clean dish towel, and let rest for 30 minutes. Meanwhile, make the filling. Boil the potatoes in lightly salted water for about 25 minutes. Drain, peel, and put them into a bowl. Mash with a potato masher, then beat in the ricotta, eggs, Parmesan, nutmeg, and brandy with a wooden spoon, and season with salt and pepper. Roll out the pasta dough on a lightly floured counter into a thin sheet. Put small mounds of the filling in even rows over one half of the pasta sheet. Fold over the other half of the sheet and press around the filling with your fingers to seal. Cut out square tortelli and press the edges together firmly. Cook the tortelli in plenty of salted boiling water until it rises to the counter and is al dente. Drain and transfer to a tureen. Pour the melted butter over, sprinkle with the Parmesan, and serve immediately.

ARTICHOKE AND CHEESE TORTELLI

TORTELLI DI CARCIOFI E FORMAGGIO

Make the pasta dough. Sift the flour into a mound on a counter and make a well in the center. Break the eggs into the well and add a pinch of salt. Knead thoroughly, shape into a ball, cover with a clean dish towel, and let rest for 30 minutes.

Meanwhile, make the filling. Melt half the butter in a shallow pan. Add the artichokes, onion, and 2 tablespoons water and cook over low heat, stirring occasionally, for 20 minutes. Remove the artichokes from the pan and chop. Transfer the artichokes and onion to a bowl. Melt the remaining butter in a small pan. Stir in the flour and cook over medium heat, stirring constantly, for 2–3 minutes until golden brown. Gradually stir in the milk, a little at a time. Bring to a boil, stirring constantly, lower the heat, and simmer gently, stirring constantly, for 20 minutes until thickened and smooth. Remove the pan from the heat and add to the artichokes with the eggs and the grated cheese. Mix well and season with salt.

Roll out the pasta on a lightly floured counter into a thin sheet. Put small mounds of the filling in even rows over one half of the pasta sheet. Fold over the other half of the sheet and press around the filling with your fingers to seal. Cut out the tortelli and press the edges together firmly. Cook in plenty of salted boiling water until it rises to the counter and is al dente. Drain, pour the melted butter over, and sprinkle with Parmesan. Serve immediately.

Preparation time: 1 hour 20 minutes,
plus 30 minutes resting
Cooking time: 50 minutes
Serves 6
3½ cups all-purpose flour, plus extra for dusting
4 eggs
salt
For the filling
4 tablespoons butter
6 young globe artichokes, trimmed
1 onion, thinly sliced
¼ cup all-purpose flour
2¼ cups lukewarm milk
3 eggs, lightly beaten
⅓ cup grated Parmesan cheese
salt
For the sauce
3 tablespoons butter, melted
½ cup grated Parmesan cheese

TORTELLI

PUMPKIN TORTELLI

TORTELLI DI ZUCCA

Preheat the oven to 350°F. Put the pumpkin in a roasting pan, drizzle with the oil, cover with aluminium foil and bake for about 1 hour. Pass the pumpkin through a food mill into a bowl, or process to a purée. Add the Parmesan and eggs, and season with salt and pepper. Stir in enough bread crumbs to make a fairly firm mixture. Roll out the pasta dough into a sheet and stamp out 3-inch rounds with a cookie cutter. Spoon a little of the pumpkin filling into the center of each round, fold in half, and crimp the edges. Cook the tortelli in a large pan of salted boiling water for 10 minutes. Meanwhile, melt the butter in a skillet, add the sage, and cook for a few minutes. Drain the tortelli, place in a warmed serving dish, and sprinkle with the sage butter and extra Parmesan. Serve immediately.

Preparation time: 50 minutes

Cooking time: 1 hour 15 minutes

Serves 4

4 cups peeled, seeded, and chopped pumpkin

2 tablespoons olive oil

⅔ cups grated Parmesan cheese,

plus extra to serve

2 eggs, lightly beaten

1½–2 cups fresh bread crumbs

1 quantity Fresh Pasta Dough (see page 163)

4 tablespoons butter

8 fresh sage leaves

salt and pepper

RADICCHIO AND ROBIOLA TORTELLI

TORTELLI AL RADICCHIO E ROBIOLA

First make the pasta dough. Heat the oil in a shallow pan. Add the radicchio, season lightly with salt, and cook over low heat, stirring occasionally, for a few minutes until wilted. Remove from the heat and set aside. Sift the flour into a mound on a counter and make a well in the center. Break the eggs into the well and add the radicchio, wine, and a pinch of salt. Knead thoroughly, shape into a ball, cover with a clean dish towel, and let rest for 1 hour. Meanwhile, make the filling. Beat the robiola in a bowl, then beat in the Parmesan, and season with salt and pepper.

Roll out the pasta dough on a lightly floured counter into a thin sheet. Cut out 3-inch squares with a pasta wheel. Put a small mound of filling in the center of each one and fold over, pressing the edges together firmly. To make the sauce, put the butter and thyme into a heatproof bowl, set over a pan of simmering water and melt, stirring occasionally. Meanwhile, cook the tortelli in plenty of salted boiling water until it rises to the counter and is al dente. Drain, transfer to a warmed serving dish, and pour the herb-flavored melted butter over. Serve immediately.

Preparation time: 1 hour 15 minutes,

plus 1 hour resting

Cooking time: 18 minutes

Serves 4

2 tablespoons olive oil

9 ounces radicchio, cut into strips

2¾ cups all-purpose flour, plus extra for dusting

2 eggs

2 tablespoons dry white wine

salt

For the filling

7 ounces robiola cheese

¼ cup grated Parmesan cheese

salt and pepper

For the sauce

1½ tablespoons butter

1 tablespoon chopped fresh thyme

TORTELLINI

Tortellini is a type of small ring-shaped filled pasta, originally from the Emilia-Romagna region of northern Italy. The inspiration for tortellini is supposed to be the navel of Venus. Home-made tortellini is made mainly for festive occasions, as it takes a long time to prepare. Tortellini is made by filling square sheets of dough, folding them into triangles, then wrapping each triangle around the index finger. The points are then pressed together and the rest of the dough gently pushed backward to make the classic tortellini shape. Tortellini can have various fillings and is typically filled with ground meat and served in stock. The bigger version of tortellini is called tortelloni, which can also sometimes refer to large tortelli.

TORTELLINI BOLOGNESE

TORTELLINI ALLA BOLOGNESE

Preparation time: 1 hour 20 minutes
Cooking time: 20 minutes
Serves 4

2 tablespoons butter
2 ounces ground veal
2 tablespoons grated Parmesan cheese
½ cup prosciutto, diced
¼ diced mortadella, cup
1 egg, lightly beaten
1 quantity Fresh Pasta Dough (see page 163)
1 quantity tomato sauce (see Angel Hair Mold, page 30)

Melt the butter in a small pan, add the veal, and cook over high heat, stirring frequently, until browned. Transfer to a bowl, let cool, then stir in the Parmesan, prosciutto, mortadella, and egg. Roll out the pasta dough into a thin sheet, put small mounds of the filling at regular intervals on the sheet, and cut into squares. Fold the squares corner to corner into triangles, then wrap each triangle around your index finger, press the points together, and gently push the rest of the dough backward to make the classic tortellini shape. Make 20 tortellini per person. Serve with hot tomato sauce.

CURRIED TORTELLINI

TORTELLINI AL CURRY

Preparation time: 15 minutes

Cooking time: 25 minutes

Serves 4

4 tablespoons butter • 1¾ cups shelled peas

⅓ cup cooked ham, diced

2 teaspoons curry powder

14 ounces fresh tortellini (see Tortellini
Bolognese, page 314)

⅔ cup grated Parmesan cheese

scant 1 cup heavy cream

salt

Melt half the butter in a pan, add the peas and ham, and cook over low heat, stirring occasionally, for 10 minutes. Stir in the curry powder and cook for another 10 minutes. Cook the tortellini in a large pan of salted boiling water until al dente. Drain and toss with the remaining butter, the Parmesan, and cream, and then with the curry sauce. Transfer to a warmed serving dish.

MUSHROOM TORTELLONI

TORTELLONI DI FUNGHI

Preparation time: 50 minutes

plus 30 minutes resting

Cooking time: 30 minutes

Serves 4

1 quantity Fresh Pasta Dough (see page 163)

4 tablespoons olive oil

1 small onion, chopped

scant 4½ cups porcini mushrooms, thinly sliced

generous 1 cup crumbled ricotta cheese

⅔ cup grated Parmesan cheese,
plus extra to serve

1 sprig chopped fresh flat-leaf parsley

3 tablespoons butter

10 fresh sage leaves

salt and pepper

Heat the oil in a pan, add the onion and porcini, and cook over low heat, stirring occasionally, for 5 minutes. Season with salt and cook for another 15 minutes. Transfer the mixture to a food processor, add the ricotta, Parmesan, and parsley, and process to a purée. Season with salt and pepper to taste.

Roll out the pasta dough on a lightly floured counter to make a thin sheet and cut out 2-inch squares. Put a little ricotta mixture into the center of each square. Fold the squares corner to corner into triangles, then wrap each triangle around your index finger, press the points together, and gently push the rest of the dough backward to make the classic tortelloni shape. Melt the butter in a large skillet, add the sage leaves, and cook for a few minutes. Cook the tortelloni in a large pan of salted boiling water until al dente. Drain, add to the skillet, and stir over high heat. Transfer to a warmed serving dish, sprinkle with Parmesan, and serve.

PESTO TORTELLONI WITH SQUID →

PESTO TORTELLONI WITH SQUID

Make the pasta dough (see Fresh Pasta Dough, page 163) with the flour, eggs, and a pinch of salt. For the pesto, put the basil, parsley, pine nuts, walnuts, and oil into a food processor and process until combined, then scrape into a bowl. Season with salt and stir in the ricotta. Roll out the pasta dough on a lightly floured counter to make a thin sheet and cut out 2-inch squares. Put a little pesto mixture into the center of each square. Fold the squares corner to corner into triangles. If you like, wrap each triangle around your index finger, press the points together, and gently push the rest of the dough backward to make the classic tortelloni shape.

For the sauce, heat 3 tablespoons of the oil in a skillet, add the squid and garlic, and cook, stirring frequently, for a few minutes until the squid are light golden brown. Season with salt and pepper to taste, sprinkle with the wine, and cook until it has evaporated. Remove the squid from the skillet, leaving the cooking juices in the pan and slice into fairly thin rounds. Cook the pasta in a large pan of salted boiling water until al dente, drain, and tip into the skillet. Remove and discard the garlic, add the remaining oil, the tomatoes, and squid rounds, and mix well. Sprinkle with the parsley and basil and mix again. Transfer to a warmed serving dish and serve immediately.

Preparation time: 50 minutes

Cooking time: 30 minutes

Serves 4

2¾ cups all-purpose flour, preferably Italian type 00, plus extra for dusting

3 eggs, lightly beaten

salt

For the pesto

scant 2 cups fresh basil leaves

¾ cup fresh flat-leaf parsley

3 tablespoons pine nuts

1 tablespoon shelled walnuts

½ cup olive oil

scant 1 cup ricotta cheese

salt

For the sauce

4 tablespoons olive oil

7 ounces small squid, cleaned

1 garlic clove

5 tablespoons dry white wine

2 tomatoes, peeled and diced

1 tablespoon chopped fresh flat-leaf parsley

6 torn fresh basil leaves

salt and pepper

LIST OF RECIPES

INDEX

Page numbers in *italic* refer to the illustrations

Phaidon Press Limited
180 Varick Street
New York, NY 10014

www.phaidon.com

© 2009 Phaidon Press Limited

ISBN 9 780 7148 5726 8 (US edition)

The Silver Spoon: Pasta originates from
Il cucchiaio d'argento, first published in
1950, Eighth edition (revised, expanded
and redesigned 1997)
© Editoriale Domus S.p.a

A CIP catalogue record for this book is
available from the British Library.

All rights reserved. No part of this
publication may be reproduced, stored
in a retrieval system or transmitted, in
any form or by any means, electronic,
mechanical, photocopying, recording or
otherwise, without the prior permission
of Phaidon Press Limited.

Photographs by Edward Park
Drawings by Francesca Bazzurro
Designed by Italo Lupi with Blandine Minot

Printed in China

The Publishers would also like to thank
Attilio Bergamaschi, Mary Consonni,
Linda Doeser, Carmen Figini, Meaghan
Kombol, Margot Levy, Clelia d'Onofrio and
Jane Rollason, for their contributions to
the book.

Recipe Notes

- Butter should always be sweet.

- Pepper is always freshly ground black pepper,
  unless otherwise specified.

- Eggs, vegetables and fruits are assumed to be
  medium size, unless otherwise specified.

- Milk is always whole, unless otherwise specified

- Garlic cloves are assumed to be large; use two
  if yours are small.

- Ham means cooked ham, unless otherwise
  specified.

- Prosciutto refers exclusively to raw, dry-cured
  ham, usually from Parma or San Daniele in
  northern Italy.

- Cooking and preparation times are for guidance
  only, as individual ovens vary. If using a fan
  oven, follow the manufacturer's instructions
  concerning oven temperatures.

- To test whether your deep-frying oil is hot
  enough, add a cube of stale bread. If it browns
  in thirty seconds, the temperature is 350–375°F,
  about right for most frying. Exercise caution
  when deep frying: add the food carefully to
  avoid splashing, wear long sleeves, and never
  leave the pan unattended.

- Some recipes include raw or very lightly cooked
  eggs. These should be avoided particularly
  by the elderly, infants, pregnant women,
  convalescents, and anyone with an impaired
  immune system.

- All spoon measurements are level.
  1 teaspoon = 5 ml; 1 tablespoon = 15 ml.
  Australian standard tablespoons are 20 ml,
  so Australian readers are advised to use
  3 teaspoons in place of 1 tablespoon when
  measuring small quantities.